2-D and 3-D Geometry

Quilt Squares and Block Towns

Grade 1

Also appropriate for Grade 2

Susan Jo Russell

Douglas H. Clements

Julie Sarama

Developed at TERC, Cambridge, Massachusetts

Dale Seymour Publications®
Menlo Park, California

The *Investigations* curriculum was developed at TERC (formerly
Technical Education Research Centers) in collaboration with Kent State
University and the State University of New York at Buffalo. The work was
supported in part by National Science Foundation Grant No. ESI-9050210.
TERC is a nonprofit company working to improve mathematics and sci-
ence education. TERC is located at 2067 Massachusetts Avenue,
Cambridge, MA 02140.

This project was supported, in part,
by the
National Science Foundation
Opinions expressed are those of the authors
and not necessarily those of the Foundation

Managing Editor: Catherine Anderson
Series Editor: Beverly Cory
ESL Consultant: Nancy Sokol Green
Production/Manufacturing Director: Janet Yearian
Production/Manufacturing Manager: Karen Edmonds
Production/Manufacturing Coordinators: Barbara Atmore and Amy Changar
Design Manager: Jeff Kelly
Design: Don Taka
Composition: Andrea Reider
Illustrations: DJ Simison, Carl Yoshihara, Rachel Gage
Cover: Bay Graphics

This book is published by Dale Seymour Publications®, an imprint of
Addison Wesley Longman, Inc.

Dale Seymour Publications
2725 Sand Hill Road
Menlo Park, CA 94025
Customer Service: 800-872-1100

Order number DS43705
ISBN 1-57232-469-4
3 4 5 6 7 8 9 10-ML-01 00 99 98

Printed on Recycled Paper

T E R C

Principal Investigator   Susan Jo Russell

Co-Principal Investigator   Cornelia C. Tierney

Director of Research and Evaluation   Jan Mokros

Director of K–2 Curriculum   Karen Economopoulos

Curriculum Development

Karen Economopoulos
Marlene Kliman
Jan Mokros
Megan Murray
Susan Jo Russell
Tracey Wright

Evaluation and Assessment

Mary Berle-Carman
Jan Mokros
Andee Rubin

Teacher Support

Irene Baker
Megan Murray
Judy Storeygard
Tracey Wright

Technology Development

Michael T. Battista
Douglas H. Clements
Julie Sarama

Video Production

David A. Smith
Judy Storeygard

Administration and Production

Irene Baker
Amy Catlin

**Cooperating Classrooms
for This Unit**

Nancy Frane
Joe Reilly
Brookline Public Schools
Brookline, MA

Elizabeth A. Pedrini
Arlington Public Schools
Arlington, MA

Mayra L. Cuevas
Boston Public Schools
Boston, MA

Jill Heuss
Westwood Public Schools
Westwood, MA

Consultants and Advisors

Deborah Lowenberg Ball
Michael T. Battista
Marilyn Burns
Douglas H. Clements
Ann Grady

CONTENTS

WHERE TO START

The first-time user of *Quilt Squares and Block Towns* should
read the following:

When you next teach this same unit, you can begin to read more of the
background. Each time you present the unit, you will learn more about
how your students understand the mathematical ideas.

Investigations in Number, Data, and Space® is a K–5 mathematics curriculum with four major goals:

- to offer students meaningful mathematical problems
- to emphasize depth in mathematical thinking rather than superficial exposure to a series of fragmented topics
- to communicate mathematics content and pedagogy to teachers
- to substantially expand the pool of mathematically literate students

The *Investigations* curriculum embodies an approach radically different from the traditional textbook-based curriculum. At each grade level, it consists of a set of separate units, each offering 2–8 weeks of work. These units of study are presented through investigations that involve students in the exploration of major mathematical ideas.

Approaching the mathematics content through investigations helps students develop flexibility and confidence in approaching problems, fluency in using mathematical skills and tools to solve problems, and proficiency in evaluating their solutions. Students also build a repertoire of ways to communicate about their mathematical thinking, while their enjoyment and appreciation of mathematics grow.

The investigations are carefully designed to invite all students into mathematics—girls and boys, members of diverse cultural, ethnic, and language groups, and students with different strengths and interests. Problem contexts often call on students to share experiences from their family, culture, or community. The curriculum eliminates barriers— such as work in isolation from peers, or emphasis on speed and memorization—that exclude some students from participating successfully in mathematics. The following aspects of the curriculum ensure that all students are included in significant mathematics learning:

- Students spend time exploring problems in depth.
- They find more than one solution to many of the problems they work on.

- They invent their own strategies and approaches, rather than relying on memorized procedures.
- They choose from a variety of concrete materials and appropriate technology, including calculators, as a natural part of their everyday mathematical work.
- They express their mathematical thinking through drawing, writing, and talking.
- They work in a variety of groupings—as a whole class, individually, in pairs, and in small groups.
- They move around the classroom as they explore the mathematics in their environment and talk with their peers.

While reading and other language activities are typically given a great deal of time and emphasis in elementary classrooms, mathematics often does not get the time it needs. If students are to experience mathematics in depth, they must have enough time to become engaged in real mathematical problems. We believe that a minimum of 5 hours of mathematics classroom time a week—about an hour a day—is critical at the elementary level. The plan and pacing of the *Investigations* curriculum are based on that belief.

We explain more about the pedagogy and principles that underlie these investigations in Teacher Notes throughout the units. For correlations of the curriculum to the NCTM Standards and further help in using this research-based program for teaching mathematics, see the following books:

- *Implementing the* Investigations in Number, Data, and Space® *Curriculum*

- *Beyond Arithmetic: Changing Mathematics in the Elementary Classroom* by Jan Mokros, Susan Jo Russell, and Karen Economopoulos

This book is one of the curriculum units for *Investigations in Number, Data, and Space.* In addition to providing part of a complete mathematics curriculum for your students, this unit offers information to support your own professional development. You, the teacher, are the person who will make this curriculum come alive in the classroom; the book for each unit is your main support system.

Although the curriculum does not include student textbooks, reproducible sheets for student work are provided in the unit and are also available as Student Activity Booklets. Students work actively with objects and experiences in their own environment and with a variety of manipulative materials and technology, rather than with a book of instruction and problems. We strongly recommend use of the overhead projector as a way to present problems, to focus group discussion, and to help students share ideas and strategies.

Ultimately, every teacher will use these investigations in ways that make sense for his or her particular style, the particular group of students, and the constraints and supports of a particular school environment. Each unit offers information and guidance for a wide variety of situations, drawn from our collaborations with many teachers and students over many years. Our goal in this book is to help you, a professional educator, implement this curriculum in a way that will give all your students access to mathematical power.

Investigation Format

The opening two pages of each investigation help you get ready for the work that follows.

What Happens This gives a synopsis of each session or block of sessions.

Mathematical Emphasis This lists the most important ideas and processes students will encounter in this investigation.

What to Plan Ahead of Time These lists alert you to materials to gather, sheets to duplicate, transparencies to make, and anything else you need to do before starting.

Building a Block Town

What Happens

Sessions 1 and 2: Drawing Geoblocks Students build small constructions with Geoblocks and then draw what they built as accurately as they can. They discuss what was easy and difficult about making a 2-D picture of a 3-D object and talk about what makes a picture look 3-D. Students trade their pictures and build constructions to match the pictures.

Sessions 3 and 4: Planning a Town Students discuss buildings in their neighborhood, in their community, and other buildings they have seen. The class then makes plans for building their own town and decides what buildings they might want to include. Each pair of students chooses a building for the town and draws a plan for it.

Session 5: Building a Town Students build their buildings on a large street grid. They write a few sentences about the building they designed and how it is used. The class decides on a name for the town.

Sessions 6 and 7: Giving Directions Students give directions to get from one place to another in the classroom, using paces and turns. Then, on a map of the class town, students plan trips and record directions for moving from one location to another. The class develops a code for giving directions, and students use this code to record trips through the class town. Students also create paths of different lengths to connect the same two locations.

Routines Refer to the section About Classroom Routines (pp. 127–134) for suggestions on integrating into the school day regular practice of mathematical skills in counting, exploring data, and understanding time and changes.

Mathematical Emphasis

- Observing and describing characteristics of 3-D shapes
- Observing shapes in the environment
- Creating and using 2-D representations of 3-D shapes
- Building 3-D constructions from 2-D representations
- Developing vocabulary for describing 3-D shapes
- Putting 3-D shapes together to make other shapes
- Visualizing, describing, and comparing paths between two locations in space and on a grid
- Estimating distances
- Visualizing and describing direction of turns

What to Plan Ahead of Time

Materials

- Geoblocks: 2 sets, each divided equally into half-sets (Sessions 1–7)
- Drawing materials (Sessions 1–4)
- 5-by-8-inch index cards (or half-sheets of letter-size paper): 1 per pair (Sessions 3–4)
- Children's books about unusual buildings or houses (Sessions 3–4, optional)
- Toy people or cars, small blocks or counters, or small cardboard pointers: 1 per pair (Sessions 6–7)
- Overhead projector (Sessions 6–7)

Other Preparation

- Make simple building shapes with 3–5 Geoblocks (see p. 100 for examples). You will need one building for every 4 students. They need not be identical. (Session 1)
- Make a large street grid for the class town on poster board or large paper. Use the Street Grid (p. 228) as the model. Your large grid should be a 6-by-6 array of rectangles, each measuring at least 5 by 8 inches for a total size of 30 by 48 inches. If students are using half-sheets of letter-size paper instead of 5-by-8 index cards as the "land" for their buildings, make your grid slightly larger (33 by 51 inches). Find a location—perhaps a table, or a space on the floor or in the hall—where you can leave the large grid for several days as students work on the class town. (Sessions 3–7)
- Geoblocks do not include some shapes, such as cylinders, cones, and arches that students should become familiar with. If you

can borrow some other sets of building blocks, students will have a wider range to choose from; add these to the available tools for making buildings. Some students may have sets at home that they are willing to lend. Sets should be small enough for table-top building. (Sessions 3–7, optional)

- Make a small "traveler" for showing paths on the overhead projector. Use a small block or counter. Cut out a small cardboard arrow (pointer) and attach it to the block or counter so that it sticks out horizontally from the counter. When you put this on the overhead projector, students will be able to see the object with the arrow pointing out from it, indicating which way the traveler is going (see the illustration on p. 121). (Sessions 6–7)
- Duplicate the following student sheets and teaching resources, located at the end of this unit. If you have Student Activity Booklets, copy only items marked with an asterisk.

For Sessions 1 and 2
Student Sheet 28, Draw a Building (p. 225): 1 per student, homework
Ways to Draw Blocks (p. 227): about 6 for the class

For Session 5
Street Grid* (p. 228): one copy, to create a map of your class's block town (see p. 121)

For Sessions 6 and 7
Student Sheet 29, Robot Paces (p. 226): 1 per student, homework
Street Grid, as prepared after Session 5 to show your block town: 1 per student*, and 1 transparency*

Sessions Within an investigation, the activities are organized by class session, a session being at least a one-hour math class. Sessions are numbered consecutively through an investigation. Often several sessions are grouped together, presenting a block of activities with a single major focus.

When you find a block of sessions presented together—for example, Sessions 1, 2, and 3—read through the entire block first to understand the overall flow and sequence of the activities. Make some preliminary decisions about how you will divide the activities into three sessions for your class, based on what you know about your students. You may need to modify your initial plans as you progress through the activities, and you may want to make notes in the margins of the pages as reminders for the next time you use the unit.

Be sure to read the Session Follow-Up section at the end of the session block to see what homework assignments and extensions are suggested as you make your initial plans.

While you may be used to a curriculum that tells you exactly what each class session should cover, we have found that the teacher is in a better position to make these decisions. Each unit is flexible and may be handled somewhat differently by every teacher. While we provide guidance for how many sessions a particular group of activities is likely to need, we want you to be active in determining an appropriate pace and the best transition points for your class. It is not unusual for a teacher to spend more or less time than is proposed for the activities.

Activities The activities include pair and small-group work, individual tasks, and whole-class discussions. In any case, students are seated together, talking and sharing ideas during all work times. Students most often work cooperatively, although each student may record work individually.

Choice Time In most units, some sessions are structured with activity choices. In these cases, students may work simultaneously on different activities focused on the same mathematical ideas. Students choose which activities they want to do, and they cycle through them. You will need to decide how to set up and introduce these activities and how to let students make their choices. Some

---

Sessions 1 and 2

Drawing Geoblocks

Materials

- Geoblocks (4 half-sets)
- Prepared Geoblock buildings (1 per 4 students)
- Drawing materials
- Ways to Draw Blocks (about 6 for the class)
- Student Sheet 28 (1 per student, homework)

What Happens

Students build small constructions with Geoblocks and then draw what they built as accurately as they can. They discuss what was easy and difficult about making a 2-D picture of a 3-D object and talk about what makes a picture look 3-D. Students trade their pictures and build constructions to match the pictures. Their work focuses on:

- observing and describing characteristics of 3-D shapes
- making a 2-D representation of a 3-D object
- building a 3-D construction from a 2-D representation

Activity

Drawing a Geoblock Building

Set up the small buildings, made with 3–5 Geoblocks, where students can see to draw them. If students are sitting at tables, set up one building at each table. If students sit at individual desks, push desks together in groups of four for this activity. It's not necessary for every building to be identical, but each should include a variety of blocks that are quite different from each other. For example:

100 ■ *Investigation 3: Building a Block Town*

---

teachers set up choices as stations around the room, while others post the list of available choices and allow students to collect their own materials and choose their own work space. You may need to experiment with a few different structures before finding a setup that works best for you.

Extensions These follow-up activities are opportunities for some or all students to explore a topic in greater depth or in a different context. They are not designed for "fast" students; mathematics is a multifaceted discipline, and different students will want to go further in different investigations. Look for and encourage the sparks of interest and enthusiasm you see in your students, and use the extensions to help them pursue these interests.

Excursions Some of the *Investigations* units include excursions—blocks of activities that could be omitted without harming the integrity of the unit. This is one way of dealing with the great depth and variety of elementary mathematics—much more than a class has time to explore in any one year. Excursions give you the flexibility to make different choices from year to year, doing the excursion in one unit this time, and next year trying another excursion.

Tips for the Linguistically Diverse Classroom At strategic points in each unit, you will find concrete suggestions for simple modifications of the teaching strategies to encourage the participation of all students. Many of these tips offer alternative ways to elicit critical thinking from students at varying levels of English proficiency, as well as from other students who find it difficult to verbalize their thinking.

The tips are supported by suggestions for specific vocabulary work to help ensure that all students can participate fully in the investigations. The Preview for the Linguistically Diverse Classroom (p. I-20) lists important words that are assumed as part of the working vocabulary of the unit. Second-language learners will need to become familiar with these words in order to understand the problems and activities they will be doing. These terms can be incorporated into students' second-language work before or during the unit. Activities that can be used to present the words are found in the appendix, Vocabulary Support for Second-Language Learners (p. 135). In addition, ideas for making connections to students' language and cultures, included on the Preview page, help the class explore the unit's concepts from a multicultural perspective.

Classroom Routines Activities in counting, exploring data, and understanding time and changes are suggested for routines in the grade 1 *Investigations* curriculum. Routines offer ongoing work with this important content as a regular part of the school day. Some routines provide more practice with content presented in the curriculum; others extend the curriculum; still others explore new content areas.

Plan to incorporate a few of the routine activities into a standard part of your daily schedule, such as morning meeting. When opportunities arise, you can also include routines as part of your work in other subject areas (for example, keeping a weather chart for science). Most routines are short and can be done whenever you have a spare 10–15 minutes, such as before lunch or recess or at the end of the day.

You will need to decide how often to present routines, what variations are appropriate for your class, and at what points in the day or week you will include them. A reminder about classroom routines is included on the first page of each investigation. Whatever routines you choose, your students will gain the most from these routines if they work with them regularly.

Materials

A complete list of the materials needed for teaching this unit is found on p. I-16. Some of these materials are available in kits for the *Investigations* curriculum. Individual items can also be purchased from school supply dealers.

Classroom Materials In an active mathematics classroom, certain basic materials should be available at all times: interlocking cubes, pencils, unlined paper, graph paper, calculators, and things to count with. Some activities in this curriculum require scissors and glue sticks or tape. Stick-on notes and large paper are also useful materials

throughout. So that students can independently get what they need at any time, they should know where these materials are kept, how they are stored, and how they are to be returned to the storage area. Many teachers have found that stopping 5 minutes before the end of each session so that students can finish their work and clean up is helpful in maintaining classroom materials. You'll find that establishing such routines at the beginning of the year is well worth the time and effort.

Technology Calculators are introduced to students in the first unit of the grade 1 sequence, *Mathematical Thinking at Grade 1*. By freely exploring and experimenting, students become familiar with this important mathematical tool.

Computer activities at grade 1 use a software program, called *Shapes*, that was developed especially for the *Investigations* curriculum. This program is introduced in the geometry unit, *Quilt Squares and Block Towns*. Using *Shapes*, students explore two-dimensional geometry while making pictures and designs with pattern block shapes and tangram pieces.

Although the software is linked to activities only in the geometry unit, we recommend that students use it throughout the year. Thus, you may want to introduce it when you introduce pattern blocks in *Mathematical Thinking at Grade 1*. How you use the computer activities depends on the number of computers you have available. Suggestions are offered in the geometry unit for how to organize different types of computer environments.

Children's Literature Each unit offers a list of suggested children's literature (p. I-16) that can be used to support the mathematical ideas in the unit. Sometimes an activity is based on a specific children's book, with suggestions for substitutions where practical. While such activities can be adapted and taught without the book, the literature offers a rich introduction and should be used whenever possible.

Student Sheets and Teaching Resources Student recording sheets and other teaching tools needed for both class and homework are provided as reproducible blackline masters at the end of each

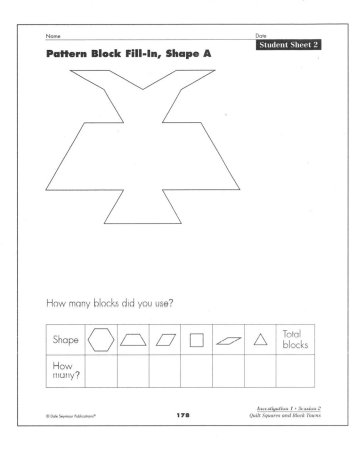

unit. They are also available as Student Activity Booklets. These booklets contain all the sheets each student will need for individual work, freeing you from extensive copying (although you may need or want to copy the occasional teaching resource on transparency film or card stock, or make extra copies of a student sheet).

We think it's important that students find their own ways of organizing and recording their work. They need to learn how to explain their thinking with both drawings and written words, and how to organize their results so someone else can understand them. For this reason, we deliberately do not provide student sheets for every activity. Regardless of the form in which students do their work, we recommend that they keep a mathematics notebook or folder so that their work is always available for reference.

Homework In *Investigations,* homework is an extension of classroom work. Sometimes it offers review and practice of work done in class, sometimes preparation for upcoming activities, and sometimes numerical practice that revisits work in earlier units. Homework plays a role both in supporting students' learning and in helping inform families about the ways in which students in this curriculum work with mathematical ideas.

Depending on your school's homework policies and your own judgment, you may want to assign more homework than is suggested in the units. For this purpose you might use the practice pages, included as blackline masters at the end of this unit, to give students additional work with numbers.

For some homework assignments, you will want to adapt the activity to meet the needs of a variety of students in your class: those with special needs, those ready for more challenge, and second-language learners. You might change the numbers in a problem, make the activity more or less complex, or go through a sample activity with those who need extra help. You can modify any student sheet for either homework or class use. In particular, making numbers in a problem smaller or larger can make the same basic activity appropriate for a wider range of students.

Another issue to consider is how to handle the homework that students bring back to class—how to recognize the work they have done at home without spending too much time on it. Some teachers hold a short group discussion of different approaches to the assignment; others ask students to share and discuss their work with a neighbor, or post the homework around the room and give students time to tour it briefly. If you want to keep track of homework students bring in, be sure it ends up in a designated place.

Investigations at Home It is a good idea to make your policy on homework explicit to both students and their families when you begin teaching with *Investigations*. How frequently will you be assigning homework? When do you expect homework to be completed and brought back to school? What are your goals in assigning homework? How independent should families expect their children to be? What should the parent or guardian's role be? The more explicit you can be about your expectations, the better the homework experience will be for everyone.

Investigations at Home (a booklet available separately for each unit, to send home with students) gives you a way to communicate with families about the work students are doing in class. This booklet includes a brief description of every session, a list of the mathematics content emphasized in each investigation, and a discussion of each homework assignment to help families more effectively support their children. Whether or not you are using the *Investigations* at Home booklets, we expect you to make your own choices about homework assignments. Feel free to omit any and to add extra ones you think are appropriate.

Family Letter A letter that you can send home to students' families is included with the blackline masters for each unit. Families need to be informed about the mathematics work in your classroom; they should be encouraged to participate in and support their children's work. A reminder to send home the letter for each unit appears in one of the early investigations. These letters are also available separately in Spanish, Vietnamese, Cantonese, Hmong, and Cambodian.

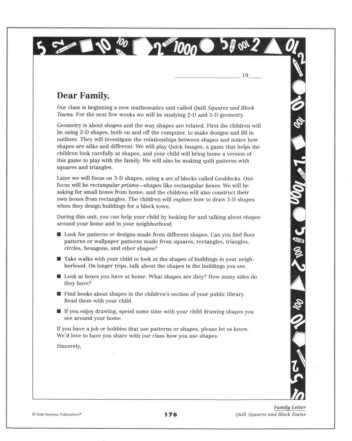

Help for You, the Teacher

Because we believe strongly that a new curriculum must help teachers think in new ways about mathematics and about their students' mathematical thinking processes, we have included a great deal of material to help you learn more about both.

About the Mathematics in This Unit This introductory section (p. I-17) summarizes the critical information about the mathematics you will be teaching. It describes the unit's central mathematical ideas and how students will encounter them through the unit's activities.

Teacher Notes These reference notes provide practical information about the mathematics you are teaching and about our experience with how students learn. Many of the notes were written in response to actual questions from teachers, or to discuss important things we saw happening in the field-test classrooms. Some teachers like to read them all before starting the unit, then review them as they come up in particular investigations.

Dialogue Boxes Sample dialogues demonstrate how students typically express their mathematical ideas, what issues and confusions arise in their thinking, and how some teachers have guided class discussions. These dialogues are based on the extensive classroom testing of this curriculum; many are word-for-word transcriptions of recorded class discussions. They are not always easy reading; sometimes it may take some effort to unravel what the students are trying to say. But this is the value of these dialogues; they offer good clues to how your students may develop and express their approaches and strategies, helping you prepare for your own class discussions.

Where to Start You may not have time to read everything the first time you use this unit. As a first-time user, you will likely focus on understanding the activities and working them out with your students. Read completely through each investigation before starting to present it. Also read those sections listed in the Contents under the heading Where to Start (p. vi).

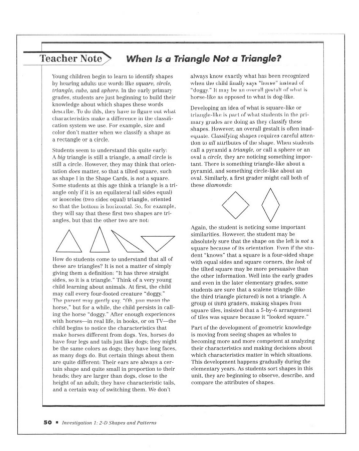

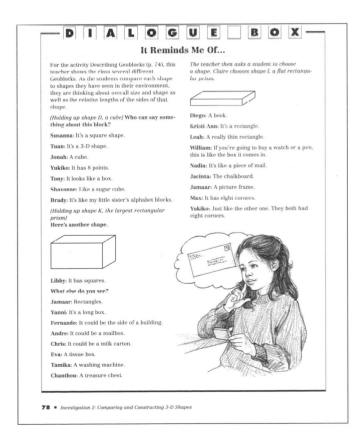

The *Investigations* curriculum incorporates the use of two forms of technology in the classroom: calculators and computers. Calculators are assumed to be standard classroom materials, available for student use in any unit. Computers are explicitly linked to one or more units at each grade level; they are used with the unit on 2-D geometry unit at each grade, as well as with some of the units on measuring, data, and changes.

Using Calculators

In this curriculum, calculators are considered tools for doing mathematics, similar to pattern blocks or interlocking cubes. Just as with other tools, students must learn both *how* to use calculators correctly and *when* they are appropriate to use. This knowledge is crucial for daily life, as calculators are now a standard way of handling numerical operations, both at work and at home.

Using a calculator correctly is not a simple task; it depends on a good knowledge of the four operations and of the number system, so that students can select suitable calculations and also determine what a reasonable result would be. These skills are the basis of any work with numbers, whether or not a calculator is involved.

Unfortunately, calculators are often seen as tools to check computations with, as if other methods are somehow more fallible. Students need to understand that any computational method can be used to check any other; it's just as easy to make a mistake on the calculator as it is to make a mistake on paper or with mental arithmetic. Throughout this curriculum, we encourage students to solve computation problems in more than one way in order to double-check their accuracy. We present mental arithmetic, paper-and-pencil computation, and calculators as three possible approaches.

In this curriculum we also recognize that, despite their importance, calculators are not always appropriate in mathematics instruction. Like any tools, calculators are useful for some tasks, but not for others. You will need to make decisions about when to allow students access to calculators and when to ask that they solve problems without them, so that they can concentrate on other tools and skills. At times when calculators are or are not appropriate for a particular activity, we make specific recommendations. Help your students develop their own sense of which problems they can tackle with their own reasoning and which ones might be better solved with a combination of their own reasoning and the calculator.

Managing calculators in your classroom so that they are a tool, and not a distraction, requires some planning. When calculators are first introduced, students often want to use them for everything, even problems that can be solved quite simply by other methods. However, once the novelty wears off, students are just as interested in developing their own strategies, especially when these strategies are emphasized and valued in the classroom. Over time, students will come to recognize the ease and value of solving problems mentally, with paper and pencil, or with manipulatives, while also understanding the power of the calculator to facilitate work with larger numbers.

Experience shows that if calculators are available only occasionally, students become excited and distracted when they are permitted to use them. They focus on the tool rather than on the mathematics. In order to learn when calculators are appropriate and when they are not, students must have easy access to them and use them routinely in their work.

If you have a calculator for each student, and if you think your students can accept the responsibility, you might allow them to keep their calculators with the rest of their individual materials, at least for the first few weeks of school. Alternatively, you might store them in boxes on a shelf, number each calculator, and assign a corresponding number to each student. This system can give students a sense of ownership while also helping you keep track of the calculators.

Using Computers

Students can use computers to approach and visualize mathematical situations in new ways. The computer allows students to construct and manipulate geometric shapes, see objects move according to rules they specify, and turn, flip, and repeat a pattern.

This curriculum calls for computers in units where they are a particularly effective tool for learning mathematics content. One unit on 2-D geometry at each of the grades 3–5 includes a core of activities that rely on access to computers, either in the classroom or in a lab. Other units on geometry, measurement, data, and changes include computer activities, but can be taught without them. In these units, however, students' experience is greatly enhanced by computer use.

The following list outlines the recommended use of computers in this curriculum:

Grade 1
Unit: *Survey Questions and Secret Rules*
  (Collecting and Sorting Data)
Software: Tabletop, Jr.
Source: Broderbund

Unit: *Quilt Squares and Block Towns*
  (2-D and 3-D Geometry)
Software: *Shapes*
Source: provided with the unit

Grade 2
Unit: *Mathematical Thinking at Grade 2*
  (Introduction)
Software: *Shapes*
Source: provided with the unit

Unit: *Shapes, Halves, and Symmetry*
  (Geometry and Fractions)
Software: *Shapes*
Source: provided with the unit

Unit: *How Long? How Far?* (Measuring)
Software: *Geo-Logo*
Source: provided with the unit

Grade 3
Unit: *Flips, Turns, and Area* (2-D Geometry)
Software: *Tumbling Tetrominoes*
Source: provided with the unit

Unit: *Turtle Paths* (2-D Geometry)
Software: *Geo-Logo*
Source: provided with the unit

Grade 4
Unit: *Sunken Ships and Grid Patterns*
  (2-D Geometry)
Software: *Geo-Logo*
Source: provided with the unit

Grade 5
Unit: *Picturing Polygons* (2-D Geometry)
Software: *Geo-Logo*
Source: provided with the unit

Unit: *Patterns of Change* (Tables and Graphs)
Software: *Trips*
Source: provided with the unit

Unit: *Data: Kids, Cats, and Ads* (Statistics)
Software: Tabletop, Sr.
Source: Broderbund

The software provided with the *Investigations* units uses the power of the computer to help students explore mathematical ideas and relationships that cannot be explored in the same way with physical materials. With the *Shapes* (grades 1–2) and *Tumbling Tetrominoes* (grade 3) software, students explore symmetry, pattern, rotation and reflection, area, and characteristics of 2-D shapes. With the *Geo-Logo* software (grades 3–5), students investigate rotations and reflections, coordinate geometry, the properties of 2-D shapes, and angles. The *Trips* software (grade 5) is a mathematical exploration of motion in which students run experiments and interpret data presented in graphs and tables.

We suggest that students work in pairs on the computer; this not only maximizes computer resources but also encourages students to consult, monitor, and teach one another. Generally, more than two students at one computer find it difficult to share. Managing access to computers is an issue for every classroom. The curriculum gives you explicit support for setting up a system. The units are structured on the assumption that you have enough computers for half your students to work on the machines in pairs at one time. If you do not have access to that many computers, suggestions are made for structuring class time to use the unit with five to eight computers, or even with fewer than five.

Assessment plays a critical role in teaching and learning, and it is an integral part of the *Investigations* curriculum. For a teacher using these units, assessment is an ongoing process. You observe students' discussions and explanations of their strategies on a daily basis and examine their work as it evolves. While students are busy recording and representing their work, working on projects, sharing with partners, and playing mathematical games, you have many opportunities to observe their mathematical thinking. What you learn through observation guides your decisions about how to proceed. In any of the units, you will repeatedly consider questions like these:

■ Do students come up with their own strategies for solving problems, or do they expect others to tell them what to do? What do their strategies reveal about their mathematical understanding?

■ Do students understand that there are different strategies for solving problems? Do they articulate their strategies and try to understand other students' strategies?

■ How effectively do students use materials as tools to help with their mathematical work?

■ Do students have effective ideas for keeping track of and recording their work? Does keeping track of and recording their work seem difficult for them?

You will need to develop a comfortable and efficient system for recording and keeping track of your observations. Some teachers keep a clipboard handy and jot notes on a class list or on adhesive labels that are later transferred to student files. Others keep loose-leaf notebooks with a page for each student and make weekly notes about what they have observed in class.

Assessment Tools in the Unit

With the activities in each unit, you will find questions to guide your thinking while observing the students at work. You will also find two built-in assessment tools: Teacher Checkpoints and embedded Assessment activities.

Teacher Checkpoints The designated Teacher Checkpoints in each unit offer a time to "check in" with individual students, watch them at work, and ask questions that illuminate how they are thinking.

At first it may be hard to know what to look for, hard to know what kinds of questions to ask. Students may be reluctant to talk; they may not be accustomed to having the teacher ask them about their work, or they may not know how to explain their thinking. Two important ingredients of this process are asking students open-ended questions about their work and showing genuine interest in how they are approaching the task. When students see that you are interested in their thinking and are counting on them to come up with their own ways of solving problems, they may surprise you with the depth of their understanding.

Teacher Checkpoints also give you the chance to pause in the teaching sequence and reflect on how your class is doing overall. Think about whether you need to adjust your pacing: Are most students fluent with strategies for solving a particular kind of problem? Are they just starting to formulate good strategies? Or are they still struggling with how to start? Depending on what you see as the students work, you may want to spend more time on similar problems, change some of the problems to use smaller numbers, move quickly to more challenging material, modify subsequent activities for some students, work on particular ideas with a small group, or pair students who have good strategies with those who are having more difficulty.

Embedded Assessment Activities Assessment activities embedded in each unit will help you examine specific pieces of student work, figure out what it means, and provide feedback. From the students' point of view, these assessment activities are no different from any others. Each is a learning experience in and of itself, as well as an opportunity for you to gather evidence about students' mathematical understanding.

The embedded assessment activities sometimes involve writing and reflecting; at other times, a discussion or brief interaction between student and teacher; and in still other instances, the creation and explanation of a product. In most cases, the assessments require that students *show* what they did, *write* or *talk* about it, or do both. Having to explain how they worked through a problem helps students be more focused and clear in their mathematical thinking. It also helps them realize that doing mathematics is a process that may involve tentative starts, revising one's approach, taking different paths, and working through ideas.

Teachers often find the hardest part of assessment to be interpreting their students' work. We provide guidelines to help with that interpretation. If you have used a process approach to teaching writing, the assessment in *Investigations* will seem familiar. For many of the assessment activities, a Teacher Note provides examples of student work and a commentary on what it indicates about student thinking.

Documentation of Student Growth

To form an overall picture of mathematical progress, it is important to document each student's work in journals, notebooks, or portfolios. The choice is largely a matter of personal preference; some teachers have students keep a notebook or folder for each unit, while others prefer one mathematics notebook, or a portfolio of selected work for the entire year. The final activity in each *Investigations* unit, called Choosing Student Work to Save, helps you and the students select representative samples for a record of their work.

This kind of regular documentation helps you synthesize information about each student as a mathematical learner. From different pieces of evidence, you can put together the big picture. This synthesis will be invaluable in thinking about where to go next with a particular child, deciding where more work is needed, or explaining to parents (or other teachers) how a child is doing.

If you use portfolios, you need to collect a good balance of work, yet avoid being swamped with an overwhelming amount of paper. Following are some tips for effective portfolios:

- Collect a representative sample of work, including some pieces that students themselves select for inclusion in the portfolio. There should be just a few pieces for each unit, showing different kinds of work—some assignments that involve writing, as well as some that do not.

- If students do not date their work, do so yourself so that you can reconstruct the order in which pieces were done.

- Include your reflections on the work. When you are looking back over the whole year, such comments are reminders of what seemed especially interesting about a particular piece; they can also be helpful to other teachers and to parents. Older students should be encouraged to write their own reflections about their work.

Assessment Overview

There are two places to turn for a preview of the assessment opportunities in each *Investigations* unit. The Assessment Resources column in the unit Overview Chart (pp. I-13–I-15) identifies the Teacher Checkpoints and Assessment activities embedded in each investigation, guidelines for observing the students that appear within classroom activities, and any Teacher Notes and Dialogue Boxes that explain what to look for and what types of student responses you might expect to see in your classroom. Additionally, the section About the Assessment in This Unit (p. I-19) gives you a detailed list of questions for each investigation, keyed to the mathematical emphases, to help you observe student growth.

Depending on your situation, you may want to provide additional assessment opportunities. Most of the investigations lend themselves to more frequent assessment, simply by having students do more writing and recording while they are working.

Quilt Squares and Block Towns

Content of This Unit Students observe, describe, compare, classify, represent, and build with 2-D and 3-D shapes. Using pattern blocks and the *Shapes* computer software, students put together shapes to make patterns and designs. As they work with these materials, they learn about the characteristics of a variety of 2-D shapes and the relationships among these shapes. Using a set of Shape Cards, they sort and describe groups of shapes.

Students work with 3-D objects and a variety of 2-D representations of those objects. They match Geoblocks to 2-D outlines of their faces, to pictures, and to drawings. They investigate rectangular prisms, including boxes they collect and boxes that they construct from different sizes of rectangles. They make their own drawings of Geoblock buildings and plan and construct a town made from Geoblocks. Students also work with directions and paths as they plan routes through their town. Throughout these activities, students develop vocabulary for naming and describing 2-D and 3-D shapes.

Connections with Other Units If you are doing the full-year *Investigations* curriculum in the grade 1 sequence, this is the fourth of six units. In the introductory unit, *Mathematical Thinking at Grade 1,* students explored some of the geometric materials used in this unit, including pattern blocks and Geoblocks. The work with patterns in that unit is continued here as students create repeating quilt designs. Counting and adding pattern blocks in their designs connects to strategies for addition problems that students encountered in *Building Number Sense* and will continue working on in *Number Games and Story Problems.* Students will work further with measuring lengths of paths in the unit *Bigger, Taller, Heavier, Smaller.*

This unit also can be used successfully at grade 2, depending on the previous experience and needs of your students.

Investigations Curriculum ▪ Suggested Grade 1 Sequence

Mathematical Thinking at Grade 1 (Introduction)

Building Number Sense (The Number System)

Survey Questions and Secret Rules (Collecting and Sorting Data)

▶ *Quilt Squares and Block Towns* (2-D and 3-D Geometry)

Number Games and Story Problems (Addition and Subtraction)

Bigger, Taller, Heavier, Smaller (Measuring)

Investigation 1 ■ 2-D Shapes and Patterns

Class Sessions	Activities	Pacing
Session 1 (p. 5) WHAT SHAPES DO YOU SEE?	Talking About 2-D and 3-D Shapes Drawing Classroom Objects Homework: Draw an Object	minimum 1 hr
Session 2 (p. 13) SAME SHAPE, DIFFERENT PIECES	Sharing Homework Pattern Block Shapes	minimum 1 hr
Sessions 3, 4, 5, and 6 (p. 17) DESCRIBING 2-D SHAPES	Quick Images with Shapes Choice Time How Many Pattern Blocks? Homework: Looking for Shapes	minimum 4 hr
Session 7 (p. 31) THREE WAYS TO FILL AN OUTLINE	Three Ways to Fill an Outline Teacher Checkpoint: How Many Blocks Did You Use?	minimum 1 hr
Sessions 8, 9, and 10 (p. 34) FILLING SHAPES	Quick Images Choice Time Finding the Most and Fewest Blocks Homework: Quick Images with Shapes Extension: Filling with the Same Block Extension: Quick Images with Pattern Blocks	minimum 3 hr
Sessions 11 and 12 (p. 43) SORTING 2-D SHAPES	Guess My Rule with Shape Cards Assessment: Sorting with Shape Cards Sharing the Shape Posters Triangles on the Shape Cards	minimum 2 hr
Sessions 13, 14, and 15 (p. 56) QUILTS WITH SQUARES AND TRIANGLES	Quick Images Looking at Quilt Patterns Designing a Quilt Square Creating a Quilt Pattern	minimum 3 hr

Classroom Routines (see pp. 127–134)

Mathematical Emphasis

- Observing, describing, and comparing 2-D shapes
- Developing vocabulary to describe 2-D shapes
- Grouping shapes according to common characteristics
- Becoming familiar with the names of 2-D shapes
- Composing and decomposing shapes
- Noticing relationships between shapes
- Using rotation and reflection to arrange shapes
- Filling a certain region with shapes
- Visualizing and representing 2-D shapes
- Counting and adding
- Building a pattern by repeating a unit square

Assessment Resources

Observing the Students (pp. 14, 22, 37)

"7 and 2 Is 9 and 1 Is 10" (Dialogue Box, p. 30)

Assessment: Sorting with Shape Cards (p. 44)

When Is a Triangle Not a Triangle? (Teacher Note, p. 50)

Sorting the Shape Cards (Teacher Note, p. 51)

What's a Triangle? (Dialogue Box, p. 54)

Materials

Pattern blocks

Paper pattern blocks

Computers with *Shapes* software installed

Crayons

Glue sticks or paste

Counters

Overhead projector, pens

Student Sheets 1–24

Teaching resource sheets

Family letter

Investigation 2 ▪ Comparing and Constructing 3-D Shapes

Class Sessions	Activities	Pacing
Sessions 1 and 2 (p. 65) DESCRIBING AND COMPARING SHAPES	Describing Geoblocks Choice Time Homework: Mystery Footprints	minimum 2 hr
Session 3 (p. 73) BLOCK PICTURES	Sharing Mystery Footprints from Home Describing Geoblocks Introducing Block Pictures Teacher Checkpoint: Block Pictures Homework: Boxes for Our Collection	minimum 1 hr
Sessions 4, 5, and 6 (p. 80) BLOCKS IN A SOCK	Introducing Blocks in a Sock Choice Time Homework: Mystery Objects Extension: Mystery Objects in Class	minimum 3 hr
Session 7 (p. 85) WHAT KIND OF BOX IS IT?	Looking at Mystery Boxes How Many Sides? Making Boxes with Cards Extension: Paper Boxes	minimum 1 hr
Sessions 8, 9, and 10 (p. 90) MAKING BOXES	Making Boxes with Cards Comparing Cardboard Boxes Revealing the Mystery Boxes Extension: Making Boxes with Cubes	minimum 3 hr

Classroom Routines (see pp. 127–134)

Mathematical Emphasis

- Observing, describing, and comparing 3-D shapes

- Creating and using 2-D representations of 3-D shapes

- Developing vocabulary for describing 3-D shapes

- Constructing 3-D shapes from 2-D faces

- Visualizing and describing rectangular prisms

Assessment Resources

Observing the Students (pp. 69, 83, 91)

Teacher Checkpoint: Block Pictures (p. 75)

Comparing Blocks to Pictures (Dialogue Box, p. 79)

Students Create Their Own Boxes (Teacher Note, p. 96)

Materials

Interlocking cubes

Geoblocks

Stick-on notes

Small bags or socks

Clear tape

Scissors

Index cards, 3 by 5 inches and 5 by 8 inches

Envelopes

Trays or boxes

Student Sheets 25–27

Teaching resource sheets

Investigation 3 ▪ Building a Block Town

Class Sessions	Activities	Pacing
Sessions 1 and 2 (p. 100) DRAWING GEOBLOCKS	Drawing a Geoblock Building Building and Drawing Building from Pictures Homework: Draw a Building Extension: Building from a Plan Extension: Using Objects with Curved Sides Extension: 2-D Pictures of 3-D Constructions	minimum 2 hr
Sessions 3 and 4 (p. 109) PLANNING A TOWN	What Buildings Have You Seen? What Kind of Buildings Do We Need? Designing Buildings for Our Town Extension: Buildings Around the World	minimum 2 hr
Session 5 (p. 113) BUILDING A TOWN	Names for Our Town Describing Our Buildings Assessment: Putting Up Our Buildings Naming Our Town Extension: A Story About Our Town	minimum 1 hr
Sessions 6 and 7 (p. 119) GIVING DIRECTIONS	Robot Paths in the Classroom Paths Through Town Long Paths and Short Paths Choosing Student Work to Save Homework: Robot Paces Extension: Short and Long Robot Paths Extension: Robot Paces in Bigger Spaces Extension: A New Town Grid	minimum 2 hr

Classroom Routines (see pp. 127–134)

Mathematical Emphasis

- Observing and describing 3-D shapes

- Creating and using 2-D representations of 3-D shapes

- Building 3-D constructions from 2-D representations

- Visualizing, describing, and comparing paths between two locations

- Visualizing and describing direction of turns

Assessment Resources

Observing the Students (p. 116)

Students Draw in 3-D (Teacher Note, p. 106)

Making It Look 3-D (Dialogue Box, p. 108)

Assessment: Putting Up Our Buildings (p. 114)

Materials

Geoblocks

Drawing materials

Index cards, 5 by 8 inches (or half-sheets of paper)

Toy people or cars, or small blocks, counters

Student Sheets 28–29

Teaching resource sheets

Following are the basic materials needed for the activities in this unit. Many items can be purchased from the publisher, either individually or in the Teacher Resource Package and the Student Materials Kit for grade 1. Detailed information is available on the *Investigations* order form. To obtain this form, call toll-free 1-800-872-1100 and ask for a Dale Seymour customer service representative.

Pattern blocks: 1 bucket per 6–8 students

Paper pattern blocks: class set

Geoblocks: 2 sets per classroom

Interlocking cubes: 20 per student

Computers: Macintosh II or above, with 4 MB of internal memory (RAM) and Apple System Software 7.0 or later.

Apple Macintosh disk, *Shapes—Quilt Squares /Block Towns* (packaged with this book)

Overhead projector and overhead pens

Index cards: 200 of the 3-by-5-inch size, 100 of the 5-by-8-inch size

Collection of familiar objects with a variety of shapes, for example: a paper cup, a baseball, a book, a candle, a salt shaker, a roll of paper towels, a crayon

Small bags or socks (1 per pair)

Small blocks or counters (1 per pair)

Trays or boxes (7 for the class)

Large paper, 11 by 17 inches or larger (1 sheet per pair)

Half sheets of paper or index cards (5 by 8 inches): 1 per pair

Crayons

Scissors

Clear tape or masking tape (several rolls)

Envelopes, at least 5 by 8 inches (1 per pair)

Glue sticks or paste

String or ribbon (about 12 feet)

Stick-on notes

The following materials are provided at the end of this unit as blackline masters. A Student Activity Booklet containing all student sheets and teaching resources needed for individual work is available.

Family Letter (p. 176)

Student Sheets 1–29 (p. 177)

Teaching Resources:

    Pattern Block Cutouts (p. 201)

    Shape Cards (p. 207)

    Combination Shapes (p. 210)

    Geoblock Footprints (p. 214)

    Geoblock Pictures (p. 221)

    Ways to Draw Blocks (p. 227)

    Street Grid (p. 228)

Practice Pages (p. 229)

Related Children's Literature

Books About Shapes

Burns, Marilyn. *The Greedy Triangle*. New York: Scholastic, 1994.

Felix, Monique. *The House*. Columbus, OH: American Educational Publishing, 1993.

Friedman, Aileen. *A Cloak for the Dreamer*. New York: Scholastic, 1994.

Hoban, Tana. *Shapes, Shapes, Shapes*. New York: Greenwillow Books, 1986.

Rogers, Paul. *The Shapes Game*. New York: Holt, 1989.

Books About Quilts

Jonas, Ann. *The Quilt*. New York: Greenwillow Books, 1984.

Paul, Ann Whitford. *Eight Hands Round: A Patchwork Alphabet*. New York: Harper Collins, 1991.

Books About Buildings

Angelou, Maya. *My Painted House, My Friendly Chicken, and Me*. New York: Clarkson Potter, 1994.

Cooper, Jason. *Skyscrapers: Man-Made Wonders*. Vero Beach, FL: Rourke Enterprises, 1991.

Dorros, Arthur. *This Is My House*. New York: Scholastic, 1992.

Karavasil, Josephine. *Houses and Homes Around the World*. Minneapolis: Dillon Press, 1986.

Morris, Ann. *Houses and Homes*. New York: Lothrop, Lee & Shepard, 1992.

Seltzer, Isadore. *The House I Live In: At Home in America*. New York: Macmillan, 1992.

Zelver, Patricia. *The Wonderful Tower of Watts*. New York: Tambourine Books, 1994.

Geometry is a part of mathematics that students experience every day. Shapes, angles, motions, and patterns are everywhere in the child's world. Part of young students' work in developing mathematical understandings is to begin to observe, describe, compare, and represent the shapes they see around them.

This unit emphasizes careful observation and description of geometric shapes. When students first learn to identify shapes, they usually depend on an overall picture of what different shapes look like. A square is a square because it has a "squarish" look. Students can identify something as a square before they can say exactly why it *is* a square. They may not yet be able to articulate that a square has four sides, that the four sides are equal, and that the shape has a particular kind of angle, but they have an overall sense of what looks square. However, if they see a square that is turned 45 degrees so that one of its corners is pointed down, they may say that it is a diamond, not a square, because it no longer looks "squarish." We might say to these students, "No, see, it has four equal sides and square corners. Look what happens if I turn it this way. It's a square." However, first and second grade students may still adhere to their belief that this is an entirely different shape. As students use 2-D and 3-D shapes in this unit, they engage in activities that require them to begin to take a closer look at shapes. What makes a square a square? How are squares different from triangles?

Students in the primary grades are just beginning work on identifying and describing shapes. In this unit, they look for shapes in their own environment and they work with several sets of 2-D and 3-D shapes. Students don't complete this work in these grades. In fact, students much older than first or second grade are still working on how to define and classify shapes. A primary goal for this unit is to engage all students in looking carefully at shapes, describing them, and seeing similarities and differences. When they sort shapes, they make groups of shapes that "go together." They describe these groups and justify why a shape goes in one group and not in another. Students often don't use the conventional classifications, and they may develop categories that seem unusual to adults. Nonetheless, through justifying why certain shapes go together, students are learning to carefully observe, describe, and compare shapes.

Another emphasis in this unit is how shapes can go together or be taken apart to make other shapes. Students at this age are learning relationships among numbers by pulling them apart and putting them back together: 10 can be broken up into 5 and 5 or into 6 and 4. Similarly, they are learning about geometric relationships by composing and decomposing shapes. They become familiar with many equivalencies in the pattern block set: a hexagon can be broken up into six triangles; a rhombus and a triangle can be put together to make a trapezoid. When they try to fill in an outline with a certain number of pattern blocks, students need to break apart or combine shapes to get the target number of blocks. The Geoblock set also has many blocks that can be put together to make other blocks: two cubes can be put together to make a rectangular prism; two triangular prisms can be put together to make a cube. As students work with these materials, they become more aware of relationships among shapes. Look for evidence that students are thinking about these relationships as they come up with their own ideas:

"A trapezoid is a triangle with the top cut off."

"If you put two squares together, you get a rectangle."

As students use triangles and rectangles to make quilt patterns or use the Duplicate or Glue tools on the computer, they have the opportunity to build a unit out of shapes and then repeat that unit to create a pattern. These activities provide further experience in how shapes can go together to create other shapes and patterns.

Students also investigate the relationship between 3-D shapes and 2-D representations of those shapes. Through matching 3-D objects to their outlines, to pictures, and to drawings, they learn about identifying shapes by looking carefully at some parts of the shape and then visualizing what the whole shape must look like. When they draw their own representations of 3-D blocks and buildings, they have to pay attention to the parts of these shapes and how they are put together. As students draw their buildings, they are encouraged to think carefully about the shapes and relative sizes of the blocks. By constructing their own boxes out of different sizes of rectangles, they explore how a rectangular prism (a box shape) is made out of pairs of congruent rectangles that form the opposite sides of the prism. Moving back and forth between 3-D objects and 2-D representations helps students describe and compare the characteristics of common 3-D shapes.

Finally, this unit introduces students to the idea of motion through space. As they plan short "trips" through their classroom and on maps of the class town, they estimate distance, choose directions, and decide how to turn to change directions.

Throughout the unit, as students become more familiar with geometric shapes and their relationships, they begin to be able to visualize these. Visualization of geometric relationships provides an important part of the foundation for working with geometric models in a wide range of mathematical content, including whole numbers, fractions, operations, area, and volume.

Mathematical Emphasis At the beginning of each investigation, the Mathematical Emphasis section tells you what is most important for students to learn about during that investigation. Many of these understandings and processes are difficult and complex. Students gradually learn more and more about each idea over many years of schooling. Individual students will begin and end the unit with different levels of knowledge and skill, but all will learn more about the geometric shapes, their relationships, and their properties.

Throughout the *Investigations* curriculum, there are many opportunities for ongoing daily assessment as you observe, listen to, and interact with students at work. In this unit, you will find two Teacher Checkpoints:

> Investigation 1, Session 7:
> How Many Blocks Did You Use? (p. 32)
>
> Investigation 2, Session 3:
> Block Pictures (p. 75)

This unit also has two embedded assessment activities:

> Investigation 1, Sessions 11 and 12:
> Sorting with Shape Cards (p. 44)
>
> Investigation 3, Session 5: Putting Up Our Buildings (p. 114)

In addition, you can use almost any activity in this unit to assess your students' needs and strengths. Listed below are questions to help you focus your observations in each investigation. You may want to keep track of your observations for each student to help you plan your curriculum and monitor students' growth.

Investigation 1: 2-D Shapes and Patterns

■ Are students noticing attributes of 2-D shapes? Do they observe and describe straight sides and curved sides, the number of sides or corners in a shape?

■ Are students developing vocabulary to describe and compare 2-D shapes? Are they learning to use some conventional terms for shapes as well as descriptive terms based on their own experience?

■ Do students become flexible in filling in outlines with shapes? Are they able to use equivalencies among shapes, for example, substituting six triangles for a hexagon, to change their designs?

■ Are students beginning to describe shapes in terms of their relationships to each other? For example, do they see a trapezoid as a "triangle with the top cut off" or notice that they can put two squares together to make a rectangle?

■ Do students use similarities and differences among shapes to group them? Are students able to describe their categories? How do students justify which shapes do or don't fit in their groups?

Investigation 2: Comparing and Constructing 3-D Shapes

■ Are students noticing attributes of 3-D shapes? Do they observe and describe the shapes of the faces, the number of faces, their relative sizes?

■ Can students match 3-D shapes to 2-D representations of those shapes, including outlines, pictures, and drawings? How do students represent 3-D shapes on paper? How do they represent 3-D shapes in a way that someone else can understand?

■ Are students developing vocabulary to describe and compare 3-D shapes? Are they learning some conventional terms for shapes as well as descriptive terms based on their own experience?

■ Are students able to construct a box (a rectangular prism) by putting its faces together? What ideas do they have about how flat pieces become the faces of 3-D shapes?

■ Are students able to describe some of the common features of a rectangular prism, such as the number and shapes of its faces?

Investigation 3: Building a Block Town

■ Do students notice that some 3-D shapes have triangular faces, some have rectangular faces, and some have both? Do they describe how some blocks are the same shape, but different sizes? Are they developing vocabulary to describe both size and shape?

■ Do students find ways of representing a 3-D shape in an understandable way on paper? How do their drawings show differences in size and shape among blocks?

■ Can students interpret 2-D drawings of 3-D constructions reasonably?

■ Can students describe a path between two locations? Can they reasonably estimate or count the number of steps in the classroom or "blocks" on a map? Can they visualize and describe which way to turn to go in a different direction?

In the *Investigations* curriculum, mathematical vocabulary is introduced naturally during the activities. We don't ask students to learn definitions of new terms; rather, they come to understand such words as *triangle, add, compare, data,* and *graph* by hearing them used frequently in discussion as they investigate new concepts. This approach is compatible with current theories of second-language acquisition, which emphasize the use of new vocabulary in meaningful contexts while students are actively involved with objects, pictures, and physical movement.

Listed below are some key words used in this unit that will not be new to most English speakers at this age level, but may be unfamiliar to students with limited English proficiency. You will want to spend additional time working on these words with your students who are learning English. If your students are working with a second-language teacher, you might enlist your colleague's aid in familiarizing students with these words, before and during this unit. In the classroom, look for opportunities for students to hear and use these words. Activities you can use to present the words are given in the appendix, Vocabulary Support for Second-Language Learners (p. 135).

shape, straight, curved Although students will learn many shape names during this unit, they need some basic vocabulary to describe common shapes.

lowest, highest, fewest, most As students compare the number of pattern blocks used to fill in shape outlines, they identify the lowest and highest number of blocks, and whether these are the fewest and most possible blocks.

building, town Students look at buildings in their neighborhood, decide what buildings they need to make for a class town, and then construct block buildings to make the town.

Multicultural Extensions for All Students

■ When students work on quilt patterns in Investigation 1, select books that show quilt patterns from a variety of cultures.

■ Make a poster with some of the common shape names—square, circle, triangle—written in all the languages represented in your classroom. Work with your class to learn all the ways to say these shapes.

■ In Investigation 3, show pictures of houses and other buildings from different parts of the world. Ask students to bring in pictures of buildings from parts of the world where they or their families have lived. Some resources are suggested in the list of related children's literature (p. I-16).

■ When planning the class town, take into account the variety of cultures of the students in the class. Encourage students to talk about places and buildings in the community that are important to them and their families.

Investigations

2-D Shapes and Patterns

What Happens

Session 1: What Shapes Do You See? As an introduction to the unit, the class discusses the shapes of things in their classroom. Each student chooses an object to draw and describe.

Session 2: Same Shape, Different Pieces Students find different ways to fill a shape with pattern blocks. They record which pattern blocks they use, how many of each shape, and the total number of blocks used.

Sessions 3, 4, 5, and 6: Describing 2-D Shapes In the Quick Images activity, students try to draw shapes and discuss how to describe them. During Choice Time, students again fill shapes with pattern blocks. They also make designs with a specified number of blocks. Using the *Shapes* software, students create pattern block designs on the computer. Two class discussions focus on strategies for finding the total number of blocks used to fill an outline.

Session 7: Three Ways to Fill an Outline Given an outline of a pattern block design, students find two or three different ways to fill it. The class discusses the different numbers of blocks they used and the most and least blocks that would fill a particular outline.

Sessions 8, 9, and 10: Filling Shapes The class repeats Quick Images with shapes. For Choice Time, students continue to fill outlines with pattern blocks, on paper and on the computer.

Sessions 11 and 12: Sorting 2-D Shapes The class plays Guess My Rule with the Shape Cards, sorting the shapes according to two rules. Then, as an assessment, students work in pairs to sort the Shape Cards and make a poster to show their favorite way of sorting. Finally they discuss what a triangle is, and identify which of the Shape Cards are triangles.

Sessions 13, 14, and 15: Quilts with Squares and Triangles Students design quilt squares using squares and triangles and repeat their squares to create quilt designs, both on paper and on the computer. The class again works on Quick Images with single and combination shapes. A discussion about their quilt patterns ends the investigation.

Routines Refer to the section About Classroom Routines (pp. 127–134) for suggestions on integrating into the school day regular practice of mathematical skills in counting, exploring data, and understanding time and changes.

Mathematical Emphasis

- Observing, describing, and comparing 2-D shapes
- Developing vocabulary to describe 2-D shapes
- Grouping shapes according to common characteristics
- Becoming familiar with the names of 2-D shapes
- Composing and decomposing shapes
- Noticing relationships between shapes (e.g., a hexagon can be made from six triangles)
- Using rotation and reflection to arrange shapes
- Filling a certain region with shapes
- Visualizing and representing 2-D shapes
- Counting and adding
- Building a pattern by repeating a unit square

What to Plan Ahead of Time

Materials

- Books about shapes (Session 1, optional)
- Pattern blocks: 1 bucket per 6–8 students (Sessions 2–10)
- Paper pattern blocks or stickers (Sessions 2–10)
- Crayons (Sessions 1–10, 13–15)
- Glue sticks or paste (Sessions 2–12)
- Counters: class supply (Sessions 3–6)
- Computers with *Shapes* software installed (Sessions 3–6, 8–10, 13–15)
- Overhead projector (Sessions 3–15)
- Transparent overhead pattern block shapes (Sessions 7–10, optional)
- Piece of string or ribbon (about 12 feet) or draw a large circle on paper (Session 11)
- Chart paper or other large paper, at least 18 by 24 inches (Sessions 11–12, 1 sheet per pair)
- Overhead pens in 2 colors (Sessions 13–15)
- Stories about quilts; books with quilt patterns (Sessions 13–15, optional)

Other Preparation

- Collect familiar objects in a variety of shapes, for example: a paper cup, a ball, a book, a candle, a salt shaker, a roll of paper towels, a crayon. (Session 1)
- Before Session 2, familiarize yourself with the pattern blocks. If you have not used the materials before, spend some time exploring them.

- If you do not have manufactured paper pattern blocks or stickers, duplicate pages 201–206 on construction paper in the appropriate colors and enlist adult help in cutting apart the shapes.
- Install *Shapes* on each available computer. Read and try the activities presented in the *Shapes* tutorial (p. 137). See the Teacher Note, Introducing *Shapes* Software (p. 28), for suggestions on introducing the software to your class. (Sessions 3–10, 13–15)
- Make about a dozen "quilt frames" to help students color their quilt designs. Cut a square hole in the center of an index card, making the hole very slightly larger than 2 inches on each side. (Sessions 13–15)

- Duplicate the following student sheets and teaching resources, located at the end of this unit. If you have Student Activity Booklets, copy only items marked with an asterisk.

For Session 1

Student Sheet 1, Draw an Object (p. 177): 1 per student, homework

Family letter (p. 176): 1 per student

For Session 2

Student Sheet 2, Pattern Block Fill-In, Shape A (p. 178): 1–2 per student

Continued on next page

For Sessions 3–6

Shape Cards (pp. 207–209): 1 set of transparencies,* cut apart

Student Sheets 3–6, Pattern Block Fill-In, Shapes B–E (pp. 179–182): 1 of each per student

Student Sheets 7–10, Pattern Block Counts A–D (pp. 183–186): 1 of each per student

For Session 7

Student Sheet 11, Different Ways to Fill, Shapes A (p. 187): 1–2 per pair

For Sessions 8–10

Student Sheets 12–15, Different Ways to Fill, Shapes B–E (pp. 188–191): 1 per pair, plus some extras, and 1 transparency* of Shapes D

Student Sheet 16, Quick Images (p. 192): 1 per student, homework

Student Sheet 17, Shapes for Quick Images (p. 193): 1 per student, homework

Combination Shapes (p. 210): 1 transparency,* cut apart.

For Sessions 11–12

Shape Cards (pp. 207–209): 1 set per pair, cut apart

For Sessions 13–15

Student Sheet 18, Quilt Squares (p. 194): 1–2 per student, and 1 transparency*

Student Sheets 19–24, Quilt Patterns A–F (pp. 195–200): copy an assortment; each student will choose 1 or 2; plus 1 transparency* of Quilt Pattern A

■ If you plan to provide folders in which students will save their work for the entire unit, prepare these for distribution.

What Shapes Do You See?

What Happens

As an introduction to the unit, the class discusses the shapes of things in their classroom. Each student chooses an object to draw and describe. Their work focuses on:

- noticing shapes in their environment
- using informal language to describe geometric shapes
- becoming familiar with the names of 2-D and 3-D shapes

Materials

- Unlined paper and crayons
- Children's books about shapes (optional)
- A set of familiar objects displayed on a table
- Student Sheet 1 (1 per student, homework)
- Family letter (1 per student)

Activity

For the next few weeks, we're going to be learning about a part of mathematics called geometry. Who can tell us something about geometry?

Geometry includes the study of shapes and their relationships, patterns, and symmetry, as well as turns, angles, and other motions in space. Listen to students' ideas about geometry, then use one or both of the following approaches to introduce this unit on shapes:

- **Books of Shapes** There are many children's books about shapes (see p. I-16 for a list). If you have one, read it aloud to your class as a way of introducing the unit and getting students to think about shapes in their environment. As you show the pictures, ask students what shapes they see and what objects in the classroom some of the shapes remind them of.

  The book *Shapes* by John J. Reiss (Bradbury Press, 1974; out of print but available in libraries) shows colorful pictures of squares, cubes, triangles, pyramids, circles, spheres, rectangles, ovals, and other shapes, along with pictures of familiar objects made of these shapes. You can ask students what other objects they can think of that have each shape. This book is an especially good introduction to the unit because it includes both 2-D and 3-D shapes.

Talking About 2-D and 3-D Shapes

■ **Drawing Shapes** Sketch several shapes, one at a time, on the board or overhead. Ask students what objects each shape reminds them of. For example, when you sketch a cylinder, students might think of a drinking glass, a chimney, or a pretzel stick.

Other shapes you might draw include a cube, a cone, a rectangular prism (a box shape), a sphere (like a ball), or a hemisphere (like a ball cut in half).

See the **Teacher Notes,** Types of 2-D Shapes (p. 10) and Types of 3-D Shapes (p. 71), for background information on the kinds of shapes students will encounter in this unit and for definitions of terms that may be unfamiliar to you.

If you have or can borrow a set of solid geometric shapes (wood or plastic), you might show these shapes instead of drawing them. (Geoblocks have prisms, but lack cylinders, cones, spheres, and other shapes that are good for this activity.)

Whichever approach you take, try to present a variety of both 2-D and 3-D shapes for students to consider. As students think about familiar objects in terms of their shapes, they begin to form mental images of different shapes. As they hear you and other students use vocabulary about these shapes, they begin to develop meaning for the words that name and describe shapes.

One important way your students acquire vocabulary about geometric shapes is by hearing you use these words frequently. Throughout this unit, be alert to ways you can use shape names correctly in context. For example, as one teacher organized students for a class meeting, he said, "Everyone come and sit in a circle on the rug." Then he paused and added, "Actually, it's more of an *oval*, isn't it?"

See the **Teacher Notes,** Types of 2-D Shapes (p. 10), and Types of 3-D Shapes (p. 71), to review names for 2-D and 3-D shapes so that you can use them correctly in context as they come up. Keep in mind that learning geometric vocabulary is not simply a matter of memorizing the names of objects. Understanding that a word such as *triangle* or *sphere* describes an entire class of objects is a long process that is just begun in this unit. The **Dialogue Box,** Talking about Shapes (p. 12), demonstrates the kind of discussion that helps students gradually acquire ways to describe, compare, and name shapes. The **Teacher Note,** When Is a Triangle Not a Triangle? (p. 50), describes how students begin to develop meaning for shape names.

Drawing Classroom Objects

Explain that students are going to be drawing something in the room, paying particular attention to its shape. Draw attention to the objects you have collected (for example, a paper cup, a ball, a book, a candle, a salt shaker, a roll of paper towels, a crayon, and so forth). Ask them to look for other objects in the room that have a special shape, either like shapes they saw in the previous activity or other shapes.

When you think students have enough ideas, hand out drawing materials. Each student chooses one object in the classroom, draws it, and writes a sentence or two about its shape.

As you watch students work, engage them in conversation about the shapes of their objects. If they are having a hard time thinking about what to write, ask them to describe the object to you in words. Accept students' own vocabulary. For example, one student described a crayon box by pointing to its edges and saying, "It's got lines like this." Another student, describing a cube, said "It has boxes on it," meaning the square faces.

Many students will use words for 2-D and 3-D shapes interchangeably, for example, calling a cube a *square* or a sphere a *circle*. Accept their wording and encourage them to write down their own descriptions in their own words. However, continue to use shape names correctly yourself as they come up in the discussion.

Pensil

The Pensil is oval witha triangal on top.

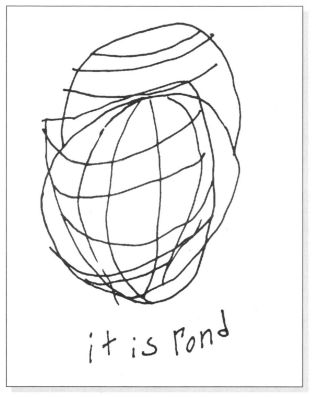

it is rond

Some students may become interested in counting the corners and edges, as shown in the first grader's drawing of a dot cube (opposite page). Encourage students to think about how many corners (or "points") and edges (or "lines") certain shapes have, even though they may not always count correctly. First grade students begin to notice, for example, that all "boxes" have eight corners.

You will undoubtedly have a wide range of drawing and writing ability in your class, from students who can copy objects quite well to students who find it very difficult. Help students choose objects that are simple enough for them to draw. For example, for a student who is struggling, you might suggest a penny or an apple. Some students may want to trace around their objects.

You may want to end this session or begin the next one with a discussion of what techniques students use to draw a 3-D object on a flat piece of paper. Students are interested in describing what makes a two-dimensional picture look three-dimensional. As one student put it, it "pops out at you." Students will continue this discussion and do more activities that involve creating and using 2-D representations of 3-D shapes in Investigation 3.

Homework

Draw an Object Distribute Student Sheet 1, Draw an Object. Students choose an object at home to draw and write about in the same way that they did in class. Students who are not comfortable writing their descriptions may get help from a family member.

❖ **Tip for the Linguistically Diverse Classroom** Family members may record their children's responses in their native language.

Also send home the signed family letter or the *Investigations* at Home booklet to introduce your work in this unit.

1. it has dots
2. it has five boxis.
3. it has 9 lines
4. it has 8 Korners

One of the important ways your students acquire vocabulary about geometric shapes is to hear you use words about shapes correctly in context. In this unit, students encounter many 2-D and 3-D shapes by using the pattern blocks, the Geoblocks, and the Shape Cards, as well as identifying shapes they encounter in their environment. Our society has developed a particular classification system for shapes, and shapes are named according to this system. Here is some information to help you review the conventions of classifying 2-D shapes.

Two-dimensional shapes are split into two major groups: shapes called *polygons* and shapes that are *not* polygons. All simple closed shapes with straight sides are polygons. ("Simple" shapes are shapes with sides that don't cross each other.)

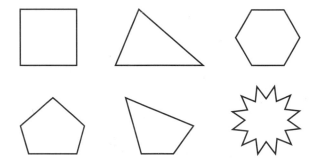

Students will also encounter closed shapes that are not polygons. These shapes have all or some curved sides, such as circles, ovals, or semicircles.

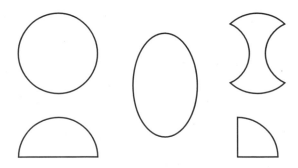

Polygons are further classified by the number of their sides.

Number of sides	Name of polygon	Examples
3	triangle	
4	quadrilateral	
5	pentagon	
6	hexagon	
7	heptagon	
8	octagon	
9	nonagon	
10	decagon	

For a straight-sided shape, the number of sides determines what it is called, no matter how odd the shape may be. Shapes with equal sides are called *regular* or *equilateral* (a regular shape also has all angles equal, while an equilateral shape may not); shapes with unequal sides are *irregular*. For example, here are a regular hexagon, like the one in the pattern block set, and two irregular hexagons.

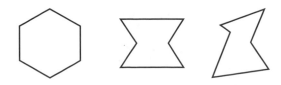

Quadrilaterals are divided into a number of categories, some of which overlap with or are contained in others. The most familiar category to you and your students is probably *rectangles*. These are quadrilaterals with four 90° or right angles. A *square* is an equilateral rectangle: a rectangle with four equal sides. Many of your students, as well as many older students, have a hard time thinking of a square as a rectangle. Don't make an issue of this for your primary grade students. However, if the opportunity arises, help students notice what attributes of squares and rectangles are the same (they have four straight sides and four "square corners").

Other quadrilaterals you will encounter are the two rhombuses in the pattern block set. A *rhombus* is a quadrilateral with equal sides, no matter what the angles are. (Since a square must have equal sides, it is also a rhombus, so there are actually three rhombuses in the pattern block set.)

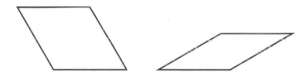

The other quadrilateral in the pattern block set is a *trapezoid*. A trapezoid is a quadrilateral with exactly one pair of parallel sides. (By an alternative definition, a trapezoid is a quadrilateral with *at least* one pair of parallel sides.) The other quadrilaterals in the pattern block set—the square and the two rhombuses—are all *parallelograms,* with two pairs of parallel sides.

As students use the Shape Cards and the pattern blocks, they will develop some of this vocabulary as they hear you use it. However, it is fine for students to use other informal language of their own, such as *diamond* for rhombus.

Notice that in this unit, we usually name the pattern block shapes as if they were two-dimensional, even though they actually have three dimensions. The block we call a *square* is not actually a square; it is a rectangular prism. (See the **Teacher Note,** Types of 3-D Shapes, p. 71, for more information about prisms and other 3-D shapes.) Since the pattern blocks are all the same thickness, most activities involving them focus attention only on one face of the block—the triangle, square, rhombus, trapezoid, or hexagon. The convention is to name the blocks by these faces, which is both convenient and sensible for the way they are used. However, your students may notice that they are, in fact, 3-D shapes.

Talking About Shapes

This class is looking at a book about shapes. They have just looked at a page of circular objects.

What other things are shaped like circles?

Leah: The magnets on my refrigerator at home.

Tamika: There are circles on Susanna's shirt.

Donte: A ring is a circle.

Jamaar: An eight has two circles in it.

Nadia: And a zero.

[The teacher draws an eight and a zero on the board.]

Actually, what is the shape of a zero? It's not quite a circle.

Luis: An oval.

Who can say what an oval is?

Mia: It's a squooshed circle.

Claire: It's curvy but not as much.

[The teacher turns the page to show pictures of spheres.]

When circles are three-dimensional, they're called *spheres*. Can you think of anything that's a sphere?

Diego: I don't know what a sphere is, but I know what else is a circle.

What?

Diego: A clock and a watch.

OK, good additions to our circle list. Does anyone know something that's a sphere?

Nathan: Well, heads, sort of.

Shavonne: I think a ball is a sphere.

Do you agree with Shavonne? Is a ball a sphere?

Kaneisha: Yes. I think a sphere is round with no corners.

Like a circle?

Kaneisha: But not flat. It takes up a lot more space.

William: Our globe is a sphere.

Garrett: Your glasses are ovals!

Kristi Ann: A gum ball is a circle.

What shape would you say a gum ball is?

Jacinta: No, it's not a circle because it's not flat. It's that other word. I forget.

Who remembers the 3-D shape that's sort of like a circle, but isn't flat? The shape like a ball?

Several students: A sphere.

Making clear distinctions between 2-D and 3-D shapes is difficult, even for older students. Using terms such as *flat* and *solid* may be helpful.

Same Shape, Different Pieces

What Happens

Students find different ways to fill a shape with pattern blocks. They record which pattern blocks they use, how many of each shape, and the total number of blocks used. Their work focuses on:

- filling an outline with shapes
- finding combinations of shapes that fill a region
- counting and adding

Materials

- Pattern blocks
- Student Sheet 2 (1–2 per student)
- Paper pattern blocks and glue sticks or paste, or pattern block stickers, or crayons

---

Activity

Spend a few minutes sharing students' drawings of objects at home. One way to include all students in a short period of time is to do a quick sort: Have one student hold up and describe the picture he or she drew. Then ask any students who have a picture that is similar in shape to stand with that student and hold up their pictures.

So Fernando drew his baseball, and he says it's kind of round. Michelle says it's like a globe. Did anyone else draw something that is kind of round or like a globe?

Next ask for a picture that is very different in shape and start a new group; students with pictures that are similar in shape join that student and all hold up their pictures. Gradually sort all the pictures in the classroom into several groups of shapes that go together.

Sharing Homework

Activity

If your students are familiar with pattern blocks, they will only need a brief introduction to get started on this activity. If they have not used pattern blocks much this year, arrange for some free exploration time before you begin this activity, so that students become familiar with the pattern block shapes and how they fit together. You might also add time for free exploration with pattern block shapes, on and off the computer, during Choice Time in Sessions 3–6. See the **Teacher Note,** Pattern Block Shapes (p. 16), for more information.

Pattern Block Shapes

Students use the pattern blocks to fill in the shape on Student Sheet 2, Pattern Block Fill-In, Shape A. Students may work alone or in pairs, depending on your supply of pattern blocks. If you have enough blocks, you may want to let students make the choice to work alone or with another student.

When they have filled in the outline, students record their work by gluing paper pattern blocks or putting stickers in the shapes, or by tracing the outlines of their blocks and coloring in. (If you have pattern block templates, some students can successfully use them to record designs, although others at this age find it difficult to use a template.) In the chart, students fill in how many of each kind of block and the total number of blocks they used.

Students who finish one pattern can take another copy of Student Sheet 2 and find a different way to fill in the outline.

Observing the Students

Observe and talk with students during this first experience filling in shapes with pattern blocks to get a sense of how they use the blocks to fill in an outline and how they record their work.

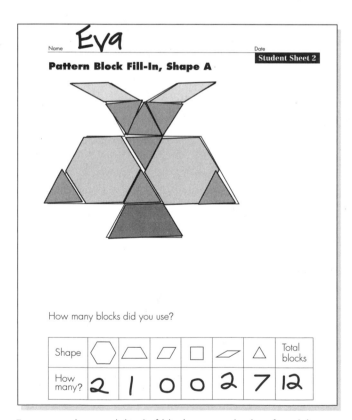

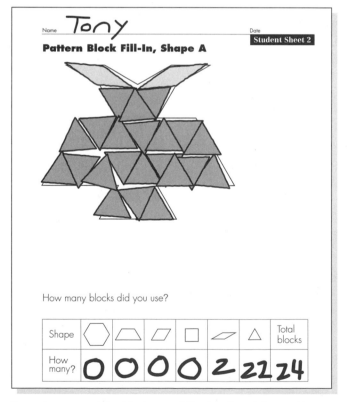

Eva counted up each kind of block accurately, then found the total this way: "7 + 2 is 8, 9, and 2 more is 10, 11, then 1 is 12."

Tony also counted the blocks carefully, then found the total by adding 2 onto 22.

- Do students easily find shapes to fill in different parts of the outline? For example, do they see immediately that the "ears" at the top of the shape on Student Sheet 2 can be filled with tan rhombuses? Do they see that a trapezoid can fill the bottom section of the outline?

- Do students seem fluent in finding ways to fit shapes together in the interior of the outline where it is not so obvious which shapes to choose?

- Do you see evidence that students know how to make the same shape in different ways? For example, do some students fill the trapezoidal shape with three triangles or with a blue rhombus and a triangle?

- Can students find ways to keep track of how many of each kind of pattern block they used? Do they double-check their counts?

- How do students find the total number of blocks? Do they count all the blocks by 1's? Do they use the numbers in the chart? How do they add the numbers in the chart?

If some students have difficulty finding ways to fill in the outline and don't have a sense of how to put together shapes to make other shapes, give them opportunities to freely explore the pattern blocks, either during Choice Time in Sessions 3–6 or at other times during the school day.

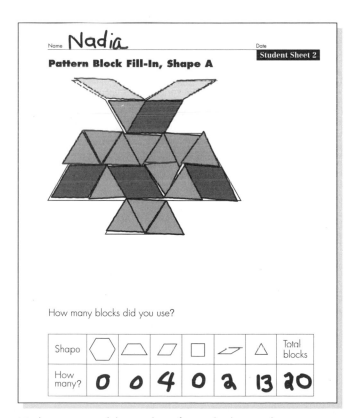

Shape	⬡	▱	◇	☐	▱	△	Total blocks
How many?	0	0	4	0	2	13	20

Nadia miscounted the number of triangles but got the correct total by recounting all the blocks in the design.

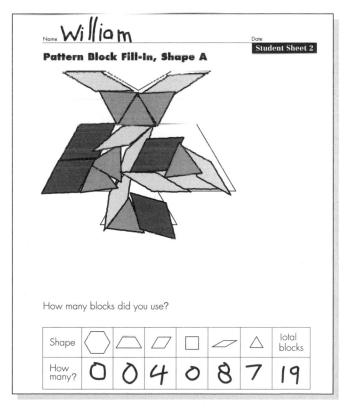

Shape	⬡	▱	◇	☐	▱	△	Total blocks
How many?	0	0	4	0	8	7	19

William had difficulty fitting blocks into the outline and found it hard to record what he did. However, he counted the shapes accurately and figured out the total by starting with 4, then counting on 8, and then 7, by 1's.

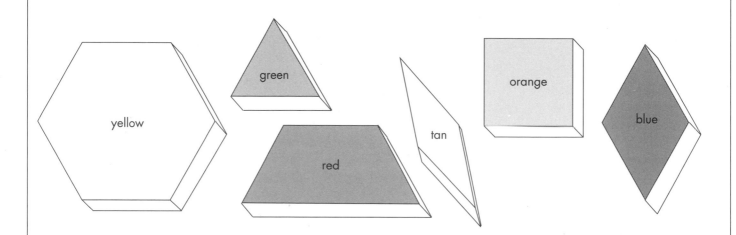

The pattern block set is made up of six shapes: a hexagon, a trapezoid, a square, a triangle, and two rhombuses. In most sets each shape comes in one color: the hexagons are yellow; the trapezoids are red; the squares are orange; the triangles are green; the narrower rhombuses are tan; and the wider rhombuses are blue. Since all pattern blocks of the same color are the same shape, it is very natural for students to identify them by color. In fact, teachers and students often name the blocks by using both color and shape, for example, "the yellow hexagon," "the orange square."

Many first grade students easily identify the green block as a triangle and the orange block as a square. The terms *trapezoid* and *hexagon* will be new to many first graders. They will learn to use the terms readily if you use them consistently yourself and help them remember the words when they forget. Young children typically refer to the blue and tan blocks as diamonds. This is fine, and there's no need to stop students from using this familiar term. As long as they are communicating effectively, let them use the language they are comfortable with while you continue to model the correct language. These shapes are both parallelograms and rhombuses. The pattern

block convention is to call them "the tan rhombus" and "the blue rhombus," because that identifies these shapes more precisely, focusing on their four equal sides. Following this convention, we identify these blocks as rhombuses in this unit. (See the **Teacher Note,** Types of 2-D Shapes, on p. 10 for more about the classification of 2-D shapes.)

The pattern block set provided in the computer software with this unit, *Shapes,* which students begin using in Sessions 3–6, includes the six standard pattern block shapes and a seventh shape, a quarter circle. The straight sides of the quarter circle are the same length as the sides of the square, so that it fits easily with the other shapes. The addition of the quarter circle extends students' exploration of shape to include semicircles, circles, and other curved shapes.

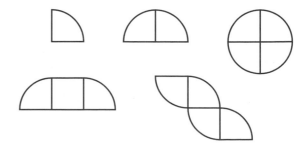

Describing 2-D Shapes

What Happens

In the Quick Images activity, students try to draw shapes and discuss how to describe them. During Choice Time, students again fill shapes with pattern blocks. They also make designs with a specified number of blocks. Using the *Shapes* software, students create pattern block designs on the computer. Two class discussions focus on strategies for finding the total number of blocks used to fill an outline. Students' work focuses on:

- visualizing and representing 2-D shapes
- filling an outline with shapes
- finding combinations of shapes that fill an area
- fitting shapes together or breaking them apart to make other shapes
- counting and adding
- visualizing what shape to select to continue a design
- visualizing how to move a shape so that it is oriented correctly to fit into a design

Organizing These Sessions

How you organize these sessions will depend on your computer setup. Here are some options to help you plan:

- **With Computers in the Classroom** Follow the investigation structure as written. That is, begin Sessions 3 and 4 with whole-group work on Quick Images, then spend the remainder of each session on Choice Time, including the computer activity. Choice Time continues through Sessions 5 and 6; at the end of each of these sessions, you hold whole-group discussions on finding the total number of blocks used in designs (How Many Pattern Blocks? p. 25).

- **With a Computer Lab** You will offer no computer work during Choice Time in Sessions 3, 4, and 6. Instead, everyone works in the lab on the computer activities for all of Session 5. Move up the first whole-group discussion to the end of Session 4.

- **With No Access to Computers** Reduce Choice Time to three sessions and hold the whole-group discussions at the end of Sessions 4 and 5.

A chart of these options appears on the following page. For further ideas, see the **Teacher Note,** Managing the Computer Activities (p. 29).

Materials

- Shape Card transparencies
- Overhead projector
- Pattern blocks
- Student Sheets 3–6 (1 of each per student)
- Student Sheets 7–10 (1 of each per student)
- Paper pattern blocks and glue sticks or paste, or pattern block stickers, or crayons
- Counters (available)
- Computers with *Shapes* software installed

	Session 3	Session 4	Session 5	Session 6
Computers in the classroom (4 sessions)	Quick Images Choice Time (including computers)	Quick Images Choice Time (including computers)	Choice Time (including computers) Discussion: How Many Pattern Blocks?	Choice Time (including computers) Discussion: How Many Pattern Blocks?
Access to a computer lab (4 sessions)	Quick Images Choice Time (no computers)	Quick Images Choice Time (no computers) Discussion: How Many Pattern Blocks?	Computer lab: Free Explore in Shapes	Choice Time (no computers) Discussion: How Many Pattern Blocks?
No access to computers (3 sessions)	Quick Images Choice Time (no computers)	Quick Images Choice Time (no computers) Discussion: How Many Pattern Blocks?	Choice Time (no computers) Discussion: How Many Pattern Blocks?	

Activity

Quick Images with Shapes

Quick Images was introduced in the *Investigations* unit *Building Number Sense*. If you have presented that unit, your students have played Quick Images with dot patterns and will need only a brief introduction here. This time they will be looking at *shapes* instead of dots.

Students need to have pencil and paper and a surface on which they can draw. From the Shape Card transparencies, select a familiar shape, such as a square or circle. Advise students to put their pencils down and watch carefully because you will show the shape for just a few seconds; then you will hide it and they will try to draw the shape they saw.

Note: Quick Images is designed for use with an overhead projector, but if none is available, you can sketch the shape on the chalkboard or on chart paper, then cover it or flip the paper over to hide the image.

Show the shape for about 5 seconds—no more. Then turn off the projector to hide the shape and ask students to quickly sketch what they saw. When students are ready, show them the shape for another 5 seconds while they put their pencils down and look carefully again. They can then revise their shape based on their second look. Finally, turn on the projector and leave the image visible while students make any final revisions to their drawing.

When students have finished, ask them to describe the shape.

What did you notice about the shape? Libby says it's a square. Who can say more about that? How did you know it's a square? Who can say something else about this shape?

Try one more shape that you think will be fairly easy for your students. Repeat the same procedure. Ask the same questions again when students have finished drawing.

Next try a somewhat more difficult shape, perhaps the semicircle or the right triangle. After students have had two looks at the shape, ask the same questions as you did before. In addition, ask:

What did you notice the first time you saw the shape? Could you remember the whole shape? What happened when you saw the shape the second time? Did that help you add anything or change anything?

Before going on to the next activity, display a few more shapes on the overhead and ask students what they know about them. (Don't do Quick Images; just show the shapes individually.) This will give you a chance to assess which shapes students recognize and which shape names they know. For more information, see the **Teacher Note,** Looking at the Shape Cards (p. 27).

At the beginning of Session 4, repeat Quick Images. Use shapes you didn't use the first time. Note what vocabulary students use to describe the shapes, which shapes seem familiar to them, and which are less familiar.

Choice Time

If you are using the complete grade 1 sequence of *Investigations,* students will be familiar with Choice Time, when they choose which of several activities to work on. The Choice Time format recurs throughout the *Investigations* curriculum. See the **Teacher Note,** About Choice Time (p. 40), for information about how to set it up and how first grade students can keep track of the choices they have completed.

For the rest of these sessions, students work on three choices. Post the Choice Time list and help students choose which activity they will work on first.

Choices

1. Pattern Block Fill-Ins

2. Pattern Block Counts

12

3. Shapes on the Computer

The first activity choice was introduced in Session 1 of this investigation. The second choice, Pattern Block Counts, should need only a brief introduction. It is just the reverse of the Pattern Block Fill-In activity: Instead of making a picture and then counting the pattern blocks, students are told the number of pattern blocks to use, and they have to make a design with that number of blocks. Students should spend time on both of these activities during Sessions 3–6.

You will also be introducing the *Shapes* software to your students, either in the classroom or the computer lab. Using this software, students make pattern block designs on the computer screen. As they do this, they will be learning the basic tools of the *Shapes* software. If you have a computer lab with a large demonstration screen, you can demonstrate the basic conventions of the *Shapes* software to the whole group, then circulate as students get started to help them select, move, and erase shapes. If you have a few computers in the classroom, introduce *Shapes* to a small group of students. As some students become proficient, they can help you teach other students how to use the software. See the **Teacher Note,** Introducing the *Shapes* Software (p. 28), for detailed suggestions about how to help students get started.

If your computers are in the classroom so that working with *Shapes* is one of the daily choices, pairs of students should rotate at the computer, giving computer time to as many students as possible. If possible, also allow pairs of students to work on the computer at other times of the day. Some teachers post a list of student pairs next to each computer so that they can keep track of whose turn it is. You will need to set a time limit for each pair, but allow at least 15 or 20 minutes.

Choice 1: Pattern Block Fill-Ins

Materials: Pattern blocks; Student Sheets 3–6, Pattern Block Fill-In Shapes B–E (1 of each per student); paper pattern blocks and glue sticks or paste, or pattern block stickers, or crayons

Students work individually or in pairs. Students choose one of the Pattern Block Fill-In sheets, fill in the shape, then record what they have done with paper pattern blocks or stickers, or by tracing around the blocks. In the chart, they record the number of each kind of pattern block in their design and the total number of blocks they used. If there is time, they may choose additional shapes.

If students keep their work in a folder, they will be able to keep track of which of the sheets they have already worked on. For your own records, you may want to use a class list to record which sheets each student completes, as well as brief comments about the work.

Choice 2: Pattern Block Counts

Materials: Pattern blocks; Student Sheets 7–10, Pattern Block Counts A–D (1 of each per student); paper pattern blocks and glue sticks or paste, or pattern block stickers, or crayons

Students work individually or in pairs, using the total number of pattern blocks indicated on the student sheet to make a design. Some students may need help selecting pieces (not too many hexagons or trapezoids) so that their designs fit on Student Sheets 9 and 10. They then record their design, and record in the chart how many of each kind of pattern block they used. Again, you may want to use a class list to help keep track of which sheets each student chooses to work on.

Choice 3: Shapes on the Computer

Materials: Computers with *Shapes* installed

Students use the Free Explore option to create pattern block designs on the computer screen. As you observe students, ask them to describe what they are doing. Talk to students about the way they are moving the blocks to help them become more aware of the geometric motions they are using. If students don't have time to complete their design in one session, show them how to save their pictures on disk. You might have students walk around to view each other's work so they see a range of possibilities. Students who complete their work may want to print their final design.

Observing the Students

As you watch students using the pattern block shapes, keep in mind that the central goals of this investigation are for students to observe and describe the characteristics of 2-D shapes and to see how 2-D shapes can fit together or be broken apart to make other shapes. Observation of students at work is particularly important in activities like these, because the final result doesn't necessarily tell you how students approached the task. For the Pattern Block Fill-Ins, two completed student sheets from two different students might look identical. However, it could be the case that one student tried lots of ways to fill in the outline, easily substituting one combination of blocks for another, before deciding on a final design, while another student had a very hard time, through trial and error, finding even one way to fill the outline. You can be aware of this contrast only by watching these students at work.

Pattern Block Fill-Ins and Pattern Block Counts These two choices focus on filling in an outlined space with pattern block shapes. As you observe these activities, watch for the following:

■ How flexible are students in choosing pattern blocks to fill an outlined shape?

■ Do students easily recognize which shapes will fill a piece of the outline?

■ When students make a design from a set number of pattern blocks, do they use equivalents among the shapes to help them get the right number in their designs? For example, if they have too many blocks, do they substitute a blue rhombus for two triangles, or, if they have too few blocks, do they substitute three triangles for a trapezoid?

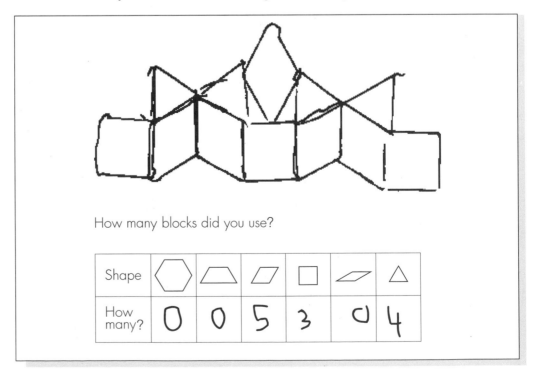

How many blocks did you use?

Shape	⬡	⬠	▱	☐	▱	△
How many?	0	0	5	3	0	4

A student's design using 12 pattern blocks

- How do students organize to record their designs? If they are using paper pattern blocks to record, can they match these to the blocks in the same arrangement, or do they start all over again with the paper shapes and make a new design? Do they fit the shapes together inside the outline, or do they overlap shapes or cut them to make them fit?

- How are students counting their blocks? How do they keep track? How do they know they counted each block once?

- What strategies do students use to find the total number of blocks they used? Do they count the blocks one by one? Do they use the numbers in their chart to help them find the total, or do they count the blocks? If they use the numbers in the chart, do they count on each number by 1's, or do they use some combinations they know to help them add?

Shapes on the Computer Using the *Shapes* software to make designs with pattern block shapes is not altogether the same task as making designs with the physical blocks. While knowledge about the shapes of the pattern blocks and their relationships is still critical, students have to figure out *how to move the blocks* on the screen to create their design. When they need to turn one of the actual blocks so that it fits in the right place, they can physically turn it until it looks right, without needing to describe to themselves what they are doing. They need not be explicit about how much they need to turn the block, nor do they need to work very hard to visualize how to turn it; they can just experiment directly until it looks right. However, when they use the *Shapes* software, students have to make deliberate decisions about moving or turning or flipping a pattern block because they have to select the right tool to make the movement they want. Since it is not so easy to simply try one piece after another to see if it fits in a certain place in their design, students begin to take more time to visualize which shapes they want in what position.

This kind of building encourages students to become more deliberate in planning a design. Instead of just selecting a block randomly and moving it around until it fits somewhere, they start to think about which block they want and how to move it so it is in the right position. Your first graders will still use plenty of trial and error as they move and turn the pieces on the screen. For example, when they rotate a piece, they will probably not think about the difference between directions of rotation or the amount of each turn. They will think about the turns visually, seeing the results of each rotation as they make it and then deciding on further adjustments based on what they see.

As students are ready, you may want to introduce some other tools to them, especially Duplicate, which allows them to make copies of the blocks that are already on the screen. This is especially useful when they have turned a block the way they want it and want another one in the same orientation. By duplicating, they don't have to start all over with a new block. See the **Teacher Note,** Introducing the *Shapes* Software (p. 28), for other tools that you can introduce to students as needed.

As you observe students using the software, the questions to keep in mind are somewhat different from those you consider when watching students with the actual pattern blocks. First, there are some basic questions about learning to use the software:

■ Are students learning how to select blocks, move them across the screen, and turn them?

■ Can students erase an individual block or the whole screen?

Then consider their ability to visualize how the blocks go together:

■ How do students decide what shapes to select? Do they select shapes randomly? Do they begin to plan what shapes they need for their design and select these deliberately?

■ Once a shape has been moved onto the screen, can students figure out how to move it into position? When a shape is in the right position but the wrong orientation for what they want, can they see that it needs to be turned? Do they begin to visualize how they will have to move and turn a shape in order to add it to their design in the way they want? When they have turned a shape one turn, can they use what they see to decide if they need to keep turning it or if they should turn it in the other direction? Do they notice what size corner, or angle, will fit in a particular location?

Students' work from Free Explore in *Shapes,* using a black and white printer. Shavonne added crayon after her picture was printed.

Student's design from Free Explore in the *Shapes* software

How Many Pattern Blocks?

Twice at the end of these Choice Time sessions, gather students to try some numerical problems based on the pattern block designs they have been making. Make available both counters and paper and pencil.

Borrow one student's design and write on the board or overhead how many of each kind of pattern block was used, but don't show the picture itself. For example:

Here is the chart Brady made for one of his pictures. He used 1 hexagon, 1 trapezoid, 4 blue rhombuses, 2 tan rhombuses, and 5 triangles. Brady already figured out how many blocks he used altogether, but I'm not going to tell you his total. You're going to figure it out for yourselves. Work with a partner for a few minutes and see if you can find out how many pattern blocks Brady used.

Students spend a few minutes figuring out the total, working individually or in pairs. Then a few students share their strategies for this problem.

If you have time, present one more problem, using another student's design.

These discussions offer an opportunity for students to use strategies they were developing in the grade 1 unit *Building Number Sense*. Since the numbers on their charts are relatively small, encourage students to develop solutions that build on addition combinations they know. See the **Dialogue Box,** "7 and 2 Is 9 and 1 Is 10" (p. 30), for examples of how one first grade class approached some of these problems.

Sessions 3, 4, 5, and 6 Follow-Up

Homework

Looking for Shapes Students choose one shape from the Shape Cards to look for at home. Some students might pick triangles; others might choose rectangles or circles or semicircles. Give each student a sheet of unlined paper. Before going home, they should draw at the top of their paper the shape they will look for. On this sheet, they can draw or list things with that shape they find at home.

Give this assignment at the end of Session 3 and remind students about it at the end of Session 4. Sometime during Sessions 5 or 6, ask students to share the shapes they found at home. You might give this assignment a second time, challenging students to search for some of the less frequently seen shapes, such as the hexagon, crescent, or trapezoid.

Looking at the Shape Cards

The Shape Cards consist of 18 single shapes, A–R. Another sheet provides six combinations of shapes. You will use all 24 shapes in Quick Images activities with the class, first single shapes, and later the combination shapes. Students will also sort the single shapes.

The 18 single shapes lend themselves to sorting and describing in a number of ways:

■ Some have only straight sides, while others have some curved parts. Two-dimensional shapes that have only straight sides are called *polygons*. Students need not use this term, but having only straight sides or not is one important characteristic they will notice as they sort.

■ Some of the straight-sided shapes (polygons) have three sides, some have four sides, and one has six sides. Polygons with three sides are *triangles*. Polygons with four sides are *quadrilaterals*. Six-sided polygons are called *hexagons*. Students will be familiar with the hexagon from the pattern block shapes.

■ Some shapes have all sides equal, while some shapes have sides that are unequal. Shapes with equal sides are called *equilateral* shapes. In this set of shapes, there is an equilateral triangle, three equilateral rectangles (we call these squares, of course), and an equilateral hexagon. Your students might not recognize that the "tilted" square is a square; they may call it a diamond. Teachers have had some interesting class discussions about whether or not this shape is a square.

■ Some shapes have only square corners (right angles), while some have other angles. Your students might describe shapes with angles that are not right angles as more *slanty* or *pointed*.

■ This set has several different kinds of quadrilaterals, including a trapezoid (a four-sided shape with only one pair of parallel sides). Students will recognize the trapezoid from the pattern block shapes. There is also a rhombus in the set, another shape students have seen in the pattern blocks.

■ There are five triangles of several different kinds. Students often think that only triangles with their bases parallel to the bottom of the paper are really triangles. Sometimes they think that only equilateral or isosceles triangles (two sides equal) are triangles. Encourage students to talk about what is the same and what is different about all the three-sided shapes. See the **Teacher Note,** When Is a Triangle Not a Triangle? (p. 50), for more discussion about how students begin to classify shapes.

The combination shapes each show two or three shapes. You will use these cards for Quick Images in Sessions 8–10 and 13–15. They provide an opportunity for students to describe shapes in relationship to each other:

The triangle is inside the square.

The square is on top of the triangle.

The points of the diamond touch the rectangle right in the middle of its edges.

You may want to make up other combination shapes to use for Quick Images once your students have tried the six in this unit.

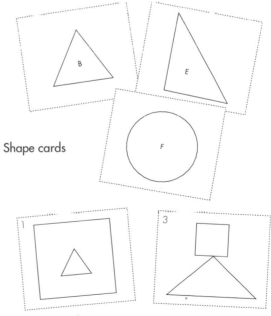

Shape cards

Combination shapes

To introduce the *Shapes* program, gather the students around the largest computer display you have. If your display is small, you may want to introduce the software to smaller groups of students over several days. Tell them that they will build pictures and designs with *Shapes* just the way they do with pattern blocks. For this introduction, demonstrate each of the following on the computer:

■ How to open *Shapes* by double-clicking on the icon.

■ How to open the Free Explore activity by clicking on it once.

■ How to get shapes from the Shapes window.

■ How to slide shapes by dragging them. (Point out that they snap into position when their sides are close.)

■ How to turn shapes with the two Turn tools.

■ How to use the Erase One tool to erase one shape at a time and the Erase All button to erase all the shapes.

Note: For complete instructions, see the *Shapes* Teacher Tutorial (p. 137).

Immediately following your introduction, give student pairs time to use Free Explore in the *Shapes* software to make their own pictures or designs.

Many students who are using computers and the *Shapes* software for the first time will need assistance. Most of their questions can be handled with short answers or simple demonstrations. For example, some students may not be aware of how to use the mouse. Often students who are more familiar with computers can assist those who need help. Encourage students to experiment and see if they can figure out what they need to do, then to share what they've found out with each other and with you. It is not unusual for students to discover things about the software that the teacher doesn't know.

As you observe students using the Free Explore activity, ask them to describe what they are doing. Talk to them about the way they are moving the shapes (sliding them and using the Turn and possibly Flip tools). This will help them become more aware of these geometric motions. Just as important, it will help them become familiar with seeing shapes in different orientations and realizing that changing the orientation does not affect the shape's name or attributes.

You can introduce more of the tools available in *Shapes* as students indicate the need for them. Some of these tools allow students to do things they can't do with the physical pattern blocks:

■ The two Flip tools flip, or reflect, shapes over a vertical or horizontal line. If you select the first flip tool and then click on a shape, the shape flips over a vertical line through the center of the shape.

■ The Duplicate tool makes copies of shapes. If you have already turned a shape so it is in the orientation that you want, you can use Duplicate to get another copy of that shape in the same orientation, rather than having to get and turn or flip a new shape. You can also use the Duplicate tool to make copies of groups of shapes that have been glued (see below).

■ The Arrow tool selects shapes. This is useful if students want to apply a tool or command such as Duplicate or Bring to Front to several shapes at the same time.

■ The Magnification tools make shapes bigger or smaller. First graders enjoy discovering this tool. *Shapes that are different sizes will not snap to each other.*

■ The Glue tool glues several shapes together into a "group," a new composite shape that can be slid, turned, and flipped as a unit.

■ The Hammer breaks apart a glued group with one click. If you hammer a shape (such as a blue rhombus) that is not part of a group, it will break that single shape into smaller shapes (in this case, two green triangles).

If you want to discuss students' work later, they should save their pictures on disk. For information about saving to a disk, see p. 173 in the *Shapes* Teacher Tutorial.

Managing the Computer Activities

In this unit, activities with the *Shapes* software are suggested throughout Investigation 1. How you incorporate these computer activities into your curriculum depends on the number of computers you have available. The activities are included as Choice Time options, but depending on your computer setup, it may not be realistic for students to use the computers during math class. For example, maybe you have a computer lab available to you once a week. Or, if you only have one or two computers in your classroom, you may need to schedule students to work at the computer throughout the day.

Regardless of the number of computers you have, we suggest that students always work in pairs. This not only maximizes computer resources, but also encourages students to consult, monitor, and teach one another. Generally, more than two students at one computer find it difficult to share. If you have an odd number of students, a threesome can be formed.

Computer Lab If you have a computer laboratory with one computer for each pair of students, all your students can do the computer activities at the same time, devoting one or two of the Choice Time sessions to work with *Shapes*.

Student work from Free Explore in *Shapes*

Three to Six Computers If you have several computers in your classroom, this setup will work for Choice Time. You might introduce the *Shapes* software to the whole class, using a large screen monitor or projection device, or to small groups. Then pairs of students can cycle through the computer activities, just as they cycle through the other choices. You may need to monitor computer use more closely than the other choices, to ensure that all students get sufficient computer time. You may need to cycle pairs through the computer choice throughout the school day, instead of just during math class, to give everyone a chance at the computer. Each pair should spend at least 15–20 minutes at the computer for each activity.

One or Two Computers If you have only one or two computers in your classroom, students will need to use the computers throughout the school day so every pair of students has fairly frequent opportunities to do the computer activities.

Using *Shapes* All Year This is the only unit in the grade 1 sequence that explicitly uses the *Shapes* software. However, we recommend that students continue using it for the remainder of the school year. With more experience, they become more fluent in the mechanics of the software itself and can better focus on the designs they want to make and how to select and arrange shapes for those designs. They can explore the tangram shapes as well as the pattern block shapes. Experience with the grade 1 *Shapes* software will benefit students going on to the grade 2 *Investigations* curriculum. Two units in the grade 2 sequence, *Mathematical Thinking at Grade 2* and *Shapes, Halves, and Symmetry*, introduce new activities using the *Shapes* software that build on the grade 1 work.

"7 and 2 Is 9 and 1 Is 10"

This class is looking at the charts of numbers of pattern blocks from some of their Pattern Block Fill-Ins (Student Sheets 2–6). The teacher puts the following chart on the board.

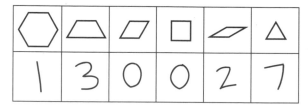

This is Yukiko's chart from one of her fill-ins. See if you can think through, in your head, how many pattern blocks she used. Don't put your hand up, just look ready when you have a way to think about this that you can share.

[After a minute or so of silence, the teacher asks for volunteers to explain their strategies.]

Eva: Start at 7. Then you go 8, 9 *[she raises two fingers]*, 10 *[raising one more finger]*, and then 11, 12, 13 *[raising three more fingers as she counts]*.

Why did you start at 7 and then count 8, 9?

Eva: Because I started with the biggest number, so then I didn't have so many to count. Then I said 8, 9 for the two skinny ones [rhombuses].

OK, who had a different way?

Tuan: I took 3 and 2 and I know that's 5 and 1 more's 6. Then I added 7. I know 7 and 7 is 14, so I took away 1 and it's 13.

Iris: I did it almost the same way as Eva, except I got mixed up. I did 1 *[puts up one finger, then pauses]*, 2, 3, 4 *[puts up three more fingers]*, 5, 6 *[two more fingers]*, so then I was up to here *[holds up 6 fingers]*. I knew I had to add on 7 more, so at first I couldn't do it, but then I used Max's hand. I did 4 more on this hand and then Max did 3 on his hand.

Chris: I started with the 7. Then I put it together with the 2. That would be 9, 7 and 2 would be 9. I skipped the 0's. Then 9 and 1 would be 10, plus 3 would be 13.

OK, that's a lot of different ways. Some of you started with the biggest number and counted up. Some of you found some combinations you already knew to help you get started, like Tuan knew that 3 and 2 is 5. Chris also used what he knew about adding something on to 10. Let's try one more.

Susanna: Well, it's sort of hard to explain. I put my hands out and then I counted in my head, but I had to use two people's hands.

Who can help Susanna explain what she is saying?

Iris: I know. It's like what I did before, when I used Max's hand.

Susanna: But I did it in my head. You kind of look at your hands while you count each number. Then you get to the end and you have to pretend there's another hand.

Yanni: I did 3 plus 4 is 7. Another 7 is 14.

How did you do the 7 plus 7 part?

Yanni: I just know it.

Andre: I have another way: 7 plus 3 is 10, and then I added 4 and I just knew it was the teen number.

Chanthou: I know there are three 0's, so I just skipped them. I know 4 and 4 is 8, so I took one away. Then I know there are two 7's. I didn't know two 7's but I heard Yanni say 7 and 7 is 14.

During this discussion, the teacher was able to observe which students were counting by 1's, which students could add on small numbers easily, which students know some number combinations, and which students know something about adding on to 10.

Three Ways to Fill an Outline

What Happens

Given an outline of a pattern block design, students find two or three different ways to fill it. The class discusses the different numbers of blocks they used and the most and fewest blocks that would fill a particular outline. Students' work focuses on:

- composing and decomposing shapes
- using different combinations of shapes to make the same larger shape
- counting and keeping track
- comparing quantities to see which are more, less, or between other quantities
- altering designs to use more or fewer pieces to cover the same space

Materials

- Pattern blocks (1 bucket per 6–8 students)
- Student Sheet 11 (1–2 per pair)
- Paper pattern blocks and glue sticks or paste, or pattern block stickers, or crayons
- Transparent overhead pattern blocks (optional)
- Overhead projector (optional)

Activity

Three Ways to Fill an Outline

Hand out a copy of Student Sheet 11, Different Ways to Fill, Shape A, to each pair of students. Students use the pattern blocks to fill each copy of the outline in a *different* way. They record each of their ways, using paper shapes or stickers, or drawing and coloring the shapes. They also count the number of blocks they used and for each design write the total on the student sheet.

As you watch students work, notice what kinds of combinations they use. Do they fill in the part of the outline that looks like the hexagon only with the hexagon, or do they sometimes use triangles or trapezoids? For example, do they replace a hexagon with two trapezoids?

As students are working, ask them if they think they can use more or fewer pattern blocks than they have used so far. For example, if you notice that a student has used mostly triangles and rhombuses, ask the student to fill the next outline using fewer pattern blocks. If a student has used a few large pieces, mostly hexagons and trapezoids, ask the student to do the next one with more pieces. If a student has one outline filled with very few blocks and one with very many blocks, you might ask the student to find a way to fill in the third outline with a number *between* the two totals.

Some students may want to try a second copy of the same student sheet, finding three additional completely different ways of filling the outline.

Teacher Checkpoint

How Many Blocks Did You Use?

Teacher Checkpoints are places to stop and gauge how the class as a whole is understanding some of the basic mathematical ideas with which they are working. For more information, see About Assessment (p. I-10).

During this class discussion, as well as during the subsequent work in Sessions 8 and 9, listen to and observe students to see how fluent they are becoming in composing and decomposing shapes. Visualizing how a larger unit can be composed of smaller ones and how shapes can be combined to form larger units is the basis for understanding many geometric ideas, from relationships among polygons to area and volume.

Gather students, asking them to bring their work on Student Sheet 11. Collect data about how many total blocks students used for various designs. As students tell you how many blocks they used for the first outline, record their numbers on the board. Ask if any students had different numbers of blocks in any of their three outlines. Record students' totals until you have all the different ways they found. For example:

5	6
8	12
7	10
14	11

What do you notice about our list of how many blocks you used for this outline? Tell me one thing you notice.

OK, there aren't any numbers in the 20's. Who notices something else?... Mia, you think the lowest number we have is 5. Is she right? Is that the lowest number?

After students have made as many observations as they can, ask:

Do you think that 5 is the fewest blocks we could have in this outline? Why do you think so?

Do you think that 14 is the most blocks we could use to fill this outline? Why do you think so?

Do you think there are other numbers that could be on this list?

If you have the transparent overhead pattern blocks, demonstrate students' ideas. As students show their designs with the lowest and highest numbers, everyone can think about whether changes could be made to make a design using more or fewer blocks.

In this discussion and the subsequent sessions, notice what students know about splitting a pattern block shape into smaller shapes, or combining shapes to make a larger shape. When you ask students about filling the same outline with more or fewer shapes, are they able to reason about whether they can use more or fewer blocks and how they would go about doing so? Which students seem very comfortable with, for example, reasoning that they can substitute six triangles for a hexagon, thereby using more blocks to cover the same space, or replacing triangles with trapezoids, thereby using fewer blocks?

If there is controversy about these questions, encourage students to try filling this outline again with fewer or more blocks during Choice Time in the next session.

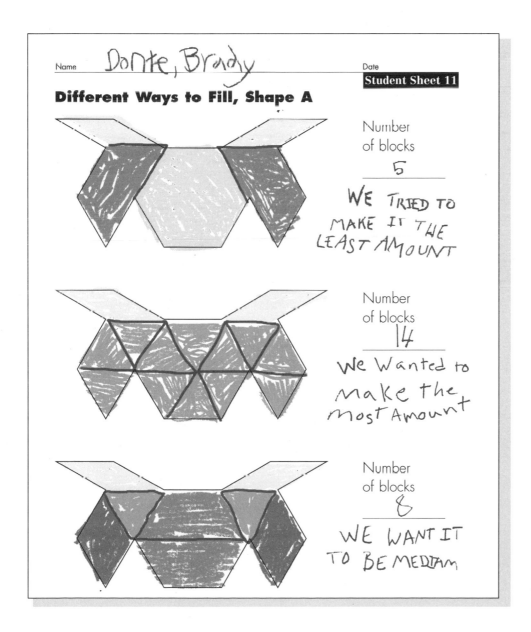

Name Donte, Brady

Date

Student Sheet 11

Different Ways to Fill, Shape A

Number of blocks

5

WE TRIED TO MAKE IT THE LEAST AMOUNT

Number of blocks

14

We Wanted to make the most Amount

Number of blocks

8

WE WANT IT TO BE MEDIUM

Filling Shapes

Materials

- Shape Card transparencies
- Combination Shapes transparencies
- Pattern blocks (1 bucket per 6–8 students)
- Paper pattern blocks and glue sticks or paste, or pattern block stickers, or crayons
- Computers with *Shapes* software installed
- Student Sheets 12–15 (1 of each per pair, plus extras)
- Transparency of Shape D (Student Sheet 14)
- Student Sheets 16–17 (1 of each per student, homework)
- Transparent overhead pattern blocks (optional)
- Overhead projector

What Happens

The class repeats Quick Images with shapes. For Choice Time, students continue to fill outlines with pattern blocks, on paper and on the computer. Their work focuses on:

- composing and decomposing shapes
- using different combinations of shapes to make the same larger shape
- altering designs to use more or fewer pieces to cover the same space
- naming and describing shapes

Organizing These Sessions

These three sessions are primarily Choice Time, as students work with pattern block shapes both on and off the computer. As a whole group, you do Quick Images with shapes at least twice during the session.

How you organize these sessions will depend on your computer setup. If you take your class to the computer lab, you will probably want to add one additional session so that students have the chance to work on the computer more than once. Here are some options to help you plan these sessions:

	Session 8	Session 9	Session 10	Extra Session
Computers in the classroom (3 sessions)	Quick Images Choice Time (including computers)	Quick Images Choice Time (including computers)	Choice Time (including computers) Finding the Most and Fewest Blocks	
Access to a computer lab (4 sessions)	Quick Images Different Ways to Fill (no Choice Time)	Computer lab: Solve Puzzles in *Shapes*	Quick Images Different Ways to Fill (no Choice Time)	Computer lab: Solve Puzzles in *Shapes* Finding the Most and Fewest Blocks
No access to computers (3 sessions)	Quick Images Different Ways to Fill (no Choice Time)	Quick Images Different Ways to Fill (no Choice Time)	Different Ways to Fill Finding the Most and Fewest Blocks (no Choice Time)	

Quick Images

Use the transparent Shape Cards and Combination Shapes for Quick Images at least twice during these three sessions, for example, at the beginning of both Sessions 8 and 9. If students are drawing the single shapes easily, you can go on to the combination shapes. You can also make up shapes or combinations of shapes of your own to provide an appropriate level of challenge for your students. Another way to challenge students is to use two of the Quick Image shapes next to each other on the overhead. If some shapes seemed to be quite unfamiliar to students when you did Quick Images before, return to these and give students another chance to draw and describe them.

Spend time asking students to describe how they thought about and remembered each shape to be sure that they are using and listening to language about shapes. Asking students to contrast two shapes can help them extend their observations and vocabulary. For example:

Tony said that he remembered that the shape I showed was a triangle, and Yanni said that he thought about three points to help him remember it. Here's another shape with three points. Why didn't you draw one like this? What's different about the one you drew?

For some examples of student work and thinking, see the **Dialogue Box, Quick Images with Combination Shapes (p. 42).**

Choice Time

Choices

1. Different Ways to Fill

2. Solve Puzzles on the Computer

Post a new Choice Time list. Explain to students that for Choice 1, Different Ways to Fill, they will be using sheets like the one in the last session, with more than one of the same outline on each sheet. Their job is to fill in each outline with pattern blocks in a different way.

In a similar activity on the computer, students choose the Solve Puzzles option in *Shapes.* Rotate pairs of students so that as many as possible have time on the computer during these three sessions. If possible, allow pairs of students to work on the computer at other times of the day as well. If you are using a computer lab, designate one of these three sessions for everyone to work on this activity in the lab. Add a second session in the lab, if possible.

Choice 1: Different Ways to Fill

Materials: Pattern blocks (1 bucket per 6–8 students); Student Sheets 12–15, Different Ways to Fill Shapes B–E (1 of each per pair, plus extras); paper pattern blocks and glue sticks or paste, or pattern block stickers, or crayons

Students select any of the remaining Different Ways to Fill sheets. They use pattern blocks to fill the two or three outlines on that sheet in different ways. As you observe students at work on their second or third outline, ask them to try making designs with more or fewer blocks than they have already used. Also ask them to speculate about the most and the fewest blocks that could be used to fill in the outline. The idea of halves and doubles will naturally come up in these discussions. By replacing each hexagon with two trapezoids, they use halves to increase the number of pieces. By replacing triangles with blue rhombuses, they combine halves into wholes to decrease the number of pieces.

Some students may want to use a second sheet with the same outline, so that they find four or six different ways in all to make a given shape. Students can also do this choice more than once, using different student sheets each time.

Choice 2: Solve Puzzles on the Computer

Materials: Computers with *Shapes* software installed

In the Solve Puzzles activity in *Shapes,* students are given multiple outlines to fill in different ways, just as they do with the actual pattern blocks. However, on the computer, they need to think more deliberately about how to move, turn, and flip the shapes in order to put them where they want them.

Students who have used Free Explore will already be familiar with the tools needed for this activity. In addition to what students learned about the software using Free Explore, they need know only the following:

- How to select Solve Puzzles by clicking on it once from the screen of activity choices.

- How to read the directions, then click on **[OK]** or press **<return>**.

- How to select a new puzzle by clicking on **Number** in the menu bar and dragging the cursor down to the number of the puzzle they want to try.

- How to use the visual **Hints** that are available to help them think of new ways when they are stuck.

Each time Solve Puzzles opens, the software presents puzzle number 1, two outlines of the blue rhombus pattern block. To get a different puzzle, students click on **Number** and select the puzzle they want.

Students do not need to do the puzzles in any order, nor do they need to do all the puzzles. To help students keep a record of each puzzle they try, post a list near the computer. When students have completed puzzle number 1, they write their names under Number 1 on your list. Alternatively, they can keep an individual record in their math notebooks or folders.

When students have found several ways to fill a shape and can't think of any more, they can use the **Hints** option, either by selecting **Hints** from the **Help** menu at the top of the screen or by pressing ⌘H. All the outlines on the screen are then filled in with possible arrangements of pattern block shapes. After a few seconds, the screen returns to show only the students' work so far. These hints are similar to Quick Images—temporary visual clues to ways of arranging shapes.

Observing the Students

Circulate to watch students at work.

- How flexible are students in choosing pattern blocks to fill in an outlined shape?

- Do students easily recognize what shapes will fill a piece of the outline?

- Can students use equivalents among the shapes to help them change their designs? For example, do they substitute a blue rhombus for two triangles or three triangles for a trapezoid? Do they use ideas about halves and doubles?

- As students fill in shapes, do they plan ahead? Can they "see" in their mind what will happen if they place blocks in certain ways? When they place a block, do they think about what they will need to fill in the remaining space?

- Do students have ways of altering their designs so that they use more or fewer blocks? Can they find ways to make a design with the fewest possible or most possible blocks (or at least get close to the fewest or most)? How do they know they have the most or fewest possible blocks?

Finding the Most and Fewest Blocks

To finish up these sessions, which are the last ones in this unit to focus on pattern blocks, show the transparency of Different Ways to Fill, Shapes D (Student Sheet 14). If you don't have an overhead projector, draw a large version of this outline on the board. Ask students to help you fill in the outline with the fewest possible blocks. Use the transparent pattern blocks, if you have them, or draw in lines to show the blocks.

Do you think this way has the fewest possible blocks? Why do you think so? How would you change the design so that it has more blocks?

Take students' ideas until they think you have the most possible blocks filling in the outline.

Why do you think this is the most possible blocks?

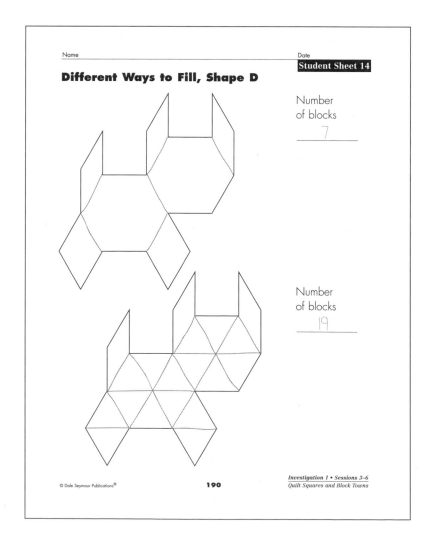

Name _____ Date _____

Student Sheet 14

Different Ways to Fill, Shape D

Number of blocks

7

Number of blocks

19

© Dale Seymour Publications®   190   *Investigation 1 • Sessions 3–6*
Quilt Squares and Block Towns

Sessions 8, 9, and 10 Follow-Up

 **Homework**

Quick Images with Shapes Send home Student Sheet 16, Quick Images, and Student Sheet 17, Shapes for Quick Images. Briefly demonstrate the activity. Show students how they can fold the paper or cut apart the four shapes to show one shape at a time, then count slowly to 5 (silently, so it doesn't interfere with the person's concentration), and finally hide the shape while the other person tries to draw it. The students (and their family members) could also draw some original shapes for the same activity.

To repeat this activity for homework another day, make up your own sheets of shapes to send home.

 **Extensions**

Filling with the Same Block As an additional challenge, ask students if they can fill in any of the outlines on Student Sheets 11–15, Different Ways to Fill Shapes A–E, with all of the same block (for example, all triangles or all trapezoids). Which outlines can they fill with all the same block? Is there more than one kind of block that will work? Are some of the outlines impossible to fill with all the same block? How do they know?

Quick Images with Pattern Blocks If you have a set of transparent pattern blocks for the overhead projector, use them for a version of Quick Images. Make a design with 3–5 pattern blocks on the overhead. Students use pattern blocks to recreate the design at their seats.

Choice Time is an opportunity for students to work on a variety of activities that focus on similar mathematical content. Choice Times are found in every unit of the grade 1 *Investigations* curriculum. These generally alternate with whole-class activities in which students work individually or in pairs on one or two problems. Each format offers different learning experiences; both are important for students.

In Choice Time the activities are not sequential; as students move among them, they continually revisit some of the important concepts and ideas they are learning. Many Choice Time activities are designed with the intent that students will work on them more than once. As they play a game a second or third time, or as they work to solve similar problems, students are able to refine their strategies, see a variety of approaches, and bring new knowledge to familiar experiences.

You may want to limit the number of students working on a particular Choice Time activity at any one time. In many cases, the quantity of materials available limits the number. Even if this is not the case, limiting the number is advisable because it gives students the opportunity to work in smaller groups. It also gives them a chance to do some choices more than one time. Often when a new choice is introduced, many students want to do it first. Assure them that, even with your limits, they will have the chance to try each choice.

Initially you may need to help students plan what they do. Rather than organizing them into groups and circulating the groups every 15 minutes, support students in making their own decisions. Making choices, planning their time, and taking responsibility for their own learning are important aspects the school experience. If some students return to the same activity over and over again without trying other choices, suggest that they make a different first choice and then do the favorite activity as a second choice.

How to Set Up Choices

Some teachers prefer to have the choices set up at centers or stations around the room. At each center students will find the materials needed to complete the activity. Other teachers prefer to have materials stored in a central location, with students taking the materials to their own desks or tables. In either case, materials should be readily accessible, and students should be expected to take responsibility for cleaning up and returning materials to their appropriate storage locations. Giving a "5 minutes until cleanup" warning before the end of any session allows students to finish what they are working on and prepare for the upcoming transition.

Decide which arrangement to use in your classroom. You may need to experiment with a few different structures before finding the setup that works best for you and your students.

The Role of the Student

Establish clear guidelines when you introduce Choice Time. Discuss students' responsibilities:

- Try every choice at least once.
- Work with a partner or alone. (Some activities require that students work in pairs, while others can be done either alone or with a partner.)
- Keep track, on paper, of the choices you have worked on.
- Keep all your work in your math folder.
- Ask questions of other students when you don't understand or feel stuck. (Some teachers establish the rule, "Ask two other students before me," requiring students to check with two peers before coming to the teacher for help.)

For each Choice Time, list the activity choices on a chart, the board, or the overhead. Sketch a picture with each choice for students who may have difficulty reading the activity names. Some teachers laminate a piece of tagboard to create a Choices board that they can easily update as new choices are added from session to session and old choices are no longer offered.

First grade students can keep track of the choices they have completed in one of these ways:

- When they have completed an activity, students record its name or picture on a blank sheet of paper.

- Post a sheet of lined paper at each station, or a sheet for each choice at the front of the room. At the top of each sheet, put the name of one activity and the corresponding picture. When students have completed an activity, they print their name on the corresponding sheet. Keep these lists throughout an investigation, as the same choices may be offered several times.

Some teachers keep a date stamp at each Choice Time station or at the front of the room, making it easy for students to record the date as well.

In any classroom there will be a range of how much work students complete. Some choices include extensions and additional problems for students who have completed their required work. Encourage students to return to choices they have done before, do another problem or two from the choice, or play a game again. You may also want to make the choices available at other times during the day.

Whenever students do any work on paper during Choice Time, they put this in their math folders at the end of the session.

At the end of a Choice Time session, spend a few minutes discussing with students what went smoothly, what sorts of issues arose and how they were resolved, and what students enjoyed or found difficult about Choice Time. Having students share the work they have been doing often sparks interest in an activity. Some days, you might ask two or three volunteers to talk about their work. On other days, you might pose a question that someone asked you during Choice Time, so that other students might respond to it. Encourage students to be involved in the process of finding solutions to problems that come up

in the classroom. In doing so, they take some responsibility for their own behavior and become involved with establishing classroom policies.

The Role of the Teacher

Choice Time provides you with the opportunity to observe and listen to students while they work. At times, you may want to meet with individual students, pairs, or small groups who need help. This gives you the chance to focus on students you haven't had a chance to observe before, or to do individual assessments. Recording your observations of students will help keep you aware of how they are interacting with materials and solving problems.

During the initial weeks of Choice Time, much of your time will probably be spent in classroom management, circulating around the room, helping students get settled into activities, and monitoring the process of moving from one choice to another. Once routines are familiar and well established, students will become more independent and responsible for their work during Choice Time. This will allow you to spend more concentrated periods of time observing the class as a whole or working with individuals and small groups.

Quick Images with Combination Shapes

This class is playing Quick Images. Many of them have become quite adept at drawing single shapes, so the teacher is using the Combination Shapes. After students have had two chances to draw the following double shape, the teacher leaves it visible and asks students to talk about their drawings.

Max: I thought about when we did a triangle, and then I drew a square inside.

Eva: I had to make the triangle big so I had room for the square.

Nadia: I was about to make the triangle small, then I realized it's the square that is supposed to be small.

Next the teacher shows this Combination Shape on the overhead:

After the first look, here are some of the students' drawings:

After the second look, more of the students draw a shape more closely resembling the original, but this Quick Image is still difficult for many students.

This one seems pretty difficult. I'm going to show it to you now so you can see how close you made it. I'll leave it here. You can try to draw it again if you want to. Who can tell me how they thought about this one?

Brady: I could remember the rectangle on the outside. But it was hard to remember how the lines went.

Shavonne: I was thinking of all the triangles in the corners.

I'm not sure I understand. Can you show us which triangles you mean?

Shavonne *[demonstrates at the overhead]*: See, it's a rectangle on the outside *[traces it]*, then you make four triangles in the corners.

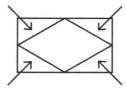

Oh, I see what you mean! That's a really interesting way of thinking about it. Did anyone think about it in a different way?

Nathan: I thought about the blue diamond in the pattern blocks for the inside shape, but I made it too little.

Leah: Me, too. I didn't make the corners touching.

Which corners should be touching?

Leah *[demonstrates at the overhead]*: See, here, here, here, and here. Each point of the diamond has to touch.

Claire: I sort of remembered that, but I made the points go too far.

Fernando: I thought it was like two arrows inside the rectangle.

Sorting 2-D Shapes

What Happens

The class plays Guess My Rule with the Shape Cards, sorting the shapes according to two rules. Then, as an assessment, students work in pairs to sort the Shape Cards and make a poster to show their favorite way of sorting. Finally they discuss what a triangle is, and identify which of the Shape Cards are triangles. Students' work focuses on:

- describing and comparing 2-D shapes
- sorting and classifying 2-D shapes
- developing vocabulary to name and describe 2-D shapes
- describing characteristics of triangles

Materials

- Shape Cards (1 set per pair)
- Chart paper or other large paper, at least 18 by 24 inches (1 sheet per pair)
- Glue or paste
- A 12-foot length of string or ribbon, or a large circle drawn on chart paper
- Shape Card transparencies
- Overhead projector

Activity

Guess My Rule with Shape Cards

Gather students in a circle where they can see an area of the floor. Hand out enough of the Shape Cards to give each student one card (some students will have the same shapes). Make a large circle on the floor with about 12 feet of string or ribbon, or draw a large circle on a sheet of chart paper.

Explain that you are thinking of a secret rule that tells which shapes can go inside this circle. You won't tell them the rule, but they can try to guess which shapes go in. A good rule to start with is SHAPES THAT HAVE ONLY STRAIGHT SIDES. To start off, place inside the circle a couple of shapes that follow your rule.

I have a secret rule for what shapes can go inside this circle. Here's a clue: These two shapes can go in the circle. I'll put them in there so you can see them. Who else thinks they might have a shape that goes in the circle?

Call on students, one at a time. If they volunteer shapes that fit your rule, ask them to place their cards inside the circle. If they offer a shape that doesn't belong, they should place that card on the floor outside the circle.

So Leah thinks her shape goes in the circle. Yes, it does go. Leah, come put your shape in the circle. Who else thinks they have a shape that goes in the circle?

Fernando? No, your shape doesn't go in. Come put your shape over here outside the circle. But that's an important clue. Look carefully at Fernando's shape. That gives important information about what can't go in the circle.

Does anyone else have a shape that you think doesn't go in the circle? Yukiko, you think you know my rule? OK, but I don't want to hear a rule yet. Do you see another shape that would go in the circle if you're right?

Don't permit students to guess your rule with words before many shapes have been placed both inside and outside the circle. When you think many students have a good idea what your rule is, ask one student to state it.

Have students take back the Shape Cards (they don't have to take back the same shape they had before), and play one more round of this game. This time use the rule TRIANGLES. As students figure out the rule and describe the shapes that can go in the circle, listen to how students describe them. Do they use the word *triangle*? Do they notice that these shapes have three sides and three "points"? Do they think some triangles are not triangles? You will return to a focus on triangles during the final activity in these sessions. The **Teacher Note,** When Is a Triangle Not a Triangle? (p. 50), provides some information for you about the mathematical thinking students are doing as they sort and classify shapes.

Activity

Assessment

Sorting with Shape Cards

Distribute a set of Shape Cards to each pair of students.

With your partner, sort your Shape Cards into groups of shapes that go together. You can use two, three, or four groups. Be sure that every shape has a place where it belongs. You can try a few different ways to put the shapes into groups, and then choose the way you like best. Later today or tomorrow, you'll make a Shape poster with the cards to show your favorite way of sorting.

Demonstrate briefly with a few shapes. Show about six shapes on the chalkboard or overhead: two different squares, a rectangle, a triangle, a circle, and a semicircle.

Do you see any shapes here that could go together?... OK, so you could put these two shapes together because they're both squares. Is there a different way?... Luis, you say you'd put all the shapes with straight sides together, and the shapes with curved sides together.

In the Shape Cards, you will have more shapes than this to sort—lots of different shapes. You'll have to find a group for every shape card. You'll need to decide on names for your groups, too.

Walk around and observe the students while they sort their cards on their desks or on the floor. Encourage them to place all the cards in the set into one category or another. If students have difficulty getting started, ask questions such as the following:

- Which shapes seem to go together? Do you see some shapes that are the same in some way?
- If you're sorting this way, where does this shape go?
- What do you call this group of shapes?
- Why did you place this shape into this category instead of that one?

When students have sorted the shapes in different ways and have decided on a favorite way of sorting them, distribute a sheet of large paper to each pair.

To show us your favorite way of sorting, make a poster. Glue your Shape Cards on this large sheet, putting them together in the groups you made. Be sure to separate the groups so we can tell which shapes are in each group. Also write a label for each category of shapes on your poster.

Note: Some students may want to cut out around the outline of the shape itself, instead of using the whole Shape Card. However, this is very difficult and time-consuming for most first graders. Suggest they use the Shape Cards as they are, but show them how they can overlap cards if necessary in order to fit them onto their poster. (An 11-by-17-inch sheet is just barely large enough to fit on all the Shape Cards in groups, with some overlapping of cards. It's better to provide 18-by-24-inch sheets, chart paper, or some other larger paper if you can.)

Student pairs arrange their set of Shape Cards and paste them down on the paper in categories. They write the name of each category (for example, "pointy and fat" or "square" or "curvy") with that group of shapes. If students have a hard time naming their categories, ask them to explain to you in their own words why the shapes in each group go together. Then help them use their own explanations as a way of naming each group. For example:

Max, why did you put these shapes together?

Max: Because these go straight and these over here don't go straight.

You said you put these together because they don't go straight. What words could we write here to tell someone looking at your poster why you put them together? Do you want to write, "don't go straight"?

Max: I could say *curvy.*

Susanna: He could write "these are straight" over here and "these are not straight" over here.

What do you think, Max?

Max: I'll say *curvy* for these and *straight* for these.

The **Teacher Note,** Sorting the Shape Cards (p. 51), includes examples of how several pairs of students sorted the shapes and how the teacher interacted with them as they worked, both to help them name their groups and to decide what to do with shapes that didn't seem to fit in their categories.

Use this activity, in combination with the activity Triangles on the Shape Cards (at the end of these two sessions), to assess your students' growing ability to describe and compare shapes. Focus on whether students are paying attention to important attributes that shapes have in common. Students are not expected to sort shapes in a way that corresponds with the conventional ways of classifying shapes. Rather, the important thing is that they are carefully observing, describing, and comparing the shapes. Consider the following questions to assess students' growth:

- Do they observe and describe some shapes as having only straight sides, while other shapes have some curved sides?
- Do they observe and describe how some shapes have different numbers of sides? For example, do they distinguish between three-sided and four-sided shapes?
- Do they observe and describe differences among shapes with the same number of sides? For example, do they compare triangles and notice that some are more "slanted" or more "pointy," or that some have equal sides while others have some longer and some shorter sides? Do they notice that some four-sided shapes have all sides equal while others do not?
- During their conversations about shapes, do they observe and describe how shapes are related to each other? For example, do they comment that two trapezoids can be put together to make a hexagon, or that a trapezoid can be broken into three triangles? Do they mention that a trapezoid could be made into a triangle by extending the non parallel sides until they meet?

In order to answer these questions for each student, you will need to observe them at work, listen to their conversations, and ask questions, as well as review their final posters. For examples of the interactions you might have while talking with students at work, as well as examples of what students say that might be used as evidence of their growing understanding, see the **Teacher Note,** Sorting the Shape Cards (p. 51), and the **Dialogue Box,** What's a Triangle? (p. 54).

Activity

Sharing the Shape Posters

Reserve about 15 minutes for students to share their posters with each other. Ask each pair to present their poster and talk about how they sorted. To save time, when one pair has presented, ask if there are any other pairs that sorted in a similar way.

Susanna and Mia have three groups—all straight, all curvy, and part straight part curvy. Did anyone else make a poster about straight sides and curvy sides?

An alternative way to share posters is to hang them up around the room. Give students a few minutes to walk around and look at the posters. Ask them to notice one way someone sorted that was different from what they did themselves. When you gather students together, ask them to share what they noticed. You may also want to focus the discussion on some of the issues that you saw coming up as students worked on their posters.

Triangles on the Shape Cards

Using the overhead projector and the Shape Card transparencies, show the six shapes A–F.

Who sees a pair of shapes that go together? Why do you think those two shapes go together?

Ask several students to put in their own words how the shapes go together, in order to elicit some of the characteristics of the shapes.

Iris said these are both triangles. Who can say something else about why these two go together? OK, Chris?… So Chris noticed that they are pointy at the top. Who else has something to add?… Jamaar says both shapes have three points.

So, so far, you think these two go together because they are triangles, they are pointy at the top, and they have three points. Can anyone add any other reason?

Once students have said all they have to say about one pair, continue the discussion by asking if they see a different pair of shapes that go together.

It is likely that students may put the two triangles together, the two rectangles together (remember, a square is a special kind of rectangle), and the circle and semicircle together. However, students may see the shapes in other ways, so follow their lead. You may want to refer to students' shape posters if they use some of the same categories here.

Once students have made their pairs, take all the shapes off the overhead except the two triangles (B and E). If students haven't identified the triangles as going together, put those two shapes up and say something like, "Here are two that I think go together. Why do you think I might put these two together?" Name the two shapes as triangles and then gradually put up some of the other Shape Cards. Ask students which of these shapes go with the two triangles and which do not, and ask for their reasons.

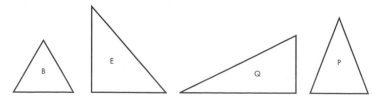

It is likely that not all students will agree about which shapes go with the two triangles. For example, some students may say that shape J doesn't go with the triangles because it is "upside down." They may also think that shape L doesn't belong because it is a "funny" shape (students might say it doesn't look like a "regular" triangle), or because it doesn't have equal sides. They might also say that shape I (the tilted square) *does* go with the triangles because "it has a point on top."

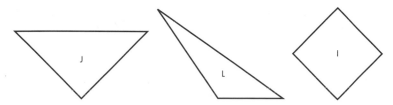

Encourage students to voice opinions and disagree with each other, but insist that students give their reasons for their ideas. The **Dialogue Box, What's a Triangle?** (p. 54), provides examples of first graders' thinking about classifying shapes.

End the discussion by making some record of students' ideas. For example, you might write three categories on a piece of chart paper or on the board: Definitely Triangles, Definitely Not Triangles, and We Are Not Sure (or "We Disagree"). Draw the shapes in each category.

❖ **Tip for the Linguistically Diverse Classroom** Add a visual clue next to each heading; for example, a triangle for Definitely Triangles, a large X through a triangle for the Not Triangles category, and a question mark inside a triangle for We Are Not Sure. For these visual clues, use a shape that your students agree is a triangle, such as an equilateral triangle.

When Is a Triangle Not a Triangle?

Young children begin to learn to identify shapes by hearing adults use words like *square, circle, triangle, cube,* and *sphere.* In the early primary grades, students are just beginning to build their knowledge about which shapes these words describe. To do this, they have to figure out what characteristics make a difference in the classification system we use. For example, size and color don't matter when we classify a shape as a rectangle or a circle.

Students seem to understand this quite early: A *big* triangle is still a triangle, a *small* circle is still a circle. However, they may think that orientation *does* matter, so that a tilted square, such as shape I in the Shape Cards, is *not* a square. Some students at this age think a triangle is a triangle only if it is an equilateral (all sides equal) or isosceles (two sides equal) triangle, oriented so that the bottom is horizontal. So, for example, they will say that these first two shapes are triangles, but that the other two are not:

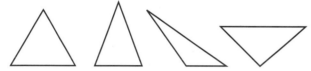

How do students come to understand that all of these are triangles? It is not a matter of simply giving them a definition: "It has three straight sides, so it is a triangle." Think of a very young child learning about animals. At first, the child may call every four-footed creature "doggy." The parent may gently say, "Oh, you mean the horse," but for a while, the child persists in calling the horse "doggy." After enough experiences with horses—in real life, in books, or on TV—the child begins to notice the characteristics that make horses different from dogs. Yes, horses do have four legs and tails just like dogs; they might be the same colors as dogs; they have long faces, as many dogs do. But certain things about them are quite different: Their ears are always a certain shape and quite small in proportion to their heads; they are larger than dogs, close to the height of an adult; they have characteristic tails, and a certain way of switching them. We don't

always know exactly what has been recognized when the child finally says "horse" instead of "doggy." It may be an overall gestalt of what is horse-like as opposed to what is dog-like.

Developing an idea of what is square-like or triangle-like is part of what students in the primary grades are doing as they classify these shapes. However, an overall gestalt is often inadequate. Classifying shapes requires careful attention to *all* attributes of the shape. When students call a pyramid a *triangle,* or call a sphere or an oval a *circle,* they are noticing something important. There is something triangle-like about a pyramid, and something circle-like about an oval. Similarly, a first grader might call both of these *diamonds:*

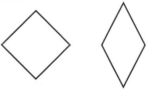

Again, the student is noticing some important similarities. However, the student may be absolutely sure that the shape on the left is *not* a square because of its orientation. Even if the student "knows" that a square is a four-sided shape with equal sides and square corners, the *look* of the tilted square may be more persuasive than the other information. Well into the early grades and even in the later elementary grades, some students are sure that a scalene triangle (like the third triangle pictured) is not a triangle. A group of third graders, making shapes from square tiles, insisted that a 5-by-6 arrangement of tiles was square because it "looked square."

Part of the development of geometric knowledge is moving from seeing shapes as wholes to becoming more and more competent at analyzing their characteristics and making decisions about which characteristics matter in which situations. This development happens gradually during the elementary years. As students sort shapes in this unit, they are beginning to observe, describe, and compare the attributes of shapes.

Sorting the Shape Cards

As students work on sorting the Shape Cards in preparation for making Shape Posters, the teacher circulates to check in with each pair of students.

Nathan and Tony first decide that all the squares should go together. They next look at the rhombus. Tony looks at it a long time, as if thinking it isn't quite a square, but he finally decides to put it with the squares. They decide to put the trapezoid with this group and they name it "four sides." They put all the rectangles (except the squares) in a second group. The teacher asks them what this group is.

Nathan: I can't remember the name. Hexagons?

Why don't you describe them to me?

Nathan: Long sides and short sides.

Does that help you name your group?

They decide to call the group "short and long."

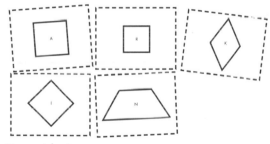

"Four sides"

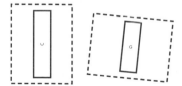

"Short and long"

Nadia and Claire have sorted the shapes into three groups, but are having trouble naming one. They call their first two groups "three sides" and "four corners." Their third group contains all the shapes that are not polygons. They have not yet placed the hexagon or the trapezoid. They ask the teacher for help with naming their third group.

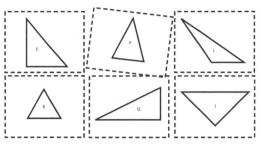

"Three sides"

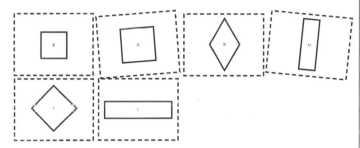

"Four corners"

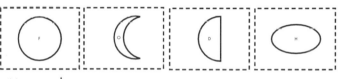

Unnamed

Nadia: We were going to call it "no sides and no corners."

Claire: But then we saw a problem.

What's the problem?

Claire: That one [the crescent] has corners.

Nadia: And this one [the half circle] has a side.

So do you still think there is something the same about all of them?

Claire: They're kind of round.

Nadia: They have round sides.

So could you call this group "round" or "round sides"?

They decide to name the group "round sides."

Continued on next page

Some time later, after talking with other pairs, the teacher comes back to Nathan and Tony who are now having trouble deciding where to place the hexagon. So are Nadia and Claire, as well as another pair, William and Shavonne, who are sitting close by. The teacher talks with all three pairs. Nadia suggests that they give their hexagon to William and Shavonne, so then they will have two hexagons and can put them together in a group.

How will that help?

Shavonne: Because then they'll have two of a kind.

Could there be a group with just one of a kind?

Tony: I think that the hexagon could go with the circles.

Claire *[groaning dramatically]:* But then we'd have sides again. And our group has to have *round* sides.

William: It could go with the circles. It's sort of like a circle but with straight sides. You could make a circle around it.

I could make a circle around this rectangle. How is it different?

Nathan: No, the rectangle has straight sides.

Nadia: If you cut a hexagon in half you have a trapezoid. We could put those two together.

Could you make up a different shape that would go with the hexagon?

At this point, the teacher leaves the groups to make their own decisions. She has offered two ideas—the possibility that the hexagon might go by itself and the possibility of making up another shape to go with the hexagon. She knows they have their own ideas about how a hexagon is related to a circle and to a trapezoid, so she doesn't want to push her ideas any further. She knows that the groups will pick up one of the ideas she has offered if it only makes sense to them, and she is curious to see what the groups will decide. Eventually, Claire and Nadia decide that the hexagon and trapezoid are in a group together. They call this group "half of one hexagon." Nathan and Tony put the hexagon in a group with the shapes with curved sides, which

William and Shavonne

Nathan and Tony

they name "all kinds of circles." William and Shavonne decide that the hexagon is a group by itself. They name it "the hexagon alone." They ignore the trapezoid.

During these interactions, the teacher has noticed these things about the students' growing understanding of 2-D shapes:

■ Even though Tony doesn't articulate this out loud, he seems to notice that the squares and the rhombus have something in common (all four sides equal).

■ Nathan and Tony are able to enlarge their original group of squares to include first the rhombus and then the trapezoid, since they all have four sides. This classification is often difficult for first graders, who are likely to be compelled to stick with "squares" as a familiar category. Other students had more difficulty placing the trapezoid, and some simply ignored it.

■ Claire and Nadia carefully think about whether the shapes in their group actually have the characteristics that are described by the name of the group. Although they at first name one group "no sides and no corners," which describes for them a general idea of something that curves, they look more carefully at each shape and realize that some of them do have sides and corners as well as curves.

■ The teacher knew that classifying the hexagon would be difficult for most students in her class. She is impressed that William and Shavonne recognize that the hexagon does not fit with any of their groups and are willing to classify it separately and that Claire and Nadia hold fast to their definition of round sides and refuse to include the hexagon in that group. She feels that all three pairs made reasonable decisions about where to place the hexagon that they were able to justify. Nadia recognizes that there is some relationship between the hexagon and trapezoid, while William notices how a polygon with more sides begins to look more "roundish."

What's a Triangle?

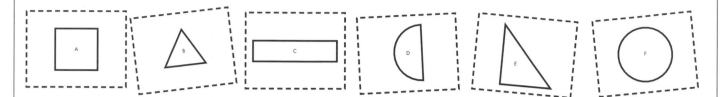

This first grade class is looking at similarities and differences among shapes on the Shape Cards. This discussion (held at the end of Session 12, Triangles on the Shape Cards, p. 48) is designed to get students to focus on the characteristics of the shapes by comparing and contrasting them.

The teacher puts transparencies of shapes A–F on the overhead, all at once.

Now that you've made your Shape Posters, you've thought a lot about what shapes can go together. Look at these six shapes. Can you find two that go together?

Diego: The circle and the half circle.

Why did you pick those two shapes?

Diego: Both are round.

Did anyone else notice anything about them?

Mia: With the circle, the whole thing is round. The other is only half round.

Iris: The half circle has a line, and the other doesn't.

Tony: It kind of has two lines. One is straight and the other is curved.

Do you see two other shapes that go together?

Garrett: *[He picks out the two triangles.]* They both have three sides.

What else can anyone say about these two?

Jacinta: They have three corners. *[She demonstrates on the overhead, pointing and counting 1, 2, 3 to show the three corners on each triangle.]*

Tuan: Both are triangles, but in different ways. This is a triangle *[he points to the right triangle]*, but it has a long side like a sailboat.

Libby: The other one looks like a regular triangle.

What is a regular triangle?

Libby: Like that one. It's not so slanty. It's like a normal triangle.

Chris: Like the one in the pattern blocks.

The teacher now shows two more triangles (shapes J and L) and the trapezoid (shape N).

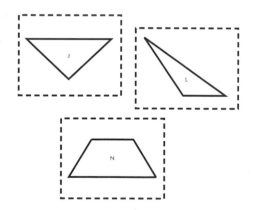

What about these shapes? Do any of these go with the two triangles we've been looking at?

Michelle: That one's too skinny. It's like an arrow.

Jamaar: That one looks like a piece of glass.

Is it a triangle?

Susanna: It's kind of like a triangle, but the top part goes up too much.

Tamika: It's thin, but it still has three corners and three sides.

Donte: One side is kind of tilted.

Luis: It doesn't have a point on the top.

Yukiko: It's like this one *[indicating the right triangle]*. It has two long sides and a short side.

Kristi Ann: A triangle has two slanted lines like the roof of a house and a straight line across the bottom.

So, do you think it's a triangle?

Students *[variously]*: Yes... No... Yes... No...

What is it if it isn't a triangle?

Jamaar: A piece of glass.

Kristi Ann: A funny triangle.

What about this one? *[The teacher points to shape J, the "upside down" isosceles triangle.]*

Andre: You'd have to turn it over. Then it would be a triangle.

Max: It's still a triangle because it has three sides.

Kaneisha: If it's on the paper, it can't change. It's still a triangle.

Is this a triangle? *[The teacher points to shape N, the trapezoid.]*

Jonah: No. It has four sides, and triangles have three sides.

Yanni: And it has four corners, see: 1, 2, 3, 4. Triangles have three corners.

Chanthou: It's missing a point at the top.

What do you mean?

Chanthou: See, you could draw it up like this *[she demonstrates]* and it would be a triangle.

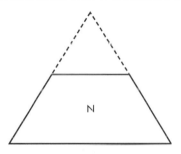

Although some students think a closed figure is a triangle if it has three sides, many others have not yet abstracted and verbalized this property. They base their judgments on how a figure looks—does it look like figures they have called triangles in the past?

Quilts with Squares and Triangles

Materials

- Transparencies of Shape Cards and Combination Shapes
- Children's literature about quilts (optional)
- Books with quilt patterns (optional)
- Student Sheet 18 (2 per student, and 1 transparency)
- Overhead projector, overhead pens in two colors
- Transparency of Quilt Pattern A
- Student Sheets 19–24 (an assortment for students to choose from)
- Crayons
- Quilt frames (10–12 for the class)
- Computers with *Shapes* software installed

What Happens

Students design quilt squares using squares and triangles and repeat their squares to create quilt designs, both on paper and on the computer. The class again works on Quick Images with single and combination shapes. A discussion about their quilt patterns ends the investigation. Students' work focuses on:

- seeing relationships between squares and triangles
- using rotation to create and change designs
- using a repeated unit to create a pattern
- seeing how changing the unit affects the whole pattern
- describing shapes and patterns

Organizing These Sessions

In these three sessions, students spend most of their time making quilt designs, both on and off the computer. In addition, you play Quick Images with Shapes once or twice during the sessions. How you organize these sessions will depend on your computer setup. The first session will be the same in any case, but if you have a computer lab, you will concentrate the Quilt Patterns on the Computer activity in one or two sessions with the whole class in the lab, while with computers in the classroom, parts of your class can be working both on and off the computer simultaneously. Without computers, students will do all their quilt design work on paper.

	Session 13	Session 14	Session 15	Extra Session
Computers in the classroom (3 sessions)	Looking at Quilt Patterns Designing a Quilt Square	Quick Images Quilt Patterns on Paper Create a Quilt in *Shapes*	Quick Images Quilt Patterns on Paper Create a Quilt in *Shapes*	
Access to a computer lab (4 sessions)	Looking at Quilt Patterns Designing a Quilt Square	Quick Images Computer lab: Create a Quilt in *Shapes*	Quick Images Quilt Patterns on Paper	Computer lab: Create a Quilt in *Shapes* Free Explore or Solve Puzzles (optional)
No access to computers (3 sessions)	Looking at Quilt Patterns Designing a Quilt Square	Quick Images Quilt Patterns on Paper	Quick Images Quilt Patterns on Paper	

If your computers are in the classroom, give students access to the *Shapes* software at other times of the day so that all students get at least two chances to work on the Create a Quilt activity on the computer. Students can also continue working on the Free Explore and Solve Puzzles activities in *Shapes.*

Quick Images

Present Quick Images with both the single Shape Cards and the Combination Shapes once or twice during these three sessions. If students are easily able to draw the single and double shapes, make up some new combination shapes.

Looking at Quilt Patterns

Introducing Quilt Patterns If you have a good children's book about quilts, such as *The Quilt* by Ann Jonas (Greenwillow Books, 1984), read it aloud to introduce these sessions. Most helpful would be a book that shows how a quilt is made from squares, and how patterns repeat on quilts. If you can, also have available a selection of books showing quilt patterns.

How Quilt Squares Make a Pattern Show the transparency of Student Sheet 18, Quilt Squares, on the overhead projector. Explain that students will be getting a copy of this sheet, which they can color in with any two colors for each square. Demonstrate by coloring in the first square, using only two colors, and possibly one other square (also with only two colors). On another square, show students that they could also leave some spaces uncolored, giving them two colors and white. Leaving some white areas is often very effective in making an interesting quilt pattern.

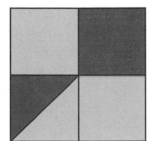 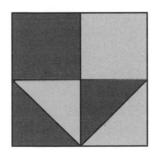 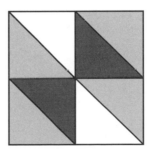

Then show students the transparency of Quilt Pattern A (Student Sheet 19). Explain that students will choose their favorite quilt square they have colored on Student Sheet 18 to make a quilt design. They'll do that by copying the square nine times, in each of the squares of the larger quilt pattern.

On the overhead, demonstrate how you could copy your first square onto each of the nine squares in Quilt Pattern A. Also demonstrate the use of a "quilt frame" to help you color in one square at a time.

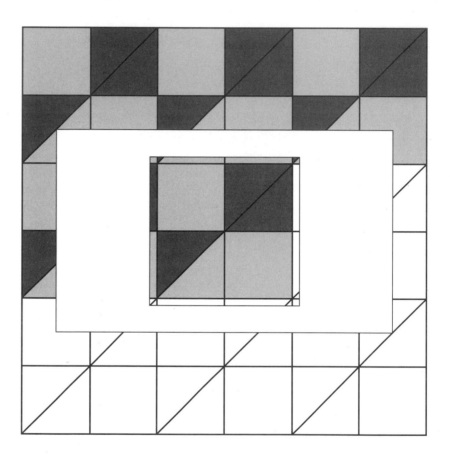

Activity

Designing a Quilt Square

Give each student a copy of Student Sheet 18. They may use any two colors to color in each square. They may also choose to leave some spaces uncolored. When they have completed one copy, give students the option of coloring a second one, using different colors in different designs.

You may want to find out from students which of their squares they are planning to reproduce as a quilt pattern, to get a sense of how many of each pattern A–F (Student Sheets 19–24) you will need.

Creating a Quilt Pattern

Quilt Patterns on Paper Students choose one of their quilt squares from Student Sheet 18 and carefully copy it into the nine squares of the corresponding quilt pattern. Help students select the correct student sheet to transfer their pattern.

Point out that if students cut out the finished quilt square they are going to use, they can hold it right next to each quilt square in the quilt design as they color. Some students may want to use a quilt frame to block out everything except the square being worked on. Show students how to put the frame over each square in the quilt design as they work.

See the **Teacher Note,** Helping Students Make a Quilt Pattern (p. 60), for a description of how to help students keep track of where they are as they copy their unit squares into the larger quilt patterns.

Create a Quilt in *Shapes* The Create a Quilt activity in *Shapes* uses the same tools and procedures as Free Explore and Solve Puzzles, so students should have little difficulty getting started. These are the only new aspects of this activity:

- From the screen of choices, select the activity Create a Quilt.
- As shapes are placed in the single square, they automatically appear in the appropriate section of each square of the nine-square quilt.

As in the other computer activities, students drag the shapes from the window at the left to fill in the single quilt square. Once placed, shapes can be moved, rotated, or erased. Shapes can also be overlapped, providing even more possibilities for quilt designs.

Students may want to print out quilt designs they make on the computer. Give them time to experiment before they decide on a final design they would like to print.

To end this unit, make a display of the quilt designs made on paper and on the computer. Ask students to describe the shapes they see in the quilt patterns. The **Dialogue Box,** Pinwheels, Windmills, and Fishy Shapes (p. 61), has examples of students' quilts and their descriptions of the patterns.

Helping Students Make a Quilt Pattern

Students commonly encounter three difficulties as they copy their unit squares nine times to make a quilt pattern: copying the original square accurately, keeping focused as they move to the second row, and dealing with mistakes.

Copying the Quilt Square Accurately It is difficult for some students to keep track of transferring each part of the original quilt square to the corresponding part of the squares on the larger pattern. Following are some ways teachers have helped students.

■ Help them describe the pattern to themselves as a way to help them transfer it accurately. For example, one student's quilt square looked like this:

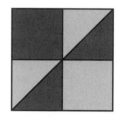

He thought about the pattern as "squares in the corners." Following this description, he always colored in the two squares first, then the triangles.

■ Suggest that they use the quilt frame to isolate each square. Some students find this useful; others find it too hard to manage the quilt frame and color at the same time. When this is an issue, students might use the quilt frame to decide which pieces to color next and make dots of the appropriate color in each shape, then take the quilt frame away and color the pattern.

■ They might outline each shape in the unit square lightly in the right color before coloring it all in, then double-check that they selected the right colors before coloring in the whole shape.

Moving to the Second Row As students begin coloring in the first square in the second row, they begin to see new patterns emerge. This can pull their eye away from their original quilt square to other patterns, and they may become confused. This commonly happens as the top half of the first square in the second row is filled in. For example:

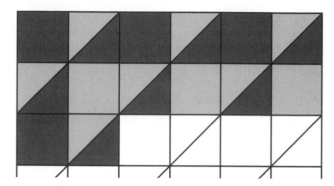

This student kept thinking he had done something wrong, even though he had colored everything correctly so far, because he was looking at a square made up of the bottom half of the first square in the first row and the top half of the first square in the second row.

Help students isolate the square they are working on by using the quilt frame, by pointing out the thicker lines between squares on the quilt pattern, or by cutting out the quilt square and positioning it right next to the square being colored.

Dealing with Mistakes It is inevitable that some students will make mistakes as they copy. Encourage students to copy carefully, but at the same time, let them know that it is difficult to keep track and that anyone can make this kind of mistake. Here are some options teachers have suggested to help students correct mistakes:

■ Cut out a square from a blank student sheet, paste it over the square that has a mistake in it, and color it again.

■ Start over again and use the quilt frame to isolate each square.

■ Leave the mistake as an interesting part of the pattern.

Different options work best for different students. Some students really want to start again. Others are happy to glue and recolor, while others are content to leave the "mistake."

Pinwheels, Windmills, and Fishy Shapes

Libby's quilt

Tamika's quilt

Kaneisha's quilt

Diego's quilt

Tuan's quilt

Chris's quilt

Libby: When I did mine, I got bigger triangles.

Diego: I got bigger triangles, too.

Iris: They're opposite.

What do you mean, opposite?

Iris: The big triangles go one way in Libby's and the other way in Diego's.

Tamika: In all of my squares, it looks like a pinwheel.

Tuan: Mine's like that, too. It's like a windmill.

Kaneisha: Mine has a fishy shape. It's like a long row of fishy bones.

Chris: Mine is all diamonds.

Comparing and Constructing 3-D Shapes

What Happens

Sessions 1 and 2: Describing and Comparing Shapes Students describe characteristics of some of the Geoblocks. They build and copy shapes made with interlocking cubes and match Geoblocks to outlines of the block faces.

Session 3: Block Pictures Students describe Geoblocks, then match Geoblocks to pictures of the blocks. They compare blocks and discuss with their partners how they decided which block is shown in the picture.

Sessions 4, 5, and 6: Blocks in a Sock Students play the game Blocks in a Sock (or Blocks in a Bag) in which they try to identify a Geoblock by feeling its shape. During Choice Time, students continue to explore the characteristics of the Geoblocks and of constructions made with interlocking cubes.

Session 7: What Kind of Box Is It? As a class, students look at Mystery Boxes they have brought from home; they talk about what kind of boxes they might be and why. After discussing how many flat sides (faces) a box has, they are introduced to a new activity: constructing their own boxes.

Sessions 8, 9, and 10: Making Boxes Students construct their own boxes out of cardboard rectangles. As boxes are finished, students compare their sizes and shapes. Over the three days, students continue writing their guesses about the Mystery Boxes. At the end of Session 10, students select some of the Mystery Boxes to be revealed.

Routines Refer to the section About Classroom Routines (pp. 127–134) for suggestions on integrating into the school day regular practice of mathematical skills in counting, exploring data, and understanding time and changes.

Mathematical Emphasis

- Observing, describing, and comparing 3-D shapes
- Creating and using 2-D representations of 3-D shapes
- Developing vocabulary for describing 3-D shapes
- Describing and comparing faces of 3-D shapes
- Constructing 3-D shapes from 2-D faces
- Relating size and shape to function
- Visualizing and describing rectangular prisms

What to Plan Ahead of Time

Materials

- Interlocking cubes: 20 per student (Sessions 1–2, 4–6, optional for 8–10)
- Geoblocks: 2 sets per class (Sessions 1–6)
- Stick-on notes or scrap paper (Session 3)
- Overhead projector (Session 3)
- Small bags or socks: 1 per pair (Sessions 4–6)
- Clear or masking tape: several rolls (Sessions 7–10)
- Scissors: 1 pair per 3–4 students (Sessions 7–10)
- Index cards for box pieces: 200 3-by-5-inch cards and 100 5-by-8-inch cards; see Other Preparation (Sessions 7–10)
- Envelopes at least 5 by 8 inches, to hold Set A box pieces: 1 per pair (Sessions 7–10)
- Trays, boxes, or paper plates, to hold Set B box pieces: 7 for the class (Sessions 8–10)

Other Preparation

- A set of Geoblocks contains 330 blocks of 25 types (see p. 72). Divide each set into two equal half-sets for distribution around the class. Parent volunteers, aides, or older students might help with this; a good approach is to search for two identical blocks and put one in each set.
- Before Session 1, make a Cube Thing with 8–10 interlocking cubes (see examples at right). You will need four or five copies of your Cube Thing, each identical in shape. Colors can vary.

- Duplicate the following student sheets and teaching resources, located at the end of this unit. If you have Student Activity Booklets, copy only the items marked with an asterisk.

For Sessions 1 and 2

Student Sheet 25, Mystery Footprints (p. 211): 1 per student, homework

Geoblock Footprints, Sets A–C (pp. 214–216): 1 of each per pair

For Session 3

Student Sheet 26, Boxes for Our Collection (p. 212): 1 per student, homework (fill in date at the bottom before copying)

Geoblock Pictures, Sheets A–D* (pp. 221–224): 2–4 copies of each, plus 1 transparency of Sheet A*

For Sessions 4, 5, and 6

Student Sheet 27, Mystery Objects (p. 213): 1 per student, homework

Geoblock Footprints, Sets D–G (pp. 217–220): 1 of each per pair

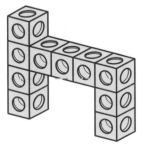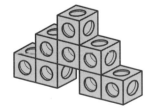

Sample "Cube Things"

Continued on next page

■ Students will be bringing in Mystery Boxes for Sessions 7–10; supplement these as needed to provide variety. There should be boxes with common sizes and shapes that students are likely to recognize, as well as some less familiar shapes. While most boxes will be rectangular prisms, try to find a few with unusual shapes. For example, look for oatmeal or corn meal in cylindrical boxes, or candy bars in boxes shaped like triangular prisms.

■ Before Sessions 8–10, cut up index cards to prepare box pieces for Sets A and B.

Set A has 12 box pieces in five shapes:

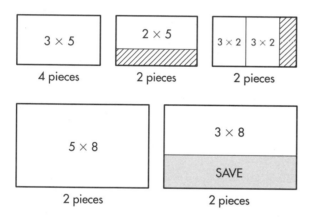

For each Set A, use seven 3-by-5 cards and four 5-by-8 cards. Cut three 3-by-5's as shown, discarding the leftover strips. Cut two 5-by-8's as shown, saving the extra for Set B.

Put the pieces for each Set A in an envelope, one per pair of students.

Set B provides seven new shapes. These will be sorted by shape, and students select the pieces they want to use. The following quantities allow 5–6 student pairs to make one new box each:

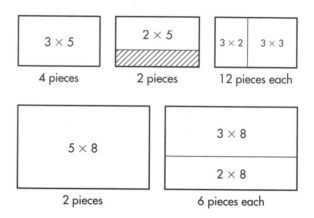

For this supply, use eighteen 3-by-5 cards and eight 5-by-8 cards. Cut fourteen 3-by-5's as shown, discarding the leftover strips. Cut six 5-by-8's as shown.

Double this quantity for a class of 20–24 students. Triple it for a class of 30–35. If students become intrigued with making boxes, you may need to replenish your supply of pieces as it is used up.

Sort the Set B box pieces by shape onto seven cardboard or plastic trays, paper plates, or flat boxes. If you staple a different shape to each tray, students can easily replace leftover pieces when they have finished working.

Describing and Comparing Shapes

What Happens

Students describe characteristics of some of the Geoblocks. They build and copy shapes made with interlocking cubes and match Geoblocks to outlines of the block faces. Their work focuses on:

- constructing and describing 3-D objects
- comparing size, shape, and orientation of objects
- developing vocabulary to describe 3-D shapes
- looking at 3-D objects as wholes and as having parts

Note About Materials

For the next few sessions, students use Geoblocks and interlocking cubes. If your students have already worked with those materials this year, they will be ready to do the specific tasks in this investigation. However, if they have not used these materials much recently, you will need to provide time for free exploration. Students need enough time to learn about the characteristics of cubes and Geoblocks and to discover relationships among the shapes. Free exploration gives students the chance to pursue their own ideas of what to make with the materials, so that later they can turn their attention to specific tasks you set for them.

You might make the cubes and Geoblocks, along with the pattern blocks (used in Investigation 1), available throughout the unit for individual exploration. As needed, include free exploration with Geoblocks as a Choice Time activity in this investigation. You will then need to add one or two sessions to give students time to explore materials as well as do the other Choice Time activities.

Materials

- Interlocking cubes (about 20 per student)
- Geoblocks (4 half-sets for the class)
- Your prepared Cube Things (4–5 for the class)
- Geoblock Footprints, Sets A–C (1 of each per student)
- Student Sheet 25 (1 per student, homework)

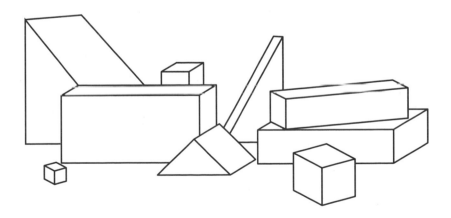
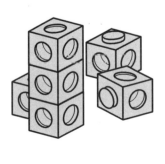

Describing Geoblocks

Note: Before introducing Geoblocks to the class, become familiar with the shapes in the set and their names by reading the **Teacher Note,** Types of 3-D Shapes (p. 71).

Seat students in such a way that everyone can reach some Geoblocks. Hold up one of the larger cubes from the Geoblock set and walk around with it so that everyone can get a look at it. Ask:

What is one thing you can say about this block?... OK, it's like a box. What else can you say?... It's smooth. It has corners. It has squares.

❖ **Tip for the Linguistically Diverse Classroom** As students name various attributes, point them out on the chosen block.

After students have described the shape, pick one of the things they said that distinguishes it from some of the other shapes in the Geoblock set:

One thing you said is that this shape looks like a box. Find another block that you think looks like a box and hold it up. It doesn't have to be exactly the same as this block, as long as it looks like a box.

Watch which blocks students select. Do some students have trouble finding a block that matches the description?

Choose one of the triangular prisms from the Geoblock set. Again, walk around to give everyone a look at it. Ask students to describe the block. Then, choose one of the characteristics mentioned by students. Use the student's own words:

Max said this block is pointy. Find another block that you think is pointy.

You might do this with one more block before introducing the Choice Time activities.

Choice Time

Post a list of the options for Choice Time, with a simple sketch as a visual reminder of each choice. If you need to include free exploration with Geoblocks during Choice Time, include optional Choice 3, Building with Geoblocks, and plan to expand Sessions 1–2 and 4–6 by one or two sessions.

Choices

1. Copying Cube Things

2. Geoblock Footprints

3. Building with Geoblocks (optional)

Briefly introduce the two main Choice Time activities to the class as described for each. Explain that students will be working on these choices for the rest of today and most of the next session. Students should work on both Choices 1 and 2 sometime during this Choice Time.

Choice 1: Copying Cube Things

Materials: Interlocking cubes (about 20 per student); 4–5 copies of the prepared Cube Thing

To introduce this activity, show one of the Cube Things you have made with 8–10 interlocking cubes. Tell students that one of their choices will be to make a Cube Thing that exactly matches this *shape* (the colors don't need to match). When they have made the shape, they should ask another student to check it, to see if they agree that it is the same.

Students begin by copying the given Cube Thing; when they have finished, they ask another student to help double-check that their Cube Thing matches the original, and make adjustments as needed.

Students may then pair up and make their own Cube Things for each other to copy. They may use no more than 10 cubes at first. You can adjust the maximum number of cubes, either for your class as a whole or for different pairs, to keep the task manageable but challenging. Your observations of students copying your first Cube Thing can help you decide on a reasonable number of total cubes for students to use. We suggest that students never use more than 20 cubes total.

Choice 2: Geoblock Footprints

Materials: Geoblocks (2 sets, divided in half and distributed at four stations); Geoblock Footprints, Sets A–C (1 of each per pair, or 2–3 copies at each Geoblock station)

To introduce the second choice, hold up a copy of Geoblock Footprints, Set A. Explain that these are "footprints" of some of the Geoblocks. The task is to find a block that fits on each footprint exactly. Demonstrate with one of the footprints. Emphasize that the challenge is to find just *one* block that fills the whole footprint.

At first, make available only the first two sets of Geoblock Footprints (A and B). Working in pairs, students choose one of these sheets. As they find blocks to match the footprints, they place each block directly on the matching print and leave it there until the whole sheet is filled. So, for example, for Geoblock Footprints, Set A, students will end up with seven blocks on the sheet. The blocks may all be different, or the same type of block may be used more than once.

If you notice that students cannot find all the shapes on a sheet and are becoming frustrated, they might move the sheet aside (leaving on it the blocks they have found so far) while they try another sheet. Everyone at the table, including the original pair, can keep an eye out for the missing blocks as they work on other sheets.

Some students may find combinations of blocks that fit inside each footprint. This approach will be more manageable at first for some students, especially those who have very little experience with the blocks. As they gain more experience, encourage them to try to identify single blocks that fill the footprint. After students have filled in all the footprints on a sheet with either a single block or a combination of blocks, you can ask them to try to find only one block that fits each footprint during another session of Choice Time.

Some students may not immediately realize that the triangular prisms have both triangular and rectangular faces. You may need to help them with the hint that sometimes rectangles are "hiding" within these triangular-looking shapes.

Geoblock Footprints, Set A is relatively easy, because many different blocks will fit each shape. For Set B, there is only one Geoblock to match some of the shapes, but the shapes are quite distinctive. Set C has eight different triangular faces. Some of these are easy to find, but again, some match only one Geoblock. It is possible to match a single block to each "footprint" on all three sheets, as long as you have a complete set of Geoblocks. Spend some time yourself finding blocks that fit the footprints. You can also use the chart of Geoblock shapes (p. 72) to figure out which blocks match a particular footprint.

Since students will return to this activity in Sessions 4–6, keep track of which footprint sets students have worked on. You can use a class list to jot down which sets they have done, or ask them to record those sets (by letter) in their math notebooks.

Observing the Students

Circulate to observe students' work on the two main activities.

Copying Cube Things

- Do students find ways to visualize the construction as made up of several parts in order to help them build it and check it? Can students find a way to get started, choosing a certain part of the Cube Thing to build first?
- Can students match their constructions to the original Cube Thing and determine if their constructions are the same or different? When their constructions don't match the original, can students adjust them by noticing differences between the two versions?
- Even if they don't have all the details exactly right, do students match the general size and shape of the original?
- Do students count the cubes as a way to help them check?

Geoblock Footprints

- Do students find block faces that match the outlines easily or with difficulty?
- Which shapes seem difficult for them to match?
- Do students notice that the triangular prisms have some rectangular faces, even though the overall shape seems to be triangular?
- Do students keep all the shapes on one sheet in mind as they work? For example, when a shape doesn't match one outline, do they check to see if it matches any of the others?
- If students can't find a single shape that matches an outline, can they put together a combination of shapes that fills the outline?
- Can students differentiate between different sizes of the same shape?
- Do students recognize differences between squares, triangles, and rectangles that are not squares?
- What vocabulary do students use to describe squares, rectangles, and triangles?

Sessions 1 and 2 Follow-Up

 **Homework**

Mystery Footprints Distribute Student Sheet 25, Mystery Footprints, which describes the homework assignment. Students choose one object at home that they think might be recognized from its outline or "footprint." As examples, draw the footprints of familiar objects, such as your hand, the chalkboard eraser, or a crayon, and ask students to guess what they are. Each student draws the outline of an object and brings it to school by Session 3, when the class will try to guess what it is. Remind students that, to keep the object a secret, they should not write its name on their footprint drawing. Some students may want to do more than one.

Types of 3-D Shapes

Your students will have their own informal ways of naming and describing the 3-D shapes they encounter. For example, they might call a cube a "box," or a sphere a "ball." They will also use names for 2-D shapes they know to describe 3-D shapes, calling a cube a "square" or a triangular prism a "triangle."

You can use the correct names for 3-D shapes so that students hear the terms, but you don't need to insist that they use them. It is more important that they focus on describing and comparing these shapes. Like the 2-D shapes, 3-D shapes are divided into two major categories, polyhedra and shapes that are not polyhedra. *Polyhedra* are shapes that have only flat faces. All the blocks in the Geoblock set are polyhedra.

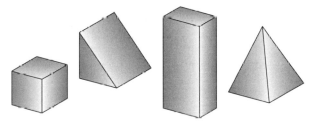

Students will also encounter, in their environment and in other building sets, shapes that are not polyhedra, such as spheres, cylinders, cones, and others.

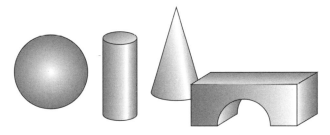

Polyhedra are sometimes classified by the number of their faces. For example, a four-faced polyhedron is called a *tetrahedron,* while an eight-faced polyhedron is an *octahedron.* However, polyhedra are also classified another way, as in the Geoblock set. Most of the blocks in the set, and many of the common 3-D shapes you and your students see in everyday life, are prisms.

Prisms are 3-D shapes that have two congruent faces connected by rectangular faces.

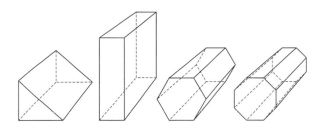

A prism is named by the two congruent faces. The first shape above is called a *triangular prism* because it has two faces that are triangles. These triangles are connected by faces that are rectangles. The second shape is called a *rectangular prism.* In a rectangular prism, all the faces are rectangles. The third shape is a *hexagonal prism.* The fourth is an *octagonal prism.*

The Geoblock set includes a variety of rectangular prisms, including cubes (rectangular prisms in which all of the faces are squares). The set also includes a variety of triangular prisms. (See the chart on the next page for examples.) Some students enjoy learning the names *triangular prism* and *rectangular prism.*

One shape in the Geoblock set is not a prism; it is a pyramid. A pyramid may have any polygon as its base, and all other faces are triangles that connect at a single vertex. Like prisms, pyramids are named by the shapes of their bases. Here are a triangular pyramid, two square pyramids, and a pentagonal pyramid.

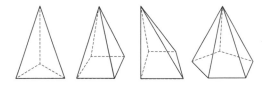

The third pyramid is like the one in the Geoblock set. A chart depicting all 25 different types of Geoblocks, and their quantities, appears on the next page.

Geoblock Set

Cube A
1 cm × 1 cm × 1 cm
Quantity: 128

Cube B
2 cm × 2 cm × 2 cm
Quantity: 32

Cube C
3 cm × 3 cm × 3 cm
Quantity: 12

Cube D
4 cm × 4 cm × 4 cm
Quantity: 8

Rectangular prism E
2 cm × 4 cm × 2 cm
Quantity: 8

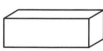

Rectangular prism F
2 cm × 6 cm × 2 cm
Quantity: 4

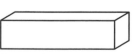

Rectangular prism G
2 cm × 8 cm × 2 cm
Quantity: 4

Rectangular prism H
2 cm × 4 cm × 4 cm
Quantity: 12

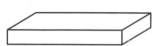

Rectangular prism I
1 cm × 8 cm × 4 cm
Quantity: 8

Rectangular prism J
2 cm × 8 cm × 4 cm
Quantity: 4

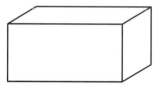

Rectangular prism K
4 cm × 8 cm × 4 cm
Quantity: 2

Triangular prism L
2 cm × 2 cm × 2 cm
Quantity: 32

Triangular prism M
4 cm × 4 cm × 4 cm
Quantity: 6

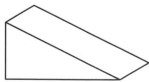

Triangular prism N
4 cm × 8 cm × 4 cm
Quantity: 2

Triangular prism O
4 cm × 4 cm × 2 cm
Quantity: 12

Triangular prism P
3 cm × 3 cm × 4 cm
Quantity: 8

Triangular prism Q
2 cm × 4 cm × 4 cm
Quantity: 2

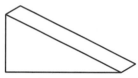

Triangular prism R
4 cm × 8 cm × 2 cm
Quantity: 6

Triangular prism S
2 cm × 8 cm × 4 cm
Quantity: 6

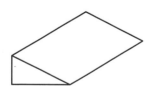

Triangular prism T
2 cm × 4 cm × 8 cm
Quantity: 6

Triangular prism U
4 cm × 8 cm × 1 cm
Quantity: 6

Triangular prism V
2 cm × 4 cm × 2 cm
Quantity: 4

Triangular prism W
4 cm × 3.5 cm × 2 cm
Quantity: 6

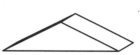

Triangular prism X
2 cm × 8 cm × 2 cm
Quantity: 6

Pyramid Y
4 cm × 4 cm × 4 cm
Quantity: 6

Block Pictures

What Happens

Students describe Geoblocks, then match Geoblocks to pictures of the blocks. They compare blocks and discuss with their partners how they decided which block is shown in the picture. Their work focuses on:

- describing characteristics of 3-D shapes
- matching a 3-D object to a 2-D picture of the object
- comparing 3-D shapes

Materials

- Stick-on notes or scrap paper
- Geoblocks (4 half-sets for the class)
- Geoblock Pictures, Sheets A–D (2–4 copies of each)
- Transparency of Geoblock Pictures, Sheet A
- Overhead projector
- Student Sheet 26 (1 per student, homework)

Activity

Sharing Mystery Footprints from Home

As students come into school today, ask them to post their "mystery footprints" somewhere in the classroom. Put stick-on notes or scrap paper near the footprints so that students can write guesses about what they think the objects might be. Encourage everyone to look at the pictures and make guesses as they are getting ready to start the day, or at any other free time they have before math class.

In a day or two, after students have had a chance to make guesses, ask the person who made each drawing to write on it the name of the object that made that footprint.

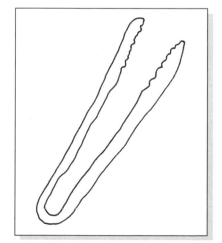 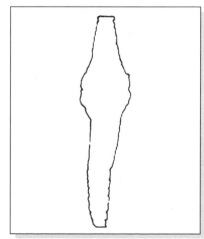 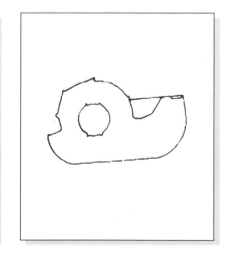

Describing Geoblocks

Spend a few minutes revisiting the activity you did to open Session 1. This time, students take turns holding up a block and naming one characteristic of that block; then everyone else finds a block that has the same characteristic. Start this activity yourself by choosing a couple of blocks with particular characteristics for students to find. For example:

My block has a side shaped like a triangle. Find a block with a side shaped like a triangle.

My block has sides that are all squares. Find a block that has all the sides shaped like squares.

❖ **Tip for the Linguistically Diverse Classroom** Show the attribute you want students to focus on. For example, as you say "My block has a side shaped like a triangle," trace the triangular outline of a side with your finger.

When students take the leader role, some will name characteristics that *all* the blocks have. For example, they might say a block is "smooth" or "made of wood" or "has corners." Accept these characteristics, but provide opportunities for others in the class to comment on whether all or just some of the blocks have the characteristic. For example, you might say:

Was it easy or hard to find a block that is smooth? Can you find a block that is *not* smooth?…Was it easy or hard to find a block that has a long, thin rectangle? Can you find a block that does not have a long thin rectangle?

Students may also enjoy talking about what the different shapes remind them of in their own experiences. An example of such a discussion appears in the **Dialogue Box,** It Reminds Me Of… (p. 78).

Introducing Block Pictures

All students should be seated where they can reach some Geoblocks. Give each pair of students a set of the Geoblock Pictures, Sheets A and B. Challenge them to find the blocks shown in the pictures. Point out to students that the blocks in the pictures are not the same size as the real blocks. You can relate this to photographs of people; in a photo, the person is smaller than in real life.

After a few minutes, call attention to Geoblock Pictures, Sheet A. If you have an overhead projector, show the transparency of this sheet. Ask students to hold up the block they think matches the rectangular prism. It is likely that students will have identified more than one possible block to match each picture. Point out some of the different blocks, and ask students to talk about how they could choose which one really matches.

Encourage students to talk about how they found the block.

Was there a block you thought was right at first, but then you decided it wasn't? How did you decide which block was the best match?

See the **Dialogue Box,** Comparing Blocks to Pictures, (p. 79) for examples of this kind of discussion.

Teacher Checkpoint

Block Pictures

For the rest of the session, students continue matching blocks to the pictures. As they complete Sheets A and B, make available copies of Geoblock Pictures, Sheets C and D.

Use this opportunity, while students are at work, to circulate among your students and listen to their conversations.

- Do students seem familiar with the Geoblock shapes? Do they seem to know what shape they are looking for? Listen for remarks like this: "I know, it's the one that's just like this one, only thinner." Do students focus on just one face at a time, or can they think about more than one? Are there some students who seem to poke around in the Geoblock container without much idea of what kind of block they are looking for?

- Do students try to match the Geoblock to the picture carefully, or do they simply select the first Geoblock that has a vague resemblance to the picture? Do some students who work carefully have a very hard time seeing which block might match? Which shapes do they have a hard time with?

- Are students using language that describes differences between shapes? For example, do they talk about shapes that are *thick* or *thin, tall* or *short*?

- Do they notice which faces are squares, rectangles, and triangles? Do they describe differences between triangular faces, for example, calling one *taller* or *pointier* than another?

What you observe will help you adjust the activity for Choice Time in Sessions 4 and 5.

If you have students who seem overwhelmed by the number and variety of blocks or have a hard time matching the shapes to the pictures, consider these options:

- Give them more time for free exploration and building with the Geoblocks.
- Give them more time with Geoblock Footprints. Allow them to find either one block or a combination of blocks to fill the outlines.
- Limit the set of blocks they use with the pictures. For example, for each sheet give them 10 or 12 blocks to choose from, including the ones pictured.

If some students are selecting Geoblocks to match the pictures too quickly, without carefully comparing blocks, you might try something like this: Put out four blocks that match one of the pictures in some way. Include the correct block. Ask students to select the block they think is the best match and to convince you that it isn't one of the other three. Remind them to take more time selecting blocks that match the pictures so that they can prove to you they've found the best match.

It is sometimes difficult to be sure about finding the "correct" block; instead, emphasize finding the "best match." Sometimes there are blocks that look quite close to the pictured block, even though they are not the "right" block, as you will see if you try matching the blocks yourself. Don't worry if some students settle on blocks that are not the *exact* match, so long as they match closely and students have thought carefully about alternative blocks.

Boxes for Our Collection In preparation for Session 7, ask students to bring small, empty boxes from home. Hand out Student Sheet 26, Boxes for Our Collection, which explains the assignment. Point out the date that tells when you will need the boxes.

Homework

Be sure students understand that they need to cover each box with heavy paper or newspaper so that no one can tell what originally came in the box. Other students will be guessing what each box might have contained by looking at its size and shape. You might show a box you have covered with paper so they have a clearer image of what you expect.

The size guideline suggests that students don't bring anything bigger than a cereal box or a shoe box. Ask students to demonstrate with their hands how big a cereal box or a shoe box is. If you have students who may have difficulty covering their boxes at home, encourage them to bring in uncovered boxes that you can help them cover.

Note: As boxes are brought in, number them consecutively by writing a number on the outside, so that the class will have a way to refer to each box. To keep track of the numbering, you could post a list of students' names and the numbers for the boxes they bring in, or use a 100 chart to mark off each number as you use it.

It Reminds Me Of...

For the activity Describing Geoblocks (p. 74), this teacher shows the class several different Geoblocks. As the students compare each shape to shapes they have seen in their environment, they are thinking about overall size and shape as well as the relative lengths of the sides of that shape.

[Holding up shape D, a cube] **Who can say something about this block?**

Susanna: It's a square shape.

Tuan: It's a 3-D shape.

Jonah: A cube.

Yukiko: It has 8 points.

Tony: It looks like a box.

Shavonne: Like a sugar cube.

Brady: It's like my little sister's alphabet blocks.

[Holding up shape K, the largest rectangular prism] **Here's another shape.**

Libby: It has squares.

What else do you see?

Jamaar: Rectangles.

Yanni: It's a long box.

Fernando: It could be the side of a building.

Andre: It could be a mailbox.

Chris: It could be a milk carton.

Eva: A tissue box.

Tamika: A washing machine.

Chanthou: A treasure chest.

The teacher then asks a student to choose a shape. Claire chooses shape I, a flat rectangular prism.

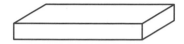

Diego: A book.

Kristi Ann: It's a rectangle.

Leah: A really thin rectangle.

William: If you're going to buy a watch or a pen, this is like the box it comes in.

Nadia: It's like a piece of mail.

Jacinta: The chalkboard.

Jamaar: A picture frame.

Max: It has eight corners.

Yukiko: Just like the other one. They both had eight corners.

Comparing Blocks to Pictures

During the activity Introducing Block Pictures (p. 74), these students have found Geoblocks that they think are matches for the two pictures on Geoblock Pictures, Sheet A. The teacher asks them to hold up the block they think matches the first picture of a rectangular prism. By encouraging them to carefully compare shapes, the teacher helps them focus on the attributes of the block in the picture and select a block that matches. To encourage discussion, she asks students to talk about blocks that *don't* match as well as blocks that do.

I see a few different blocks being held up. How did you decide which block matches the picture?

Luis: It's thin. You can see that it's real thin on the ends.

Iris: It has rectangles.

So it has rectangles and it's thin on the ends. Did anyone have a block that you thought was right at first, but then you changed your mind?

Michelle: I thought it might be this one. *[She holds up block G.]* See, it's kind of thin, too. But then I noticed it has squares on the ends and this one doesn't have squares.

OK, good observation. Anyone else have a block that they think works or a reason why a block doesn't work for this picture?

Mia: At first we picked up this one [block I], because it's kind of long. But now we don't think it works.

Why did you change your mind?

[Mia shrugs. The teacher then holds up the two blocks together.]

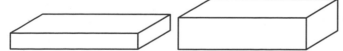

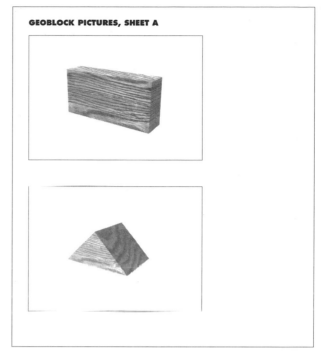

GEOBLOCK PICTURES, SHEET A

Who can help out? What can you say about these two blocks? Is there a way they're the same? Is there a way they're different?

Chris: They are kind of the same, because look, this way. *[Chris holds them together and shows how the longest dimensions are the same on the two blocks.]*

[The teacher holds the two on the overhead so that the 4-by-8 side on each block is projected.] **It's kind of like footprints. If you look at them this way, they have the same footprint. Is there a way they're different?**

Claire: If you look at it another way, it's much, much thinner.

[The teacher then shows the 1-by-8 face of block I and the 2-by-8 face of block J on the overhead.]

So if you look at them this way, they look quite different. That's what Luis was saying before. Mia, does that have anything to do with why you changed your idea about which block works?

Mia: Yeah. That one's too thin.

Blocks in a Sock

Materials

- Interlocking cubes (about 20 per student)
- Geoblocks (4 half-sets per class)
- Geoblocks J and P for demonstration
- Geoblock Pictures, Sheets A–D from Session 3 (2–4 copies of each)
- Small bags or socks (1 per pair)
- Geoblock Footprints, Sets D–G (1 of each per pair)
- Student Sheet 27 (1 per student, homework)

What Happens

Students play the game Blocks in a Sock (or Blocks in a Bag) in which they try to identify a Geoblock by feeling its shape. During Choice Time, students continue to explore the characteristics of the Geoblocks and of constructions made with interlocking cubes. Their work focuses on:

- identifying 3-D objects by matching them to outlines of their faces
- identifying the characteristics of 3-D objects by touch
- describing and comparing sizes and shapes
- becoming familiar with a variety of squares, rectangles, and triangles
- matching a 3-D object to a 2-D picture of the object

Activity

Introducing Blocks in a Sock

Show students the two blocks (block J and block P) that are pictured on Geoblock Pictures, Sheet A.

Remember you decided that these two blocks match the pictures on this sheet? I'm going to put these two blocks in this sock [bag]. One of you is going to put your hand in the sock and try to pick out this one *[indicates the top picture, the rectangular prism]* **just by feeling it. Who would like to try?**

Give several volunteers a chance to put a hand into the sock, feel the two blocks, and try to tell by feel which is the one specified. No one should pull a block out of the bag to check yet. Give several students a chance to feel the blocks and try to tell which is the one in the picture you have chosen.

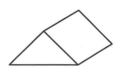

As students are feeling the blocks, encourage them to say how they can tell which block is which. For example, students might say, "I can tell which one it is because it's long and skinny," or "It's shaped like a box." Finally, ask one or two students to volunteer to reach in and pull out the block that matches the picture.

Explain that during Choice Time, students will work in pairs with one of the picture sheets. They first find the Geoblocks that match the pictures, then put those Geoblocks in a sock. One student chooses one of the pictures, and the other student tries to pull the matching block out of the sock. Then they trade roles and do it again.

Choice Time

The rest of Sessions 4, 5, and 6 is Choice Time. Post the list of choices, adding Blocks in a Sock (or Bag). Continue to include Building with Geoblocks if students seem to need more free-exploring experience to become familiar with them.

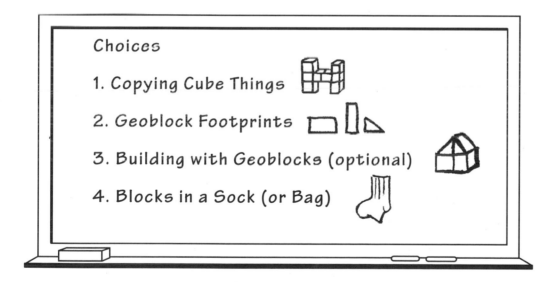

Choices

1. Copying Cube Things

2. Geoblock Footprints

3. Building with Geoblocks (optional)

4. Blocks in a Sock (or Bag)

Choice 1: Copying Cube Things

Materials: Interlocking cubes (about 20 per student)

Students work in pairs. Each student makes a Cube Thing from a small number of blocks. Partners then trade Cube Things and try to make an exact copy of each other's construction.

Choice 2: Geoblock Footprints

Materials: Geoblocks; Geoblock Footprints, Sets A–C and Sets D–G

Students who have completed Geoblock Footprints A and B can go on to Set C. For students who are easily finding matches for the footprints in Sets A–C, make available Sets D–G. Each of these sheets shows from three to six copies of the same footprint; students are to find a different block for each footprint on the sheet. (Note that students need not complete all Sets A–C before working on Sets D–G.)

Choice 3: Building with Geoblocks (optional)

Materials: Geoblocks

If you are including this choice for more free exploration of the Geoblocks, you might suggest students try Building a Wall, an activity that helps focus their attention on relationships among the Geoblocks. Start with block K (the 4-by-4-by-8 centimeter block), a rectangular prism that can be made in a variety of ways with other blocks. This is the first block of the wall. The task is to continue the wall, using any blocks from the set, but keeping the wall the same height and thickness.

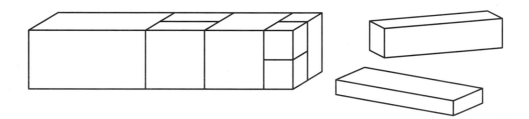

Choice 4: Blocks in a Sock

Materials: Geoblocks; socks or bags (1 per pair); Geoblock Pictures, Sheets A–D (2–4 copies of each)

Each pair of students chooses one sheet of Geoblock Pictures. First, they find the Geoblock that matches each picture; then they put the two or three blocks in a sock (or bag). One student chooses one of the pictures, and the other student feels inside the bag, without looking, and tries to pull out that block. Students take turns choosing a picture and finding the matching block.

After working with one picture sheet, they can try a different one. Here's one way to organize this: At a table with three pairs of students, put one each of the four Picture Sheets on the table. Each pair chooses one sheet to begin. After they have played with one sheet, the pair can select another sheet. Since each pair is using a different sheet, students won't need the same blocks at the same time.

Some students may feel more comfortable starting with one of the sheets that shows pairs of blocks (Sheets A and B); others may want to try a sheet with three blocks (Sheets C and D). Students who want a further level of challenge can combine a two-block with a three-block sheet and hide a total of five blocks in the sock.

Observing the Students

Circulate to observe as students work on the choices. See pp. 69–70 for guidelines on observing students' work on Choice 1, Copying Cube Things, and Choice 2, Geoblock Footprints.

Blocks in a Sock

- Are students able to find by feel a block that matches the one they are seeing? Do students identify a block by focusing on only one characteristic, or do they explore enough parts of the block to distinguish the target block? Do students examine the pictures of both blocks to help them?

- Which characteristics are they able to recognize easily? Which are more difficult? Do they notice the shapes of all the faces of the block? Do they notice the dimensions of the block (one is fat, another is thin)?

- Can they informally describe differences in size and shape?

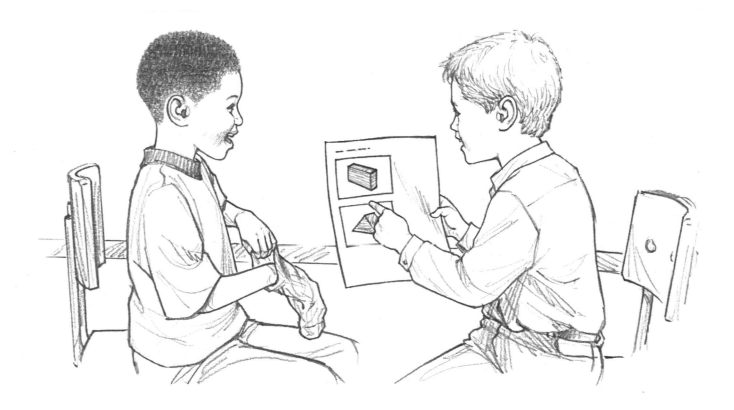

Sessions 4, 5, and 6 Follow-Up

 **Homework**

Boxes for Our Collection: Reminder Encourage students to bring in their covered Mystery Boxes. You will be starting to use them in Session 7. As boxes come in from home, keep numbering them consecutively.

Mystery Objects Give each student a copy of Student Sheet 27, Mystery Objects. This is a version of Blocks in a Sock that students play at home with someone in their families. They choose 3–5 small, common objects for which there are duplicates (two of each object). Students can make the game easier or more difficult by choosing objects that are very similar or very different. For example, an easier version might include a piece of macaroni, a penny, a straw, and a bottle cap. A more difficult version might include a penny, a dime, a nickel, a bottle cap, and a checker.

Players put one of each object in a bag or sock, and leave the other one out where they can see it. As one player points to an object, the other player tries to find it in the bag by feel and pull it out.

They finish by writing a few sentences about their experience. Students who are not comfortable writing may give their responses orally and ask a family member to record for them.

❖ **Tip for the Linguistically Diverse Classroom** Family members may record their children's responses in their native language.

> **5.** After playing the game, write about what you did. Tell what objects you used. Tell what was easy or hard.
>
> I used batteries, pennies, quarters, caps for markers and dimes, penny and dime are similar so it is hard to guess them. The cap is different from all others so it's easy to guess

 **Extension**

Mystery Objects in Class The homework activity Mystery Objects can also be played in class with common objects found in the classroom. This activity will encourage conversation about shape, size, and texture.

What Kind of Box Is It?

What Happens

As a class, students look at Mystery Boxes they have brought from home; they talk about what kind of boxes they might be and why. After discussing how many flat sides (faces) a box has, they are introduced to a new activity: constructing their own boxes. Their work focuses on:

- relating size and shape to function
- describing a rectangular prism (a rectangular box shape)
- making 3-D objects out of 2-D pieces

Materials

- Collection of Mystery Boxes
- Box pieces, set A, in envelopes (1 set per pair)
- One completed box for demonstration
- Clear tape or masking tape (several rolls)
- Scissors (1 pair per 3–4 students)

Looking at Mystery Boxes

As a whole group, look at the covered boxes that have been brought from home. Hold up about five of the boxes, one at a time, and ask students to visualize what each might have contained.

Here's one of the Mystery Boxes that you brought in. We have numbers on all the boxes so we have a way to talk about them. This one is number 4. Don't say anything yet; just look at the box carefully. Look at its size and shape. What kind of box do you think it is? What did it have inside?

Ask students for their ideas about what kind of box this one is. After a few moments, hold up a new box and ask students to imagine what could have been in this new box. Repeat with four or five boxes. Try to choose boxes that are quite different from each other in size and shape. Include a few that you think will be distinctive and recognizable for your students, and one or two that you think will be less familiar. Some good choices for this activity are a toothpaste box, a small jewelry box, an oatmeal box (a cylinder), a shoe box, and a cereal box.

❖ **Tip for the Linguistically Diverse Classroom** Suggest that second-language students respond by drawing their ideas on index cards. As they hold up a drawing, identify what they have drawn to the rest of the class. For example, a student might draw a ring to identify what he or she believed to be a jewelry box.

Record students' ideas by writing their guesses, either with marker directly on the box's wrapping or on a card taped to the box, so that you will have a list of the class's ideas on each box. (Using a separate card or piece of paper will keep the paper covering the boxes from being torn as students write their own guesses over the next few days.)

Ask some follow-up questions about students' guesses that focus their attention on the sizes and shapes of the boxes. For example:

Libby guessed that this box might have held earrings, and Andre said a bracelet. Why do you think these might be good guesses?

Iris thinks Box 5 might be a raisin box and Jacinta thought it could be cough drops. Who has a reason they think that Box 5 is or isn't a raisin box or a cough drop box?

No one thought that Box 31 could be a shoe box. Why do you think it isn't a shoe box?

Suppose I said that one of these boxes is a cereal box. Which one do you think it is? Why do you think that one rather than this one?

Choose a place in the room where all the Mystery Boxes can be displayed for the next few days. Explain that students can write (or draw) their guesses on the box (or on the card attached to the box) during Choice Time or at other times of the day. You may want to direct students to this activity when they first arrive in the morning or at other appropriate times. Let them know that in a few days, you will take the wrappings off so they can see what the Mystery Boxes really are.

How Many Sides?

Give every student or student pair a box from the Mystery Box collection. Pose the following question:

In a minute I want you to tell me how many flat sides your box has. But first, what do you think I mean when I say "a flat side"?

Let a few students give their ideas. Clarify what you mean by indicating one face on a few different boxes.

Mathematicians call each of these flat sides a *face,* but a lot of people call them *sides.* So you can use the fancy name, *face,* if you want to, or you can call them *sides.*

Now look at your box and figure out how many faces (or sides) it has. Don't tell me yet. In a minute, after you've thought about it, I want to know how you are sure. You can work with a neighbor to help you count.

Give students a minute or two to study their boxes. Then collect their ideas, asking them how many faces their boxes have and how they know for sure. Many students will say, "I counted." Follow up with questions like these:

How can you be sure you counted each face? How do you know you didn't count one twice? Who had a way of keeping track of which ones you counted?

These questions will help students think about the way the faces are arranged in relation to each other.

Most of your boxes will probably be rectangular prisms, with three pairs of opposite faces, or six faces in all. You may have some other boxes with different shapes as well. If you have any cylindrical boxes, students may be intrigued about how to count the curved side. Ask them how they think they should count it.

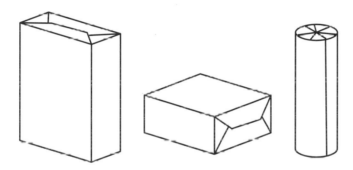

Bring this discussion to a close by summarizing the results:

A lot of you decided that your boxes have six faces. Hold up your box if you think it has six faces. OK, everyone look around at these boxes. What's the same about all the boxes with six faces?

Who has a box that doesn't have six faces? How many faces does it have?

Your students may not come up with a complete description of a rectangular prism, but they will begin to notice some of the features of this common 3-D shape.

Ask student helpers to collect all the Mystery Boxes and place them in the planned display area.

Making Boxes with Cards

As you introduce this activity, which students will be doing for the next three sessions, relate the box pieces to the faces students just counted on their boxes. Start by showing students the box you have made, along with some flat box pieces.

Now you're going to make your own box, like this one, from flat pieces and tape. Here's what the flat pieces look like. You're going to figure out how to put them together.

You and your partner will get a set of flat pieces in different sizes. These pieces won't all fit together. It's like a puzzle. You have to figure out *which* pieces you can put together to make a box. The box should have sides, a bottom, and a top.

Open one envelope of Set A box pieces and show them to the class. Ask for volunteers to suggest how you might start by indicating two pieces that could be taped together. Demonstrate the taping of those two pieces. If you think it's needed, show how to attach one more side.

It's a good idea to offer some guidelines about the use of tape. For example:

Decide what you're going to tape first. Then take small pieces of tape to attach the cards along their edges.

Many teachers precut a lot of small pieces of tape and put them on the edge of the tables where students are working, so that students can just take a piece when they are ready for it. This system helps provide students with a supply of reasonably sized pieces. Other teachers feel that they need to be the only person who cuts off pieces of tape, and they let the students know this rule.

Each pair of students works with one envelope of Set A box pieces. This gives students the pieces they need to make two different boxes: one that's 3 by 5 by 8, and another that's 3 by 5 by 2.

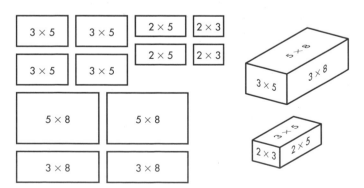

Encourage students to do some planning before they start taping by holding pieces next to each other to see how they want to put them together. If they tape some pieces and decide that it's not what they want, they can just cut through the tape to take them apart.

Decide where students can keep their boxes in progress. They will continue working on them during the next three sessions. When they set them aside, students should be sure to write their names or initials on their boxes.

Session 7 Follow-Up

Paper Boxes If you can get the book *The House* by Monique Felix (American Educational Publishing, 1993), this story without words gives a wonderful visual account of putting together a box (house) by cutting and folding paper.

 **Extension**

Making Boxes

Materials

- Set A box pieces in envelopes (from Session 7)
- Set B box pieces, sorted by size, in trays or boxes
- Clear or masking tape
- Scissors (1 pair per 3–4 students)

What Happens

Students construct their own boxes out of cardboard rectangles. As boxes are finished, students compare their sizes and shapes. Over the three days, students continue writing their guesses about the Mystery Boxes. At the end of Session 10, students select some of the Mystery Boxes to be revealed. Their work focuses on:

- visualizing and describing rectangular prisms
- constructing 3-D objects from 2-D shapes
- building rectangular prisms from 2-D pieces
- recognizing which faces of a rectangular prism are the same size and shape

Note: Keep the class collection of Mystery Boxes on display through Sessions 8–10. Remind students to continue making guesses about what the boxes held, and to record their guesses according to your plan (either on the boxes themselves or on attached cards).

Activity

Making Boxes with Cards

For most of these three class sessions, students continue their work on making boxes. You will see a range of how students put the pieces together. Some will make a standard box shape, with opposite faces the same size. Others will cut or bend pieces to *make* them fit together. This range of approaches is to be expected for students at this level. For more information about how students approach this task, see the **Teacher Note,** Students Create Their Own Boxes (p. 96). Students should be sure their names or initials are on their completed boxes.

If some students easily make both boxes with the Set A pieces, introduce the trays of Set B card pieces for making additional boxes. Let everyone know that once they have made two boxes with the Set A pieces, they can try to make some different boxes with pieces from Set B. This task is even more like a puzzle than Set A, because they have to find which pieces go together to make a new box. Some students may become interested in making several different boxes.

Set B allows six new possible boxes:

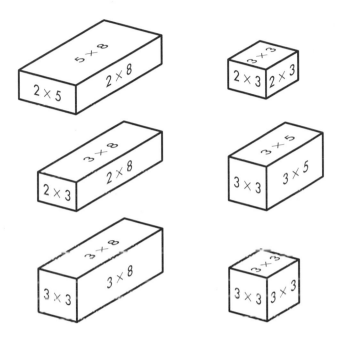

Encourage students to try to make a box that is a different size and shape
from the ones they made previously. Students might also enjoy another box-
making activity, Making Boxes with Cubes (Extension, p. 94).

Observing the Students

This activity requires students to pay attention to the characteristics of
a rectangular prism: how faces come together at edges, how opposite sides
of the prism are the same size and shape. As students build their boxes out
of flat pieces, they begin to get the feel for the parts of a box and how 2-D
shapes can be put together to make a 3-D shape. As you observe students
at work, the following questions can guide your observations and questions
to students:

- Do the students make use of the information that opposite faces of a
  rectangular box (a rectangular prism) are the same size and shape?
  Do they choose adjacent faces with edges of equal lengths?

- Do students lay out the pieces on the table and see how they can "fold"
  them up into a box?

- When students begin a box that doesn't work, do they seem stuck, or do
  they try a different combination of pieces? Do they learn from what
  doesn't work how to make better choices, or do they start again, choosing pieces randomly?

- When students run into a problem, can they figure out a way to over-
  come it to finish their box, even if the result is not a conventional box?

Comparing Cardboard Boxes

Devote about 20 minutes at the end of Session 9 to a whole-group discussion about how many different boxes have been made. Students should have their boxes in front of them. Take one box from a pair of students, and ask anyone who has a box like it to hold up their box. Repeat with a second box. In this way, gather a collection of one example of each different box that students have made so far.

If some students notice that the same boxes may look different, depending on how they are positioned, ask for some examples. The question of whether a box is in fact the same size and shape if it is positioned differently may also come up. For example, if we stand the 3-by-5-by-8 box so that the 3-by-5 card is on the bottom, it looks tall and not very wide. With the 5-by-8 card on the bottom, the same box looks different—long and wide, but not very tall. These are certainly different-looking shapes, but they do have the same dimensions.

Some students may not be able to see that a box is the same size and shape when it is turned differently. You don't need to resolve this issue for the class, but do engage them in conversation about why they think two of the same size box, in different positions, are the same or different. You might also put out three or four boxes, then show another box that is the same size and shape as one of them but in a different position, and ask which box it matches.

You may want to start a display with one of each size of box that has been made so far. Then students can compare new boxes they make to these boxes. As students go back to their box work in Session 10, you can challenge them to construct boxes that are different from those in the display.

Revealing the Mystery Boxes

At the end of Session 10, gather students where they can see the Mystery Boxes. Ask them to agree on one box they feel sure they can identify. They then share their ideas about what it held and describe what they noticed about its size and shape that gave them clues about what kind of box it is. See the **Dialogue Box,** Baby Shoes and Birdhouses (p. 95), for an example of this discussion.

After several students have given their opinions, take off the paper wrapping and reveal the box. Repeat with two or three boxes, always choosing ones that students seem to have a definite idea about.

Then ask if there are any boxes that students are particularly curious about.

Are there any boxes that are really a mystery to you? Is there one that you want me to unwrap because it was really hard to guess?

Allow several students to choose boxes and unwrap them. It's not necessary to unwrap all the Mystery Boxes during this math class. If interest is high, you might designate another time during the day when students who are interested can unwrap more of the boxes; or you may want to have one more session with the whole class to unwrap a few more. For some classes, revealing the few you have looked at in this session will be satisfying enough.

Extension

Making Boxes with Cubes If you have any students who cannot manage taping the cards together, you might introduce this as an alternative activity (or an additional activity for any students). You will need the class set of interlocking cubes (50–60 per pair) and a collection of small objects, such as pencils of different lengths, crayons, shells, small toys (cars, people, or animals).

Students make a box of interlocking cubes to hold a small object. They may work alone or in pairs. Each student (or pair) selects an object and makes a box that is *just* the right size to hold the object. (Of course, it should have a little leeway so the object can be easily put in and taken out of the box.) They should be able to actually put the object in the box when it is finished. The box doesn't need to have a top; it can be an open box, so the object inside it can be seen.

Following are some guidelines for observing students' work on cube boxes:

■ When students build their cube boxes, do they use the size of the object to estimate the length, width, and height of their boxes? Do they keep using their object to check the size of their box?

■ Do they gradually construct a reasonably box-like container? As they are building, do they evaluate their work? Do they modify their box, based on what they see? Do they make opposite faces of the box the same size and shape?

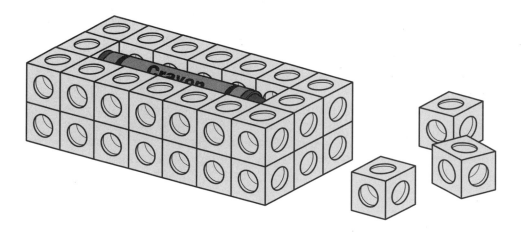

Baby Shoes and Birdhouses

This class is having a final discussion about what the Mystery Boxes might be before some of them are revealed. The teacher is holding up a large box, about 12 by 8 by 3 inches.

Brady: It's cereal. I'm positive. It's exactly like my mom's box of corn flakes.

Garrett: I think it's cereal, too, because it couldn't be like a shoe box or something, because it's tall like that and it's skinnier.

Libby: But it could be something like maybe a box that had some blocks or some building toys, because I have a box like that, and it has blocks in it.

Any more ideas?... OK, we're going to unwrap it. *[It turns out to be a cereal box.]* **You had great ideas about what might make sense for this box. You were really thinking about its size and shape. Nadia, do you want to choose one for us to unwrap?**

[Nadia chooses a box that is about 9 by 4 by 4 inches. Through the paper, it appears to have a top that fits on one of the 9-by-4 faces.]

Susanna: Baby shoes. Because it's small and has a top on it.

Tuan: I agree with Susanna because when my little sister got a pair, they came in a box like this.

[The teacher asks Nathan to unwrap it. It has a shoe brand name on it. Students call out, "Shoe box!"]

OK, we'll do one more today. Then, if you want to, we can pick a few again while we're waiting for them to call the buses at the end of the day. *[The teacher chooses a house shape: a rectangular prism with a triangular prism on top of it, like a roof.]*

Yukiko: A birdhouse.

Why do you think so?

Yukiko: Because it looks like one.

What makes it look like one?

Yukiko: The pointy end.

Luis: A doughnut box. That's the kind my dad gets when he gets doughnuts.

Eva: I know! It's a kids' meal. A hamburger box. And fries. 'Cause it's like ones I had before. The pointy part is where the handle is so you can carry it.

Shall we unwrap it now? *[Lots of "yes!" shouts.]* **Do you remember who brought this box in? Iris?** *[Iris unwraps it.]*

Various students: Animal crackers! We never guessed it!

Students at this age level have a variety of approaches to making boxes out of flat pieces. Making a box requires visualizing how 2-D pieces can go together to make a 3-D shape, selecting pieces that fit together in the right way, and enough manual dexterity to actually put the pieces together. Some students carefully lay out pieces flat on the table and can see how they will "fold up," once they are taped together, to make a box. They put on the top after the rest is taped.

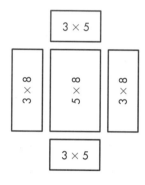

Some students who use this approach have difficulty finding the pieces that make a box. In the following example, these students have placed five sides in relationship to each other to make the bottom and sides of the box, but not all the opposite sides match in size and shape. When they tape these pieces, they will find that one side is smaller than the opposite side.

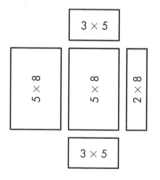

Expect students to make first attempts (such as this one) that don't work. Encourage them to find a way to fix the problem. Their approaches might include these:

- Cutting off the side that doesn't work and replacing it with a piece of a different size.
- Cutting a piece to attach onto the short side, making it closer in size to the opposite side.
- Bending a 5-by-8 card to attach the short side to its opposite side, making a curved "roof."

Making a box is a complex task for young students. You don't need to insist that students make their boxes in the conventional manner if they solve the problems posed by this task in a reasonable way. For example, in one class, a first grader ignored the precut pieces and pieced together his own box by cutting pieces the sizes he wanted.

Some students may begin with the precut pieces, then cut their own pieces to finish the box. This is a common solution when students have taped together four sides, but find there is no piece that fits for the other two sides. For example, one first grade student attached four 3-by-5 cards together, but then had no 5-by-5 pieces for the top and bottom:

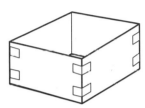

In this case, you can remind students that these pieces are like a puzzle and that they need to try a different combination of pieces if one way doesn't work. However, for some students, getting four sides together may have taken a great deal of work and attention, and you may want to let them cut a top and bottom to fit rather than starting again. One pair of students made four sides out of 5-by-8 pieces, leaving an 8-by-8 opening top and bottom. Since there were no 8-by-8 pieces, they experimented until they found that they could make an 8-by-8 piece by putting together a 5-by-8 and a 3-by-8 piece.

Some students may not be able to coordinate 2-D pieces to make a rectangular prism. These students put pieces together to make some other 3-D object, for example:

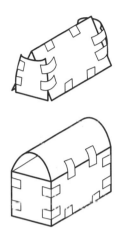

Expect a lot of variation in the approaches your students use. At this age, differences in small motor coordination will influence students' work, as well as how they visualize the way 2-D pieces can go together to make a 3-D object. The goal of this activity is not for all students to construct boxes "correctly," but for all students to gain experience in visualizing and describing the components of rectangular prisms and to see how 3-D objects can be constructed from 2-D pieces.

Building a Block Town

What Happens

Sessions 1 and 2: Drawing Geoblocks Students build small constructions with Geoblocks and then draw what they built as accurately as they can. They discuss what was easy and difficult about making a 2-D picture of a 3-D object and talk about what makes a picture look 3-D. Students trade their pictures and build constructions to match the pictures.

Sessions 3 and 4: Planning a Town Students discuss buildings in their neighborhood, in their community, and other buildings they have seen. The class then makes plans for building their own town and decides what buildings they might want to include. Each pair of students chooses a building for the town and draws a plan for it.

Session 5: Building a Town Students build their buildings on a large street grid. They write a few sentences about the building they designed and how it is used. The class decides on a name for the town.

Sessions 6 and 7: Giving Directions Students give directions to get from one place to another in the classroom, using paces and turns. Then, on a map of the class town, students plan trips and record directions for moving from one location to another. The class develops a code for giving directions, and students use this code to record trips through the class town. Students also create paths of different lengths to connect the same two locations.

Routines Refer to the section About Classroom Routines (pp. 127–134) for suggestions on integrating into the school day regular practice of mathematical skills in counting, exploring data, and understanding time and changes.

Mathematical Emphasis

- Observing and describing characteristics of 3-D shapes
- Observing shapes in the environment
- Creating and using 2-D representations of 3-D shapes
- Building 3-D constructions from 2-D representations
- Developing vocabulary for describing 3-D shapes
- Putting 3-D shapes together to make other shapes
- Visualizing, describing, and comparing paths between two locations in space and on a grid
- Estimating distances
- Visualizing and describing direction of turns

What to Plan Ahead of Time

Materials

- Geoblocks: 2 sets, each divided equally into half-sets (Sessions 1–7)

- Drawing materials (Sessions 1–4)

- 5-by-8-inch index cards (or half-sheets of letter-size paper): 1 per pair (Sessions 3–4)

- Children's books about unusual buildings or houses (Sessions 3–4, optional)

- Toy people or cars, small blocks or counters, or small cardboard pointers: 1 per pair (Sessions 6–7)

- Overhead projector (Sessions 6–7)

Other Preparation

- Make simple building shapes with 3–5 Geoblocks (see p. 100 for examples). You will need one building for every 4 students. They need not be identical. (Session 1)

- Make a large street grid for the class town on poster board or large paper. Use the Street Grid (p. 228) as the model. Your large grid should be a 6-by-6 array of rectangles, each measuring at least 5 by 8 inches for a total size of 30 by 48 inches. If students are using half-sheets of letter-size paper instead of 5-by-8 index cards as the "land" for their buildings, make your grid slightly larger (33 by 51 inches). Find a location—perhaps a table, or a space on the floor or in the hall—where you can leave the large grid for several days as students work on the class town. (Sessions 3–7)

- Geoblocks do not include some shapes, such as cylinders, cones, and arches that students should become familiar with. If you can borrow some other sets of building blocks, students will have a wider range to choose from; add these to the available tools for making buildings. Some students may have sets at home that they are willing to lend. Sets should be small enough for table-top building. (Sessions 3–7, optional)

- Make a small "traveler" for showing paths on the overhead projector. Use a small block or counter. Cut out a small cardboard arrow (pointer) and attach it to the block or counter so that it sticks out horizontally from the counter. When you put this on the overhead projector, students will be able to see the object with the arrow pointing out from it, indicating which way the traveler is going (see the illustration on p. 121). (Sessions 6–7)

- Duplicate the following student sheets and teaching resources, located at the end of this unit. If you have Student Activity Booklets, copy only items marked with an asterisk.

For Sessions 1 and 2

Student Sheet 28, Draw a Building (p. 225): 1 per student, homework

Ways to Draw Blocks (p. 227): about 6 for the class

For Session 5

Street Grid* (p. 228): one copy, to create a map of your class's block town (see p. 121)

For Sessions 6 and 7

Student Sheet 29, Robot Paces (p. 226): 1 per student, homework

Street Grid, as prepared after Session 5 to show your block town: 1 per student*, and 1 transparency*

Drawing Geoblocks

Materials

- Geoblocks (4 half-sets)
- Prepared Geoblock buildings (1 per 4 students)
- Drawing materials
- Ways to Draw Blocks (about 6 for the class)
- Student Sheet 28 (1 per student, homework)

What Happens

Students build small constructions with Geoblocks and then draw what they built as accurately as they can. They discuss what was easy and difficult about making a 2-D picture of a 3-D object and talk about what makes a picture look 3-D. Students trade their pictures and build constructions to match the pictures. Their work focuses on:

- observing and describing characteristics of 3-D shapes
- making a 2-D representation of a 3-D object
- building a 3-D construction from a 2-D representation

Activity

Drawing a Geoblock Building

Set up the small buildings, made with 3–5 Geoblocks, where students can see to draw them. If students are sitting at tables, set up one building at each table. If students sit at individual desks, push desks together in groups of four for this activity. It's not necessary for every building to be identical, but each should include a variety of blocks that are quite different from each other. For example:

Explain that students will be drawing these buildings. Talk to them a bit about trying to make their pictures look three-dimensional, but keep in mind that you'll use the students' first attempts to talk more about making 2-D representations of 3-D objects. Students will have many chances to draw during the next few sessions.

Today we're going to try to draw some of the blocks so that they look three-dimensional. Does anyone know what I mean when I say a drawing can look three-dimensional, or 3-D?

Help students understand the difference between 2-D and 3-D, and how a picture that is flat on a piece of paper (2-D) can look 3-D. Some students may understand these ideas more easily if you use words like *flat* and *solid,* or *on paper* and *the real object.* Students often offer comments that to make something look three-dimensional on paper means that it "pops out at you," "it doesn't look flat," or "it looks like you can hold it." Reassure students that this kind of drawing is rather difficult, and that you are all going to be experimenting to see how to make a picture of a block building *not* look flat.

It takes years for adults to learn how to do really good 3-D drawings. You're going to draw the building the best way you can. It probably won't look exactly the same as the building, but see if you can draw it in a way that helps us see which blocks I used. Then we'll look at some of the pictures and see if we get some ideas about how to make pictures look 3-D.

When most students have a completed picture, ask them to share their work, telling what was easy or hard for them about drawing the building. Encourage them to describe what it's like to draw something that is three-dimensional on a flat surface, and what they did to try to make it look 3-D.

You will find a wide range in students' drawings and explanations. The goal here is not improved drawing skills—although that will happen for some students—but observation and description of 3-D objects. For more about the goals of these activities and examples of students' drawings, see the **Teacher Note,** Students Draw in 3-D (p. 106).

If different students drew the same building from different angles, you might compare some of these drawings and ask students to comment on why drawings of the same building look different.

Building and Drawing

Students again work on drawing a Geoblock construction, but this time they build their own.

First, show the sheet called Ways to Draw Blocks. Post it somewhere in the room for reference, or make a few copies available for borrowing. Some young students enjoy trying these conventional representations. However, the ideas on this sheet are not meant to substitute for their own ways of making shapes look 3-D. Simply explain that this shows some of the ways people have figured out to draw blocks to make them look three-dimensional. Emphasize that while students may want to try this approach when they are drawing blocks, they can also draw in their own ways. Remind the class that some of them had good ideas about how to make something look 3-D. They can try to use some of the ideas they have heard from their classmates. Students should feel free to represent their buildings in their own ways.

Students start by constructing their own building with three or four blocks. Then they draw what they have built. This time, as you circulate and watch students work, ask questions to try to help your students think about how their drawings represent the different parts of the block building. Ask questions like these:

How were you looking at the building when you drew this? Which part of the building does this part of your drawing show?

See the **Dialogue Box,** Making It Look 3-D (p. 108), for examples of how one teacher helped students revise their drawings to take into account more of what they could see about the objects they were drawing.

Some students may have time to build and draw more than one construction. They may want to try a slightly larger building, using 6–8 blocks. See the Extensions at the end of Sessions 1 and 2 for further suggestions.

Building from Pictures

Now students will try to build a construction from a picture, as if building from a plan.

To start, each student builds a Geoblock construction, using no more than 6–10 blocks. (This limit is important to keep the task manageable.) Then each student draws a picture of his or her own construction. Encourage students to make the best plan they can so that someone could easily recognize their building from the plan. Explain that this is something like what architects do when they draw plans for a new building.

Give students only about 10 minutes to build and draw, and let them know that's the amount of time they will have. A strict time limit helps students focus on the drawing task rather than making elaborate or complicated buildings.

Collect all the drawings, mix them up, and give out one drawing to each student. Now each student tries to build the construction shown in the drawing. You don't need to keep the original buildings intact for later comparison. The goal of this activity is for students to do the best they can to reproduce the 3-D construction represented in the drawing. Since some drawings will be easier to follow than others, the emphasis should not be on how well the construction matches the original building, but how well it follows what the drawing seems to show.

If students find parts of a plan difficult to follow—for example, they're not sure which of two similarly shaped blocks is intended—tell them to make the best choice they can, using whatever clues the plan gives them.

Again, give students a fairly short time to complete their constructions— about 10 minutes (or less, if students are able to finish easily in a shorter time). To end this part of the activity, students walk around the room and look at each building next to its drawing.

In a follow-up group discussion, students talk about what was difficult or not so difficult about following the plans, and how they coped with parts of the plan they couldn't understand. Following are some issues students have mentioned:

- One student found that the way the building looked in the drawing, it couldn't stand up on a flat surface. So she modified the placement of two blocks so it would stand up.

- One student couldn't find one of the blocks in the drawing, so chose a substitute that was about the right size and shape.

- One very tall building was hard to make because it kept falling over, so the student had to make a change to make it more stable.

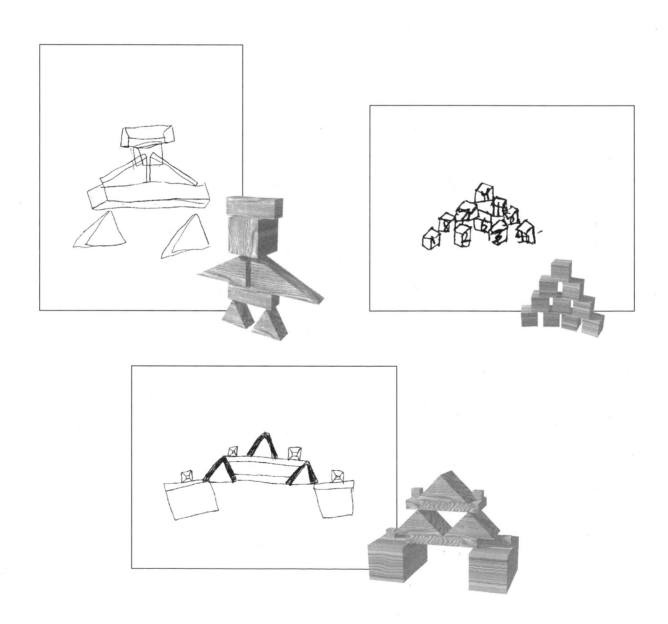

Sessions 1 and 2 Follow-Up

Draw a Building Students draw a picture of a building they have seen, either in their own neighborhood or somewhere they have visited. They write a sentence or two telling about the building. Alternatively, instead of drawing, students can cut out a picture of a building that they have seen and write about it. Student Sheet 28, Draw a Building, provides directions for students to take home. Students who are not comfortable writing their ideas may ask a family member to record their response for them.

 **Homework**

❖ **Tip for the Linguistically Diverse Classroom** Family members may record their children's responses in their native language.

Building from a Plan Pairs of students can try building and drawing simple constructions, then taking down the buildings and trying to rebuild each other's buildings, using the drawings.

Extensions

Using Objects with Curved Sides If you can, borrow some block sets that include objects with curved sides, such as cylinders, spheres, or cones. Some students will enjoy including one of these blocks in their building and drawing activity. Ask students to show and talk about how they made something look rounded on flat paper.

2-D Pictures of 3-D Constructions Show the class some books with illustrations of a variety of buildings. As you look at the pictures together, discuss what the artists did to make the pictures look 3-D. (Some suggestions are given in the list of related children's literature, p. I-16.)

When students first try to draw block constructions, most will draw a picture that looks two-dimensional. Many students draw the faces of blocks they can see in one view of the building. Some carefully draw the shapes of these faces and put these blocks in position so that they are arranged in the way they are arranged in the block construction. This is often a very effective way of showing all the blocks and how they are arranged.

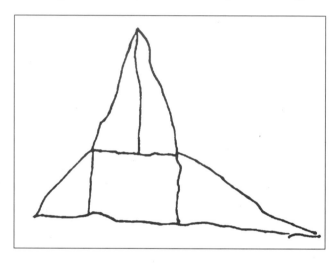

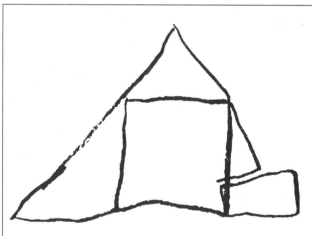

Students vary in their ability to draw the shapes of the block faces they see. Some are very careful to draw squares, rectangles, and triangles that are very close in shape to the faces of the blocks. But others have some difficulty drawing these shapes or showing how the blocks go together. Some may even show the outline of the whole construction without showing individual blocks.

Teachers can encourage these students to more carefully identify the shapes of the faces of the individual blocks, as well as how the blocks come together.

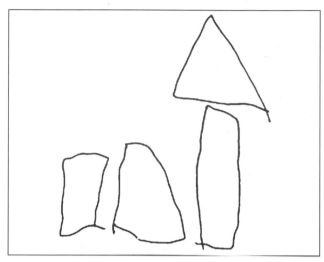

Many factors affect how well students can represent the constructions in drawings. Students' fine motor skills are developing in different ways, so that some students are simply more skilled at or more interested in drawing than others. Another factor is students' care in observing the characteristics of the 3-D blocks. The mathematics work in these sessions focuses on observing, describing, and comparing 3-D shapes. As you work with students, keep the emphasis on this careful observation and description, rather than on drawing skill. Ask questions like these:

Which part of the block does this shape on your drawing show?

How were you looking at your building as you drew this? Where were you standing?

Which blocks does this triangular prism touch in the building? Is there a way you can show that on your drawing?

For examples of a teacher working with her students as they make drawings of block constructions, see the **Dialogue Box,** Making It Look 3-D (p. 108).

Through experimenting and looking at each other's drawings, students will develop more ideas about how to make their drawings look 3-D, but you don't need to push students to do so. Let them see others' drawings and decide what techniques to try. One common method students use is to draw adjacent faces of a block next to each other.

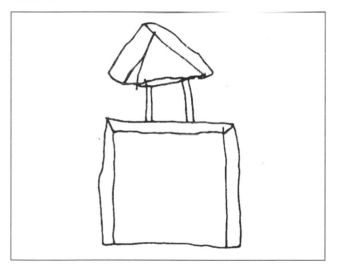

The student who made the drawing above described her work like this:

> I made the triangle first, then I added two lines to make the rectangles. Then I made a cube. Then I made more rectangles to make the top and the sides.

This kind of drawing can very clearly show which blocks are being used and their relationships to each other.

A closely related method is to draw a face of the block, then "surround" it with another outline of the same shape.

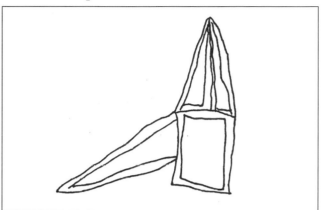

A student using this technique described his work this way:

> See, first I drew it flat on the paper. Then to make it look three-dimensional, I drew the same shape next to it.

A more unusual approach for a first grader is the use of shading.

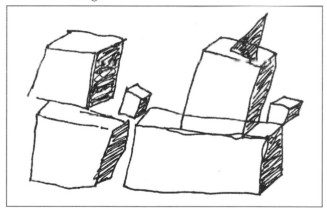

Despite the variety of skill levels, first graders in field-test classrooms enjoyed drawing block constructions and building from plans. It is important to keep these activities enjoyable by acknowledging how challenging these activities are for everyone and accepting the range of ways students represent their buildings. Through these activities, students become more aware of the different-shaped faces of 3-D objects and how these faces are connected to make a solid object.

Making It Look 3-D

These first grade students are trying for the first time to make a drawing of their own block construction (the activity Building and Drawing, p. 102). Buildings were limited to three or four blocks. The teacher circulates and interacts with students as they work, asking them to show how their drawing matches the blocks and encouraging them to experiment and revise.

Leah has drawn the front triangular face of a triangular prism, but now she is frowning and tapping her pencil on the table.

Geoblock

Leah's drawing

I can see that your drawing shows this triangular prism, but you don't seem satisfied.

Leah: It doesn't show this part *[she points to the top edge of the block].*

Is there some way you want to try to revise your drawing?

Leah: I'll put in some more lines.

Leah changes her drawing to look like this:

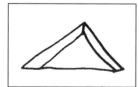
Leah's revised drawing

Donte is working on a taller, stacked building.

Block building and Donte's drawing

This is really interesting, how you drew this. I can see all four blocks. How were you looking at your building?

Donte: I was looking from the top. See, they all have squares on top and these little skinny parts are the spaces between the blocks.

Can you show me where you see this in your building? *[She points to the small square in Donte's drawing.]*

Donte: Here. *[He points to the top of the small, rectangular prism.]*

Hmm. I can see all the square parts. What if you look at your building from the side, so you can see the long rectangle on the bottom block. Could you try another drawing looking from the side?

Planning a Town

What Happens

Materials

- Large street grid for the class town
- Geoblocks (4 half-sets)
- 5-by-8-inch index cards or half-sheets of letter-size paper (1 per pair)
- Drawing materials
- Children's books about unusual buildings or houses (optional)
- Additional sets of building blocks (optional)

Students discuss buildings in their neighborhood, in their community, and other buildings they have seen. The class then makes plans for building their own town and decides what buildings they might want to include. Each pair of students chooses a building for the town and draws a plan for it. Students' work focuses on:

- recognizing a variety of shapes in the world around them
- making a 2-D representation of a 3-D structure
- planning a geometric structure with limited space and materials

Activity

What Buildings Have You Seen?

This discussion could occur during either math or social studies time, especially if your classroom has been studying your own community or other cultures.

Ask students to share some of the buildings they drew for homework. What have they noticed about the shapes of buildings in their neighborhood, in their town, or elsewhere? What are the roofs around here like? Are there different kinds of roofs? What about the shapes of the buildings themselves? Do any of the Geoblocks remind them of the shapes of buildings they have seen? What are unusual buildings they have seen? What shapes did they notice? Have they ever seen a building that was round or some other unusual shape?

If you have books about houses in other cultures or other interesting buildings, share them with your students during this session or at other times during the day. You might put them on a special table where students can look at them. One book recommended for this is *My Painted House, My Friendly Chicken, and Me* by Maya Angelou (Clarkson Potter, 1994). This book tells the story of an 8-year-old Ndebele girl from South Africa. It has beautiful photographs of the Ndebele people and the designs they use to paint their houses. You may be able to tie this discussion to social studies themes you have explored with your students.

What Kind of Buildings Do We Need?

Show the large grid of streets you have prepared and explain that the class will be building a town of their own. Each pair of students will make one building for the town. Brainstorm with students what kinds of buildings they might like to have in their town. Make a list of students' ideas on the board or on chart paper. First graders have thought about these possibilities, among others:

houses	apartment building	grocery store
school	police station	candy and toy store
pet shop	museum	ice cream store
veterinarian	zoo	restaurant
parking lot	pool	hotel
skating rink	arcade	auto repair shop
library	shelter	clothing store
stadium	fire station	filling station

❖ **Tip for the Linguistically Diverse Classroom** To ensure that the list of student ideas is comprehensible to everyone, add simple pictures that symbolize the written words. For example, you might draw a car next to *parking lot,* a book next to *library,* and so forth.

Use this discussion to help students think about different buildings that they see around them and their functions. Ask students to think about all the needs of a town. What is important so that the people in the town have what they need? If students mention very specific buildings (a specific fast-food restaurant, a particular grocery store), you might want to ask them to name the general category for that building *(restaurant, supermarket).* Sometimes students want to include specific famous buildings they know about, such as the Empire State Building. This is also a chance to explore vocabulary about types of businesses housed in the town buildings: Is there a difference between a *grocery store* and a *supermarket*? What is a hardware store? For examples of how the teacher guided this discussion in one first grade class, see the **Dialogue Box,** Arcades and Parks and Hardware Stores (p. 112).

Designing Buildings for Our Town

Once students have enough ideas about what buildings they would like to have in their town, give each pair one 5-by-8-inch index card or a half-sheet of paper. This card (or paper) is the amount of land they have on which to build. Each building must fit entirely on the card or paper and use no more than 12 blocks. If you are using other sets of building blocks along with the Geoblocks, you will need to assign different pairs of students to different sets of blocks or have a system for borrowing special blocks, such as cylinders or cones, from the other sets.

Each pair should decide on one kind of building to make out of the blocks and then draw a plan for it (on separate drawing paper, not on the card or paper that represents their land). Explain to students that they will *draw* their plans in this session, and then use their plans to actually make their buildings on the street grid in the next session. They need to draw their plans carefully so that the plan will help them remember how to put the building together. Students should have the blocks available and will probably move back and forth between actually building the building with blocks and drawing it.

As you watch students work, remind them that their building has to fit on the 5-by-8-inch lot and that they can use only 12 blocks. This limit on the number of blocks is partly to help students share scarce resources, but it is also intended to help them keep their buildings a manageable size, so that they can draw plans that they can understand and successfully rebuild their buildings on the large town grid.

Sessions 3 and 4 Follow-Up

Buildings Around the World If some of your students' families have lived in different countries, try to find pictures of houses or buildings from those areas or ask if students' families have any pictures they can send in. You can add these pictures to your display of books about buildings.

 **Extension**

DIALOGUE BOX

Arcades and Parks and Hardware Stores

This class is brainstorming what buildings they need in their class town. This is their list so far:

school	houses
apartment buildings	candy and toy store
skating rink and arcade	library
grocery store	

You said you needed both houses and apartment buildings. Why?

Fernando: Because a lot of us live in apartment buildings and some of us live in houses.

OK. And can someone explain what an arcade is?

Jacinta: It has lots of stores and you can buy fun things there.

Is the skating rink in the arcade?

William: It can be.

Pretend that this is your town. What else would you need?

Kristi Ann: You need roads and cars.

Since roads and cars aren't buildings, I'm going to start a second list for things that aren't buildings. *[She starts another list headed "Other things we need."]*

Jonah: Parks.

Why do you need parks?

Jonah: I don't know.

Shavonne: So you can go and play if you don't have a yard.

I'll put parks with roads and cars on the second list. We can decide which of the areas on our street grid should be parks.

Claire: We should put Burger Hut.

What kind of store is that?

Claire: A food store.

Well, we have a grocery store. That's a food store. Is this something different?

Tony: The food is cooked.

Andre: You eat right there.

Mia: It's a restaurant. *[The teacher adds* restaurant *to the list.]*

Diego: I know. A supermarket.

Is that a different kind of food store?

Chanthou: We have grocery store. It's the same thing.

Tamika: No, a supermarket's bigger than a grocery store.

Hmm. Do you think so? I'll put supermarket next to grocery store. Any other idea of what we need?

Chris: We should put F & S. Cause you need things to fix up all the buildings.

What kind of store is F & S?

Chris: Where you get stuff—nails, hammers, boards.

Kaneisha: A hardware store.

Building a Town

What Happens

Students build their buildings on a large street grid. They write a few sentences about the building they designed and how it is used. The class decides on a name for the town. Their work focuses on:

- building a 3-D construction from a 2-D plan
- describing shapes of their buildings

Materials

- Large street grid
- Students' building plans (from Sessions 3–4)
- Geoblocks (4 half-sets)
- Other building sets (optional)

Activity

Names for Our Town

Spend a few minutes discussing names for the class town. Write suggestions for names on a list and keep it posted. Rather than coming to a conclusion now, ask students to think about names as you build the town today and to add any new ideas to the list as they come up.

Activity

Describing Our Buildings

Note: Because there won't be room for everyone to work on the town at once, have two activities going on simultaneously in this session. Some students will be writing at their seats while others build their buildings on the town grid.

For the writing activity, each student writes a few sentences about the building that he or she designed with a partner for the class town. The sentences should describe what the building is, and might include some details about people who use the building or events that happen there. You might want to provide questions or starter sentences for this writing. For example:

What is your building?

Who uses your building?

What is your building used for?

❖ **Tip for the Linguistically Diverse Classroom** Fold a piece of paper in thirds. In the first third, students draw a picture that identifies their building; in the middle, they draw who uses their building; and in the last, they show what it is used for.

If students don't finish their writing during this session, you might have them continue their work during writing time. These descriptions can be posted with the building plans near the town.

Activity

Assessment

Putting Up Our Buildings

While the class works on the writing activity, call small groups of students to the table or floor area where the large street grid is located. Remind them to bring their building plans. Help pairs select a site for their building. Each building should fit within one of the rectangles of the grid. It will be easier to work without knocking others' buildings down if you start students building near the middle of the grid and gradually work outward to the perimeter of the town. Or, if the street grid is against a wall, build from the wall outward. Each pair of students might name one of the streets. You can write the street names along the lines of the grid. Encourage students to leave a blank rectangle between their building and other buildings, if possible.

Sears tower

MEETING BUILDING

As students erect their buildings, you can also talk with them about where certain buildings should go. Which buildings should be close to apartments or houses? Which could be further away? For example, one class decided that the school should be close to the houses and apartments because that's where the children live; that the police station should be close to the museum in case there was a robbery; and the zoo should be far away from the library because it is too noisy.

If a building does get knocked down while someone else is building, remind students that that's why they have plans for their buildings. The plans will help with repairs as needed.

You will be duplicating small grids, with the location of each building marked, for Sessions 6 and 7. You may want to have students make a sign for their buildings, so you will be able to identify each one (for example, Eva and Diego's house, Shavonne and Nathan's skyscraper, the pet store). Students may also enjoy adding details. They can make some of these, such as trees, windows, or signs, out of paper or cardboard. If you have small toy figures, such as people, animals, or cars, they might add these as well.

Observing the Students

Over the past few sessions, you have been watching students observe, describe, and compare 3-D objects. As students are putting up their buildings on the class grid, use this opportunity to review for yourself students' developing knowledge about 3-D shapes. These activities combine a wide variety of skills, some of which are mathematical and some of which are not. Remember that you are not assessing students on how good their drawings are or on whether their buildings match their drawings with complete accuracy; the focus instead is on how students are describing and comparing different 3-D shapes. As students place their buildings, ask them how they can tell from their plans which blocks go where. You might also ask questions like these:

How do you know this size cube goes here instead of a smaller cube? How did you know from your plan that this block goes here?

Here are some guidelines for assessment of student work in this investigation:

- Do students notice that some Geoblocks have only rectangular faces and some have triangular faces? Do they distinguish between these in their drawings?

- Do students notice that Geoblocks that are somewhat alike in shape can be distinguished by comparing dimensions (size and thickness)? In students' drawing and building, do they distinguish, for example, between a large cube and a smaller cube, or describe one rectangular prism as much thinner than another?

- Do students see that some 3-D objects have faces that are different shapes, for example, two triangular faces and three rectangular faces? Can you tell from their drawings and the way they match their buildings to their drawings that they are aware of the variety of faces a single block might have?

Naming Our Town

When all the buildings are in place, give students a chance to look at the whole town. Then ask if they have thought of any other ideas for naming the town. If the class seems ready, you can choose a name together. Or, you may want to give students until the next session to think about names and choose the name then.

After Session 5 When the town is complete, take a copy of the Street Grid (p. 228) and write on it the names of all the buildings in your town, in the right locations on the grid. Also put a large dot in one corner of each rectangle in the grid that has a building on it, to indicate the location of the entrance to that building (see the illustration on p. 121). You might want to add some simple drawings to help nonreaders identify each location. Then duplicate this sheet, 1 per student, for use in Sessions 6–7.

Session 5 Follow-Up

Extension

A Story About Our Town Students write a story about the class town. It might recount events that happen in the town, talk about whether they would like to live in the town, or simply describe the town to someone who hasn't seen it. You might give this assignment during your class writing time.

❖ **Tip for the Linguistically Diverse Classroom** Students might create a storyboard to visually tell a story about their town. For example, a sequence of four pictures might show (1) the town, (2) fire breaking out in a building, (3) a fire truck rushing to the scene, and (4) firefighters with hoses putting out the fire.

> _EXTRA! EXTRA!_
> Yestorday GirAffE escaPes from Zoo in copitol city. He's not cot yet. He is danqerous. and scerd. BeVare! —Loo feet tol. If you See him col Polece

Giving Directions

What Happens

Students give directions to get from one place to another in the classroom, using paces and turns. Then, on a map of the class town, students plan trips and record directions for moving from one location to another. The class develops a code for giving directions, and students use this code to record trips through the class town. Students also create paths of different lengths to connect the same two locations. Their work focuses on:

- visualizing paths between two locations in the classroom and on a map
- estimating distances between locations using paces
- following and giving directions for how to move in space
- visualizing which way to turn to go in a different direction
- comparing distances of different paths
- recording written directions for moving on a path
- counting and adding

Materials

- Prepared Street Grid with students' buildings marked (1 per pair, and 1 transparency)
- Overhead projector
- Small block or counter with cardboard arrow taped on it
- Toy people or cars, small blocks or counters, or small cardboard pointers (1 per pair)
- Student Sheet 29 (1 per student, homework)

Activity

Robot Paths in the Classroom

Choose a starting place and an ending place for a path in your classroom. For example, you might choose the door as a starting place and your desk as an ending place. Explain to students that you are going to act like a robot and they are going to direct you. This robot can only walk straight ahead and turn. To begin this activity, choose a path that will not require more than one turn.

I'm standing here in the doorway to our class, and I want to walk to my desk. Remember, I'm a robot. I only know how to walk straight ahead and to turn. Who thinks they can give me directions to walk to my desk? What should I do first?

OK, Diego, you think I should walk straight ahead. Who wants to say how many paces you think I should go?

You may need to explain to students that a pace is a normal walking step—not a giant step, not a baby step, just an ordinary step.

Try out the students' directions. If a student suggests that you go 6 paces, take that many paces and stop. Then ask for the next direction. If a student tells you too many paces, keep going so students can see where that many paces takes you. Then go back to your starting point and ask for another estimate. Point out that they now have some information to use:

So you think 10 paces was too many. That's good information to help you make a new estimate. Who wants to tell me how many paces you think I should try?

When it's time to make a turn, ask students which way you should turn. Many students won't be able to distinguish right and left; this is a good opportunity to review right and left with them. Even if they can tell their *own* right and left, they may not be able to tell what *another person's* right and left are. This requires visualizing themselves in someone else's position, which can be difficult even for adults.

There are two ways to help students tell you which way to turn, and you may want to introduce both so students can use the one that's easier for them. You can tell students which is your right hand and which is your left, and they can tell you whether to turn toward your right hand or toward your left. You could even carry two large pieces of paper, one with a large R on it in your right hand and one with a large L on it in your left hand. The other way is to use landmarks on the walls of the classroom: turn toward the chalkboard, turn toward the sink, turn toward the bookshelf, and so forth.

In this unit, students are not expected to specify how far to turn. (The concept of describing the amount of a turn is introduced in a grade 2 *Investigations* unit that can also be used at grade 1, *How Long? How Far?*) If students use the landmark method, "Turn toward the sink," how much to turn is not an issue. If they use the "turn right" or "turn left" method, 90 degrees (a quarter of a full rotation) is a convenient amount for each turn. Students may then need to say "turn right" or "turn left" more than once to get you facing in the intended direction.

Continue asking students to give you directions until you have reached the destination you indicated.

OK, I've turned as far as you told me to go. Am I ready to walk straight ahead again now? Who can tell me how many paces you think I should go?

Students need not give you the whole distance at once. For example, they could try three or four paces, then see how far you are, then tell you the next distance.

Choose a new starting point and a new ending point and repeat the activity, with students giving you directions to get from here to there.

Then ask a student volunteer to be the robot. This time the class picks a starting point and an ending point, and then gives directions to the student robot. Ask the student to walk across the classroom first so that the class can get an idea of how long this new robot's paces are. They may notice that the student's paces are shorter than yours were.

If time permits and students are still focused, repeat the activity with a different student as the robot. You will be doing a variation of this activity at the beginning of Session 7 (Long Paths and Short Paths).

Show the overhead transparency of the class town with the building locations written on the grid.

Paths Through Town

	N				
Vet					
	Apartment House		Fire Station	Police	
	Park with pool	School			
	Pet Shop		Bank	Parking Lot	Pizza
			Used Cars		
Movies		Zoo			Hospital

W ... E (left and right of the grid)
S (below the grid)

Use a small block or counter to stand for a person. You will need to indicate the front of the person in some way so that students can tell which way it is facing. A small pointer cut from cardboard and taped horizontally onto the block will show up on the overhead projector.

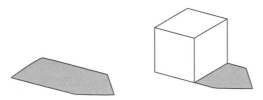

Just as you did for the Robot Paths activity, choose a starting place and an ending place in the town. Put the block at the starting place, and ask students to give directions to move this "person" to the chosen destination. Explain that the dot at the corner of each building indicates the entrance. A path will always start and end at a dot.

Students will give directions by telling how many city blocks to go (instead of paces). Like the robot, the person can either go straight ahead for a specified number of blocks or turn. Students can use the north (N), south (S), east (E), and west (W) markings on the sheet to indicate the direction of the turn they want. (Students at this age are not expected to understand compass directions; these are just convenient labels.)

Codes for Paths After completing one trip through the town with the block "person," introduce the idea of recording directions for the path. Again, choose a starting location and an ending location. This time as students give directions, record the directions in a list. For example:

Start: Pet Shop
turn east
go forward 1 block
turn north
go forward 2 blocks
turn east
go forward 1 block
End: Fire station

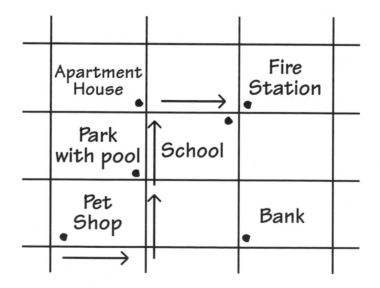

Do this once or twice. Then ask students if they can think of a shorter way
to write the directions. That is, can they make up a code that would be easy
to write? For example, students might suggest using F for forward, B to
mean block, and N, S, W, E for turns:

    E   F1B   N   F2B   E   F1B

Or they might suggest using arrows, like this:

    →   F1B   ↑   F2B   →   F1B

One class's code looked like this (T means "turn"):

    TE   1B   TN   2B   TE   1B

Whatever code everyone agrees on is fine. Use the code to help students
distinguish between the action of turning (but staying in one location) and
the action of moving forward (moving to a new location).

Using the Code Once the code is established and you have recorded a couple of trips together, give a copy of the prepared Street Grid of your class
town to each pair of students. Each pair also needs a sheet of lined paper
and a "person." If you have toy people or cars, or something like teddy bear
counters, the direction they are facing is clear. If you are using small blocks
or similar plain counters, students might draw an arrow in pencil on the
top of the block, or attach a small cardboard pointer. Or, each pair might
simply use a cardboard pointer as a "person."

Pairs now work together to take and record different trips around the town,
using the class code. Remind students to decide on and record both their
starting point and ending point before they start their trip. You might set up
a structure on the board as a model.

    Start: _____

             _____

             _____

             _____

             _____

      End: _____

Plan to continue this activity through Session 7, with a break at the beginning
of that session to consider paths of different lengths between the same starting and ending points in the classroom. Some students may enjoy finding both
a long path and a short path between the same locations in their town.

Students also enjoy adding pictures to the street grid to show more detail about the town. For example, they might draw some of the buildings, add trees, animals, and people, or write the street names.

Don't expect students to be completely consistent in using the class code to record their trips. For example, some students will have a hard time separating turns from forward movement. That is, for the sample trip between the pet shop and the fire station, a student might write directions this way:

1BE, TN, 2B, TE, 1E

This student sometimes uses 1B to mean "one block," and sometimes uses a direction to show forward movement, so that 1E means "one block east." Sometimes she combines these: 1BE also means "one block east." Nonetheless, she is carefully planning her trip and recording directions; this student is successfully creating a path from one location to another.

Activity

Long Paths and Short Paths

At the beginning of Session 7, do the Robot Path activity again with your class, using volunteers to be the robot. This time ask students to think about long paths and short paths. Pick a starting point and an ending point. In giving directions to the robot, students should look for a path that is as short as possible. As the robot follows the directions, record the number of paces and turns the robot takes:

Start: Bookshelf

9 paces

turn

5 paces

turn

5 paces

End: Jamaar's seat

Ask students how many paces the robot took for the whole path. Students might share several strategies for how they figured out the total. For example:

I know 5 and 5 is 10 and then I counted up 9 more.

I did 5 and 5 is 10 and then I just knew that 10 and 9 is 19.

I knew 9 and 5 is 14 because put 1 on the 9 and that's 10, and then 4 more is 14. Then I counted up 5 more.

Next, students give the robot directions to take a longer path from the same starting point to the same ending point.

Before, the robot was in a hurry and wanted to take the shortest path possible. This time, we're going to give Yanni directions to go from the bookshelf to where Jamaar is sitting again. But this time the robot is *not* in a hurry, so he wants to take a longer path.

Again, record the students' directions; then ask students to figure out how many paces the robot took.

Repeat this activity once or twice with a different robot each time. Then students can continue working on the Paths Through Town activity. If students have done two or three paths, ask them to find a long path and a very short path between two locations on the grid.

Choosing Student Work to Save

As the unit ends, you may want to use one of the following options for creating a record of students' work on this unit.

- Students look back through their folders or notebooks and think about what they learned in this unit, what they remember most, what was hard or easy for them. Students might discuss this with a partner or share in the whole group.

- Depending on how you organize and collect student work, students might select some examples of their work to keep in a math portfolio. In addition you may choose some examples from each student's folder to include. You might include some of the pattern block designs students have recorded (for example, any of those on Student Sheets 2–15), or students' quilt patterns, including printouts of patterns they created on the computer. You may want to keep the original and make copies of these pieces for students to take home (or vice versa). An important piece of work to include is the Shape Posters from Investigation 1; if these are too large, consider taking photographs of them. You could also include photographs of students' block buildings for the class town. Attach each photo to the student's plan for that building.

- Send a selection of work home for families to see. Some teachers include a short letter, summarizing the work in this unit. You could enlist the help of your students and together generate a letter that describes the mathematics they were involved in. This work should be returned to you if you are keeping a year-long portfolio of mathematics work for each student.

Sessions 6 and 7 Follow-Up

 **Homework**

Robot Paces Students find a family partner to do the Robot Paces activity at home with them. Send home Student Sheet 29, Robot Paces. They record one of the paths that they followed, recording in any way they wish.

 **Extensions**

Short and Long Robot Paths The Robot Paths activity offers good experience in estimating distances and visualizing paths that connect locations in space. Repeat this activity whenever you have a free 10 or 15 minutes. Vary the activity by asking students to give the student robot directions for a short path or a long path.

Robot Paces in Bigger Spaces If you have access to a large space, such as a gymnasium or outside area, have students play Robot Paths in pairs. One student is the robot, the other gives directions. You may want to specify starting points and ending points at first. In a gymnasium, you can set up folding chairs with numbers on them, pylons, or other large objects to give students starting points and destinations.

A New Town Grid Use the Street Grid to make a town "map" using familiar locations from your community (your school, neighborhood stores, community centers, parks, and so forth). You will probably not be able to place these locations so that they match where they are actually located, but simply explain to students that distances and directions won't be exactly as they are in the real world. Students can then work with this new grid to plan and record trips familiar to them.

Counting

Counting is an important focus in the grade 1 *Investigations* curriculum, as it provides the basis for much of mathematical understanding. As students count, they are learning how our number system is constructed, and they are building the knowledge they need to begin to solve numerical problems. They are also developing critical understandings about how numbers are related to each other and how the counting sequence is related to the quantities they are counting.

Counting routines can be used to support and extend the counting work that students do in the *Investigations* curriculum. As students work with counting routines, they gain regular practice with counting in familiar classroom contexts, as they use counting to describe the quantities in their environment and to solve problems based on situations that arise throughout the school day.

How Many Are Here Today?

Since you must take attendance every day, this is a good time to look at the number of students in the classroom in a variety of ways.

Ask students to look around and make an estimate of how many are here today. Then ask them to count.

At the beginning of the year, students will probably find the number at school today by counting each student present. To help them think about ways to count accurately, you can ask questions like these:

How do we know we counted accurately? What are different methods we could use to keep track and make sure we have an exact count? (For example, you could count around a circle of seated students, with each student in turn saying the next number. Or, all students could start by standing up, then sit down in turn as each says the next number.)

Is there another way we could count to double-check? (For example, if you counted around the circle one way, you could count around the circle the other way. If you are using the standing up/sitting down method, you could recount in a different order.)

You might want to count at other times of the day, too, especially when several students are out of the room. For example, suppose groups of students are called to the nurse's office for hearing examinations. Each time a new group of students leaves, you might ask the class to look around and think about how many students are in the room now:

So, this time Diego's table and Mia's table both went to the nurse. Usually we have 28 students here. Look around. What do you think? Don't count. Just tell me about how many students might be here now. Do you think there are more than 5? more than 10? more than 20?

Later in the year, some students may be able to use some of the information they know about the total number of students in the class and how many students are absent to reason about the number present. For example, suppose 26 students are in class on Monday, with 2 students absent. On Tuesday, one of those students comes back to school. How many students are in class today? Some students may still not be sure without counting from one, but other students may be able to reason by counting on or counting back, comparing yesterday and today. For example, a student might solve the problem in this way:

> "Yesterday we had 26 students, and Michelle and Chris were both absent. Today, Chris came back, so we have one more person, so there must be 27 today."

Another might solve it this way:

> "Well we have 28 students in our class when everyone's here. Now only Michelle is absent, so it's one less. So it's 27."

From time to time, you might keep a chart of attendance over a week or so, as shown below. This helps students become familiar with different combinations of numbers that make the same total. If you have been doing any graphing, you might want to present the information in graph form.

Day	Date	Present	Absent	Total
Monday	March 2	26	2	28
Tuesday	March 3	27	1	28
Wednesday	March 4	27	1	28
Thursday	March 5	27	1	28
Friday	March 6	28	0	28
Monday	March 9	28	0	28
Tuesday	March 10	26	2	28
Wednesday	March 11	25	3	28

After a week or two, look back over the data you have collected. Ask questions about how things have changed over time.

In two weeks of attendance data, what changes? What stays the same?

On which day were the most students here? How can you tell? Which day shows the least students here? What part of the [chart] gives you that information?

Another idea (for work with smaller numbers) is to keep track of the number of girls and boys present and absent each day. Again, many students will count by 1's. Later in the year, some will also reason about these numbers:

> "There are two people absent today and they're both girls. We usually have 14 girls, and Kaneisha's sick, that's 13, and Claire's sick, that's 12."

Can Everyone Have a Partner?

Attendance can be an occasion for students to think about making groups of two:

We have 26 students here today. Do you think that everyone can have a partner if we have 26 students?

Students can come up with different strategies for solving this problem. They might draw 26 stick figures, then circle them in 2's. They could count out 26 cubes, then put them together in pairs. They might arrange themselves in 2's, or count by 2's .

At the beginning of the year, many of your students will need to count by 1's from the beginning each time you add two more students, but gradually some will begin to notice which numbers can be broken up into pairs:

> "I know 13 doesn't work, because you can do it with 12, and 13's one more, so you can't do it."

Some students will begin to count by 2's, at least for the beginning of the counting sequence. Then, as the numbers get higher, they may still be able to keep track of the 2's, but need to count by 1's:

> "So, that's 2, 4, 6, 8, 10, 12, um, 13, 14 . . . 15, 16."

As you explore 2's with your students, keep in mind that many of them will need to return to 1's as a way to be sure. Even though some students learn the counting sequence 2, 4, 6, 8, 10, 12 . . . by rote, they may not connect this counting sequence to the quantities it represents at each step.

One teacher found a way to help students develop meaning for counting by 2's. She took photographs of each student, backed them with cardboard, then used them during the morning meeting as a model for making pairs. She laid out the photos in two columns, and asked about the new total after the addition of each pair:

We have 10 photos out so far. The next two photos are for William and Yanni. When we put those two photos down, how many photos will we have?

Lining up is another time to explore making pairs. Before lining up, count how many students are in class (especially if it's different from when you took attendance). Ask students whether they think the class will be able to line up in even pairs. For many first grade students, the whole class is too many people to think about. You can ask about smaller groups:

What if Kristi Ann's table lines up first? Do you think we could make even partners with the people at that table?

What about Shavonne's table? ... Do you think Shavonne's table will have an extra? How do you know?

Is there another table that would have an extra that we could match up with the extra person from Shavonne's table?

Once students are lined up in pairs, they can count off by 2's. Because most first graders will need to hear all the numbers to keep track of how the counting matches the number of people, ask them to say the first number in the pair softly and the second one loudly. Thus the first pair in line can say, "1, **2**," the second pair can say, "3, **4**," and so forth.

Counting to Solve Problems

Be alert to classroom activities that lend themselves to a regular focus on solving problems through counting. Use these situations as contexts for counting and keeping track, estimating small quantities, breaking quantities into parts, and solving problems by counting up or back. For example, take a daily milk count:

Everyone who is buying milk today stand up. Without counting yet, who has an idea how many students might be standing up? Is it more than 5? more than 10? more than 50? ... Now, let's count. How could we keep track today so that we get an accurate count?

You can make a problem out of lunch count:

We found out that 23 students are buying school lunch today. We have 27 students here. So how many students brought their own lunch from home today?

Watch for the occasional sharing situation:

Claire brought in some cookies she made to share for snack. She brought 36 cookies. Is that enough for everyone to have one cookie, including me and our student teacher? Oh, and Claire wants to invite her little brother to snack. Do we have enough for him, too? Will there be any cookies left over?

The sharing of curriculum materials can also be the basis of a problem:

Each pair of students needs a deck of number cards to share. While I'm getting things together, work on this problem with your partner. We said this morning that we have 26 students here. If I need one deck for each pair, how many decks do I need?

Exploring Data

Through data routines at grade 1, students gain experience working with categorical data—information that falls into categories based on a common feature (for example, a color, a shape, or a shared function). The data routines specifically extend work students do in the *Investigations* curriculum. The Guess My Rule game and its many variations (introduced in the unit *Survey Questions and Secret Rules*) can be used throughout the year for practice with organizing sets into categories and finding ways to describe those categories—a fundamental part of analyzing data. Students can also practice collecting and organizing categorical data with quick class surveys that focus on their everyday experiences; this practice supports the survey-taking they do in the curriculum.

Guess My Rule

Guess My Rule is a classification game in which players try to figure out the common characteristic, or attribute, of a set of objects. To play the game, the rule maker (who may be the teacher, a student, or a small group) decides on a secret rule for classifying a particular group of things. For example, a rule for classifying people might be WEARING STRIPES.

The rule maker (always the teacher when the game is first being introduced) starts the game by giving some examples of objects or people who fit the rule. The guessers then try to find other items that fit the same rule. Each item (or person) guessed is added to one of two groups—either *does fit* or *does not fit* the rule. Both groups must remain clearly visible to the guessers so they can make use of all the evidence as they try to figure out the rule.

Emphasize to the players that "wrong" guesses are as important as "right" guesses because they provide useful clues for finding the rule. When you think most students know the rule, ask for volunteers to share their ideas with the class.

Once your class is comfortable with the activity, students can choose the rules. Initially, you may need to help students choose appropriate rules.

Guess my Rule with People When sorting people according to a secret rule, always base the rule on just one feature that is clearly visible, such as WEARING A SHIRT WITH BUTTONS, or WEARING BLUE. When students are choosing the rule, they may choose rules that are too obvious (such as BOY/GIRL), so vague as to apply to nearly everyone (WEARING DIFFERENT COLORS), or too obscure (HAS AN UNTIED SHOELACE). Guide and support students in choosing rules that work.

Guess My Rule with Objects Class sets of attribute blocks (blocks with particular variations in size, shape, color, and thickness) are a natural choice for Guess My Rule. You can also use collections of objects, such as sets of keys, household container lids, or buttons. One student sorts four to eight objects according to a secret rule. Others take turns choosing an object from the collection that they think fits the rule and placing it in the appropriate group. If the object does not fit, the rule maker moves it to the NOT group. After several objects have been correctly placed, students can begin guessing the rule.

Guess My Object Once students are familiar with Guess My Rule, they can use the categories they have been identifying to play another guessing game that also involves thinking about attributes. In this routine, students guess, by the process of elimination, which particular one of a set of objects has been secretly chosen. This works well with attribute blocks or object collections.

To start, place about 20 objects where everyone can see them. The chooser secretly selects one of the objects on display, but does not tell which one (you may want the chooser to tell you, privately). Other students ask yes-or-no questions, based on attributes, to get clues to help them identify the chosen object. After each answer, students move to one side the objects that have been eliminated. That is, if someone asks "Is it round?" and the answer is yes, all objects that are *not* round are moved aside.

Pause periodically to discuss which questions help eliminate the most objects. For example, "Is it this one?" eliminates only one object, whereas "Is it red?" may eliminate several objects. For more challenge, students can play with the goal of identifying the secret object with the fewest questions.

Quick Surveys

Class surveys can be particularly engaging when they connect to activities that arise as a regular part of the school day, and they can be used to help with class decisions. As students take surveys and analyze the results, they get good practice with collecting, representing, and interpreting categorical data.

Early in first grade, to keep the surveys quick and the routine short, use questions that have exactly two possible responses. For example:

Would you rather go outside or stay inside for recess today?

Will you drink milk with your lunch today?

Do you need left-handed or right-handed scissors?

As the school year progresses, you might include some survey questions that are likely to have more than two responses:

Which of these three books do you want me to read for story time?

Who was your teacher last year?

Which is your favorite vegetable growing in our class garden?

How old are you?

In which season were you born?

Try to choose questions with a predictable list of just a few responses. A question like "What is your favorite ice cream flavor?" may bring up such a wide range of responses that the resulting data is hard to organize and analyze.

As students become more familiar with classroom surveys, invite the class to brainstorm questions with you. You may decide to avoid survey questions about sensitive issues such as families, the body, or abilities, or you might decide to use surveys as a way of carefully raising some of these issues. In either case, it is best to avoid questions about material possessions ("Does your family have a car?").

Once the question is chosen, decide how to collect and represent data. Be sure to vary the approach. One time, you might collect data by recording students' responses on a class list. Another time, you might take a red interlocking cube for each student who makes one response, a blue cube for each student who makes the other response. Another time, you might draw pictures. If you have prepared Kid Pins and survey boards for use in *Mathematical Thinking at Grade 1*, these can be used for collecting the data from quick surveys all year.

Initially, you may need to help students organize the collected data, perhaps by stacking cubes into "bars" for a "graph," or by making a tally. Over time, students can take on more responsibility for collecting and organizing the data.

Always spend a little time asking students to describe, compare, and interpret the data.

What do you notice about these data?

Which group has the most? the least? How many more students want [recess indoors today]?

Why do you suppose more would rather [stay inside]? Do you think we'd get similar data if we collected on a different day? What if we did the same survey in another class?

Understanding Time and Changes

These routines help students develop an under-standing of time-related ideas such as sequenc-ing of events, understanding relationships among time periods, and identifying important times in their day.

Young students' understanding of time is often limited to their own direct experiences with how important events in time are related to each other. For example, explaining that an event will occur *after* a child's birthday or *before* an important holiday will help place that event in time for a child. Similarly, on a daily basis, it helps to relate an event to a benchmark time, such as *before* or *after* lunch. Both calendars and daily schedules are useful tools in sequenc-ing events over time and preparing students for upcoming events. These routines help young stu-dents gain a sense of basic units of time and the passage of time.

Calendar

The calendar is a real-world tool that people use to keep track of time. As students work with the calendar, they become more familiar with the sequence of days, weeks, and months, and the relationships among these periods of time. Calendar activities can also help students become more familiar with relationships among the numbers 1–31.

Exploring the Monthly Calendar At the start of each month, post the monthly calendar and ask students what they notice about it. Some students might focus on arrangement of num-bers or total number of days, while others might note special events marked on the calendar, or pictures or designs on the calendar. All these kinds of observations help students become familiar with time and ways that we keep track of time. You might record students' observations and post them near the calendar.

As the year progresses, encourage students to make comparisons between the months. Post the calendar for the new month next to the calendar for the month just ending and ask students to share their ideas about how the two calendars are similar and different.

Months and Years To help students see that months are part of a larger whole, display the entire calendar year on a large sheet of paper. Cut a small calendar into individual monthly pages and post the sequence of months on the wall. You might decide to post the months according to the school year, September through August, or the calendar year January through December. At the start of each month, ask stu-dents to find the position of the new month on the larger display. From time to time, you might also use this display to point out dates and distances between them as you discuss future events or as you discuss time periods that span a month or more. (Last week was February vacation. How many weeks until the next vacation?)

How Many More Days? Ask students to figure out how long until special events, such as birth-days, vacations, class trips, holidays, or future dates later in the month. For example:

Today is October 5. How many more days until October 15?

How many more days until [Nathan's] birthday?

How many more days until the end of the month?

Ask students to share their strategies for finding the number of days. Initially, many students will count each subsequent day. Later, some students may begin to find their answers by using their growing knowledge of calendar structure and number relationships:

> "I knew there were three more days in this row and I added them to the three days in the next row. That's 6 more days."

Others may begin using familiar numbers such as 5 or 10 in their counting:

> "Today is the 5th. Five more days is 10, and five more is 15. That's 10 more days until October 15."

For more challenge, ask for predictions that span two calendar months. For example, you might post the calendar for next month along side of the calendar of this month and ask a question like this:

It's April 29 today. How many more days until our class trip on May 6?

Note that we can refer to a date either as October 15 or as the 15th day of October. Vary the way you refer to dates so that students become comfortable with both forms. Saying "the 15th day of October" reinforces the idea that the calendar is a way to keep track of days in a month.

How Many Days Have Passed? Ask questions that focus on events that have already occurred:

How many days have passed since [a special event]? since the weekend? since vacation?

Mixed-Up Dates If your monthly display calendar has date cards that can be removed or rearranged, choose two or three dates and change their position on the calendar so that the numbers are out of order. Ask students to fix the calendar by pointing out which dates are out of order.

Groups of two or three can play this game with each other during free time. Students can also remove all the date cards, mix them up, and reassemble the calendar in the correct order. You might mark the space for the first day of the month so that students know where to begin.

Daily Schedule

The daily schedule narrows the focus of time to hours and shows students the order of familiar events over time. Working with schedules can be challenging for many first graders, but regular opportunities to think and talk about the idea will help them begin predicting what comes next in the schedule. They will also start to see relationships between particular events in the schedule and the day as a whole.

The School Day Post a schedule for each school day. Identify important events (start of school, math, music, recess, reading, lunch) using pictures or symbols and times. Include both analog (clock face) and digital (10:15) representations. Discuss the daily schedule each day with students using words such as *before* math, *after* recess, *during* the morning, *at the end of* the school day. Later in the school year you can begin to identify the times that events occur as a way of bridging the general idea of sequential events and the actual time of day.

The Weekend Day Students can create a daily schedule, similar to the class schedule, for their weekend days. Initially they might make a "timeline" of their day, putting events in sequential order. Later in the year they might make another schedule where they indicate the approximate time of day that events occur.

Weather

Keeping track of the weather engages young students in a real-life data collection experience in which the data they collect changes over time. By displaying this ongoing collection of data in one growing representation, students can compare changes in weather across days, weeks, and months, and observe trends in weather patterns, many of which correspond to the seasons of the year.

Monthly Weather Data With the students, choose a number of weather categories (which will depend on your climate); they might include sunny, cloudy, partly cloudy, rainy, windy, and snowy.

If you vary the type of representation you use to collect monthly data, students get a chance to see how similar information can be communicated in different ways. On the following page you'll see some ways of representing data that first grade teachers have used.

At the end of each month (and periodically throughout the month), ask questions to help students analyze the data they are collecting.

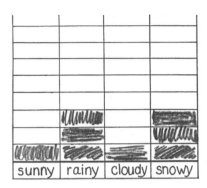

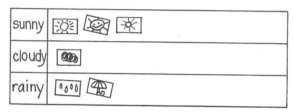

Weather data can be collected on displays like these. In the second example, a student draws each day's weather on an index card to add to the graph. The third example uses stick-on dots.

What is this graph about?

What does this graph tell us about the weather this month (so far)?

What type of weather did we have for the most days? What type of weather did we hardly ever have?

How is the weather this month different from the weather last month? What are you looking at on the graph to help you figure that out?

How do you think the weather graph for next month will look?

Yearly Weather Data If you collect and analyze weather data for some period of time, consider extending this over the entire school year. Save your monthly weather graphs, and periodically look back to see and discuss the changes over longer periods of time.

Another approach over the entire year is to prepare 10-by-10 grids from 1-inch graph paper, making one grid for each weather category your class has chosen. Post the grids, labeled with the identifying weather word. Each day, a student records the weather by marking off one square on one or more grids; that is, on a sunny day, the student marks a square on the "sunny" grid, and if it's also windy, he or she marks the "windy" grid, too.

From time to time, students can calculate the total number of days in a certain category by counting the squares. Because these are arranged in a 10-by-10 grid, some students may use the rows of 10 to help them calculate the total number of days. ("That's 10, and another 10 is 20, and 21, 22, 23.")

Making Weather Representations After students have had some experience collecting and recording data in the grade 1 curriculum (especially in *Survey Questions and Secret Rules*), they can make their own representation of the weather data. For one month, record the weather data on a piece of chart paper (or directly on your monthly calendar), without organizing it by category. At the end of the month, ask students to total the number of sunny days, rainy days, and so forth, and post this information (perhaps as a tally). Students then make their own representation of the data, using pictures, numbers, words, or a combination of these. Encourage them to use clear categories and show the number of days in each.

VOCABULARY SUPPORT FOR SECOND-LANGUAGE LEARNERS

The following activities will help ensure that this unit is comprehensible to students who are acquiring English as a second language. The suggested approach is based on *The Natural Approach: Language Acquisition in the Classroom* by Stephen D. Krashen and Tracy D. Terrell (Alemany Press, 1983). The intent is for second-language learners to acquire new vocabulary in an active, meaningful context.

Note that *acquiring* a word is different from *learning* a word. Depending on their level of proficiency, students may be able to comprehend a word upon hearing it during an investigation, without being able to say it. Other students may be able to use the word orally, but not read or write it. The goal is to help students naturally acquire targeted vocabulary at their present level of proficiency.

We suggest using these activities just before the related investigations. The activities can also be led by English-proficient students.

lowest, highest

1. Write a sequence of numbers on the board—say, 4 to 11. Identify the lowest and highest number in this series.

2. Write a different sequence of numbers; say, 6 to 15. Ask students to identify the lowest and highest numbers.

3. Write a different number on each of a set of index cards and tape a card to each student's back (students should not see their own number).

4. Students walk around, looking at each other's numbers, and decide who in the group has the lowest number. That student steps forward to face the group and holds up his or her card.

5. All students remove their numbers. Anyone who has a lower number than the one facing the group exchanges places with that student.

6. When the group confirms the student with the lowest number, challenge the rest to use their cards to place themselves in a line from the lowest to the highest number.

most, fewest

1. Place a tub of pattern blocks in front of the group. Model the following procedure: Reach into the tub, grab one handful of blocks, and then count the blocks you grabbed. Ask students to do the same.

2. When everyone has counted, each student tells how many blocks he or she got. When all have shared their amounts, ask:

Who had the *most* blocks? How do you know? Who had the *fewest* blocks? How do you know?

3. Repeat the activity, asking students to use the opposite hand this time. Before they begin, ask:

Using this hand, do you think you will get more or fewer blocks?

shape, straight, curved

1. Draw several shapes on the board. Include some with curved sides and some with straight sides. As you draw, identify these attributes. For example:

I'm going to draw a curved shape. I start here, curve my line around like this, and then curve back this way. This shape is curved.

2. Explain that you are going to point to different shapes on the board. As you point, students are to clap their hands when you point to a shape with curved sides. If you point to a shape that is not curved, students shake their heads "no."

3. Repeat the activity, having students clap for shapes with straight sides.

building, town

1. Show pictures of towns. Ask questions about the buildings in each picture. For example:

Which building is the highest?

2. Show at the same time pictures of two towns that appear quite different (for example, towns from different parts of the world, with different architecture). Ask questions that challenge students to compare the towns and the buildings. For example:

**Which town has more buildings?
Which town has taller buildings?
Which town looks more like our town?**

Teacher Tutorial

Contents

Overview

The units in *Investigations in Number, Data, and Space®* ask teachers to think in new ways about mathematics and how students best learn math. Units such as *Quilt Squares and Block Towns* add another challenge for teachers—to think about how computers might support and enhance mathematical learning. Before you can think about how computers might support learning in your classroom, you need to know what the computer component is, how it works, and how it is designed to be used in the unit.

The *Shapes* Tutorial is written for you as an adult learner, as a mathematical explorer, as an educational researcher, as a curriculum designer, and finally—putting all these together—as a classroom teacher. It is not intended as a walk-through of the student activities in the unit. Rather, it is meant to provide experience using the computer program *Shapes* and to familiarize you with some of the mathematical thinking in the unit.

The first part of the Tutorial shows how to create a picture using the pattern block shapes. Through making this picture, you become familiar with the tools available in the *Shapes* software. The later parts of the Tutorial include more detail about each component of *Shapes* and can be used for reference. There is also detailed help available in the *Shapes* program itself.

Teachers new to using computers and *Shapes* can follow the detailed step-by-step instructions. Those with more experience might not need to read each step. As is true with learning any new approach or tool, you will test out hypotheses, make mistakes, be temporarily stumped, go down wrong paths, and so on. This is part of learning but may be doubly frustrating because you are dealing with computers. It might be helpful to work through the Tutorial and the unit in parallel with another teacher. If you get particularly frustrated, ask for help from the school computer coordinator or another teacher more familiar with using computers. It is not necessary to complete the Tutorial before beginning to teach the unit. You can work through in parts, as you prepare for parallel investigations in the unit.

Although the Tutorial will help prepare you for teaching the unit, you will learn most about *Shapes* and how it supports the unit as you work side by side with your students.

About *Shapes*

Shapes is a computer manipulative, a software version of pattern blocks and tangrams, that extends what students can do with these shapes. Students create as many copies of each shape as they want and use computer tools to move, combine, and duplicate these shapes to make pictures and designs and to solve problems. In addition to the standard pattern block shapes, the pattern block set in *Shapes* includes a quarter circle, which extends students' explorations to include shapes with curved sides.

What Should I Read First?

Read the next section, Starting *Shapes*, for specific information on how to load the *Shapes* program and choose an activity.

The section Free Explore takes you step by step through an example of working with *Shapes*. Read this section for a sense of what the program can do.

The section Using *Shapes* provides detailed information about each aspect of *Shapes*. Read this to learn *Shapes* thoroughly or to answer specific questions.

Starting *Shapes*

Note: These directions assume that *Shapes* has been installed on the hard drive of your computer. If not, see How to Install *Shapes* on Your Computer, p. 171.

 1. Turn on the computer by doing the following:

    a. If you are using an electrical power surge protector, switch to the ON position.

    b. Switch the computer (and the monitor, if separate) to the ON position.

    c. Wait until the desktop or workspace appears.

 2. Open *Shapes* by doing the following:

    a. Double-click on the *Shapes* Folder icon if it is not already open. To double-click, click twice in rapid succession without moving the pointer.

Shapes—Quilt Square/Block Town

    b. Double-click on the *Shapes* icon in this folder.

c. Wait until the *Shapes* opening screen appears. Click on the bar "Click on this window to continue." when the message appears.

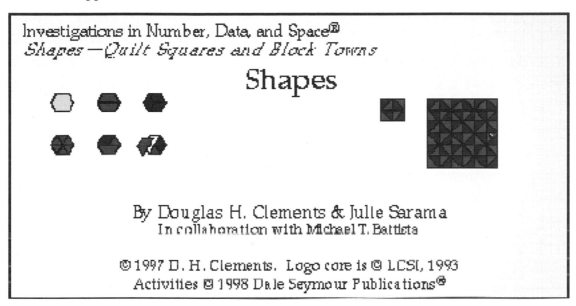

Start an activity by doing the following:

Click on Free Explore (or any activity you want).

How to Start an Activity

Solve Puzzles	Create a Quilt	Open My Work	Free Explore

When you choose an activity, the Tool bar, Shape bar, and Work window fill the screen.

The following section provides a step-by-step example of working with *Shapes*.

About Free Explore

The Free Explore activity is available for you to use as an environment to explore *Shapes*. It can also be used to extend and enhance activities.

When you choose Free Explore, you begin with an empty Work window. You can build a picture in that window with the shapes from the Shape bar. The tools in the Tool bar enable you to move, duplicate, and glue the shapes you select from the Work window.

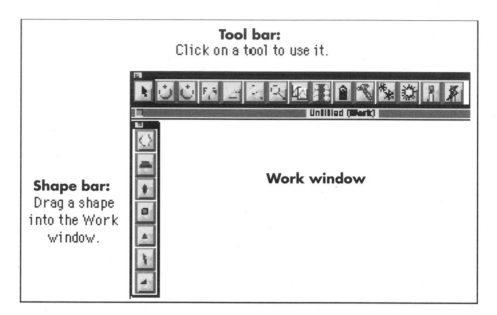

Tool bar:
Click on a tool to use it.

Shape bar:
Drag a shape into the Work window.

Work window

Building a Picture

Let's begin by making a building in the Work window.

☞ 1. Build the front of the building by doing the following:

    a. Drag an orange square shape off the Shape bar.

Move the cursor so it is on the square. It becomes a hand.	Click the mouse button and hold it down . . .	. . . while you move the square where you want it.

    b. Slide the square to the middle of the Work window.

       If you need to move the square, just click on it and drag it again.

c. Drag another orange square shape from the Shape bar and place it next to the first one.

Notice that the new square "snaps" right next to the first one.

d. Continue this procedure until the "front" of the building is finished.

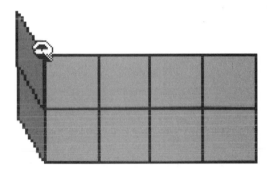

☞ **2.** Build the side of the building by doing the following:

Drag two tan rhombuses (thin diamonds) for the side of the building from the Shape bar and slide into place.

Young students might not do this, but we're going to try for a three-dimensional effect!

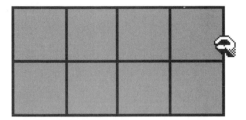

☞ **3.** Start the roof of the building by doing the following:

Drag a blue rhombus (diamond) from the Shape bar.

This shape will have to be turned to make it fit.

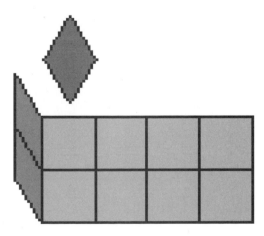

☞ **4.** Turn the blue rhombus by doing the following:

    a. Click on the Left Turn tool in the Tool bar.

    The cursor changes from an arrow to a left-turn circle.

    b. Click this new cursor on the blue rhombus.
    The rhombus turns to the left.

    c. Click on the blue rhombus a second time.
    The rhombus turns to the left again, and it is ready to be slid into place.

☞ **5.** Slide the blue rhombus into place by doing the following:

    a. Click on the Arrow tool in the Tool bar.
    The cursor changes back to an arrow.

    b. Slide the rhombus into place.

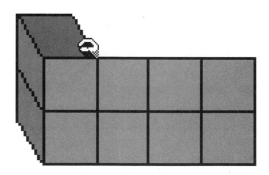

☛ **6.** Duplicate the blue rhombus three times to make three copies of it:

a. Click on the Duplicate tool in the Tool bar.

The cursor changes from an arrow to the Duplicate icon .

b. Click the Duplicate tool *on* the blue rhombus.

A duplicate is made. Using the Duplicate tool is particularly appropriate in this case because the duplicate is turned the correct way automatically.

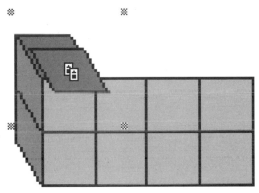

c. Click on the Arrow tool in the Tool bar.

The cursor changes back to an arrow.

d. Slide the duplicate rhombus into place.

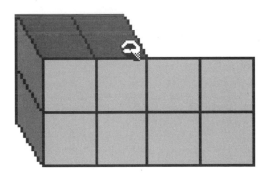

e. Repeat steps a through d to make and position two more duplicates.

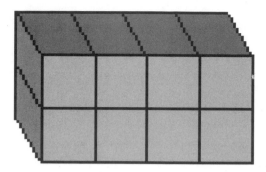

Note: To be more efficient, we could have duplicated three copies right away and then slid each into place one after the other.

☞ **7.** Make a half-circle doorway.

   a. Drag a quarter circle from the Shape bar. Slide it into place.

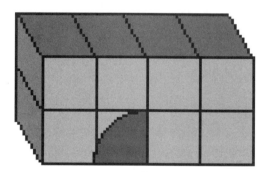

   b. Drag another quarter circle (or duplicate the first one) and slide it into place.

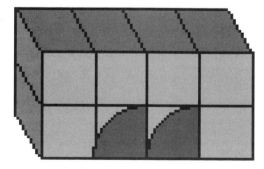

   c. Click on the Vertical Flip tool in the Tool bar.

   The cursor changes from an arrow to the Vertical Flip icon ⅎꟻ.

d. Click the Vertical Flip tool on the second quarter circle.

The shape flips over a vertical line through the center of the shape. Because the quarter circle is symmetric, we could have also turned it several times to the right, but flipping is more efficient.

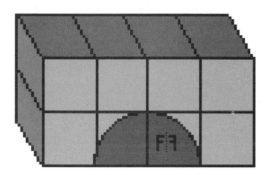

Our building is finished.

1. Make a sun.

More About Building Pictures

a. Drag a yellow hexagon from the Shape bar.

Place it in the upper right-hand corner of the Work window.

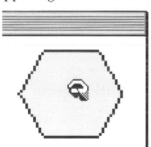

b. Get another yellow hexagon and place it right over the first one.

c. Click on the Right Turn tool in the Tool bar.

The cursor changes from an arrow to the Right Turn icon **Ↄ**.

d. Click the Right Turn tool on the second hexagon.

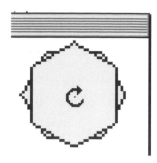

Our sun is finished. Now let's add a walkway. It will be a pattern of several shapes. First, we'll design the unit.

 1. Make a unit for the walkway.

   a. Drag a yellow hexagon, a red trapezoid, a green triangle, and a blue rhombus from the Shape bar.

   Place the shapes in the lower left-hand corner of the Work window as shown. Some shapes will have to be turned to make the pattern shown.

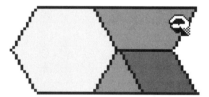

   b. Click on the Glue tool in the Tool bar.

   The cursor changes from an arrow to the Glue icon .

   c. Click in the middle of *each* of the four shapes in the unit.

   The cursor changes to a "squirt glue" icon whenever you click on a shape that has not yet been glued. Note that you have to click on each shape; even though they are "snapped" and touching sides, you must indicate each one you want glued together by clicking in the middle of each shape.

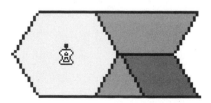

   The four shapes are now a glued group. They can be moved, turned, flipped, or duplicated as if they were one shape.

You can check that the shapes are one glued group. Move the cursor to the Glue tool in the Tool bar and hold down the mouse button. The following will appear on your screen, indicating one group.

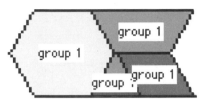

2. Duplicate the unit for the walkway.

a. Click on the Duplicate tool in the Tool bar.

The cursor changes from an arrow to the Duplicate icon ▣.

b. Click the Duplicate tool on the group of shapes.
A duplicate is made. Using the Duplicate tool is necessary because we're going to make a repeating pattern.

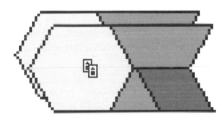

3. Define the motion for the pattern.

a. Click on the Arrow tool in the Tool bar.
The cursor changes back to an arrow.

b. Slide the duplicate of the unit where you want it to be for the start of the pattern.

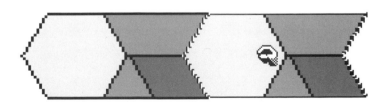

☞ **4.** Continue the pattern.

    a. Click on the Pattern button in the Tool bar.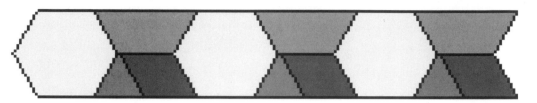

    The Pattern tool is a button. Simply clicking on a button will perform the action immediately. The next part of the pattern is put into place.

    b. Keep clicking on the Pattern button until your walkway extends across the window.

Our walkway is finished. Now let's make trees. Use the Pattern tool again to make the top of the first tree.

☞ **1.** Make a unit for the treetop.

    Get a green triangle from the Shape bar.

    Place it on the left-hand side of the Work window. We don't need to glue this time because our unit is just one shape.

☞ **2.** Duplicate it.

    a. Click on the Duplicate tool in the Tool bar.

    The cursor changes from an arrow to the Duplicate icon .

    b. Click the Duplicate tool on the triangle.

☞ **3.** Define the motion for the pattern.

    a. Click on the Right Turn tool in the Tool bar.

    The cursor changes back to the Right Turn icon ↻ .

    b. Turn the duplicate of the unit to the right two times.

c. Click on the Arrow tool in the Tool bar.
The cursor changes back to an arrow.

d. Slide the duplicate of the unit where you want it to be for the
start of the pattern.

We have now defined the motion for the pattern.

☛ **4.** Continue the pattern.

a. Click on the Pattern button in the Tool bar four times to

complete the treetop.

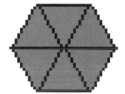

We'll finish the tree.

☞ 1. Make a trunk and ground cover.

    a. Drag two squares from the Shape bar. Place the squares below the green triangles as shown.

    b. Drag three tan rhombuses from the Shape bar. Turn them left three times and place them as ground cover. (You could also get one, turn it left three times, then use the Duplicate tool to make two copies.)

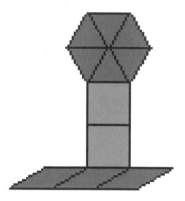

We need ground cover in back of the tree too.

    c. Drag three more tan rhombuses from the Shape bar. Place them in "back" of the others. (You could use the Duplicate tool to do this.)

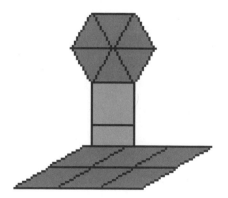

The tree shouldn't be behind the ground cover.

☞ 2. Bring the tree trunk to the front of the ground cover.

a. Select the bottom orange square by clicking in the middle of it one time.

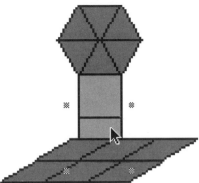

The small gray "selection" squares show that the bottom orange square is "selected." You can choose menu items to apply to selected shapes.

b. Choose **Bring To Front** from the **Edit** menu.

Edit Font Wini				**Edit** Font Winc		
Undo	⌘Z			Undo	⌘Z	
Cut	⌘H			Cut	⌘H	
Copy	⌘C			Copy	⌘C	
Paste	⌘U			Paste	⌘U	
Clear				Clear		
Select All	⌘A			Select All	⌘A	
Bring To Front				Bring To Front		

Point to the menu you want and press the mouse button . . .

. . . then move the cursor to **Bring To Front.**

The orange square is brought to the front of the picture.

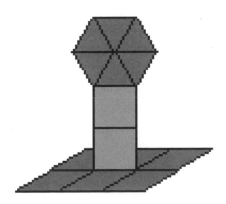

☛ 3. Glue the tree and ground cover together.

In Step 2, you selected a single shape, the orange square, and applied the action (**Bring To Front**) to it. You can also select a *group* of shapes and apply a tool or action to the entire group at one time. This will make gluing all these shapes together easier.

a. Place the arrow at the top left corner of the group of shapes in the tree.

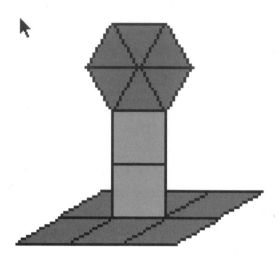

b. Drag diagonally to enclose the shapes in a dotted rectangle . . .

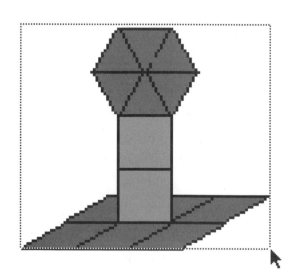

c. . . . and release the mouse button.

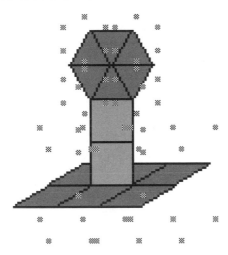

d. Use the Glue tool to glue all the shapes into a group at once by clicking in the middle of any one of them.

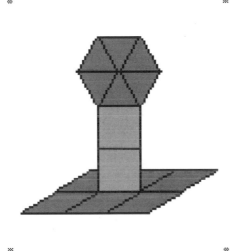

Click on the Arrow tool in the Tool bar. Now the small gray "selection" squares will surround a whole group instead of each individual shape.

You can now do something to all these shapes at once: duplicate them, slide them, turn them, or flip them as one shape. Note that if you click on one of the selected group and slide the whole group, there may be a delay while the *Shapes* program builds an outline of the group.

Next let's try duplicating a group.

☞ 1. Duplicate the tree.

Use the Duplicate tool to make several copies of the tree and place them where you like.

☞ 2. Add any finishing touches.

In the picture below, blue rhombuses connecting the building and the walkway were added, some shapes were moved, and the **Bring To Front** command was applied to add a few finishing touches.

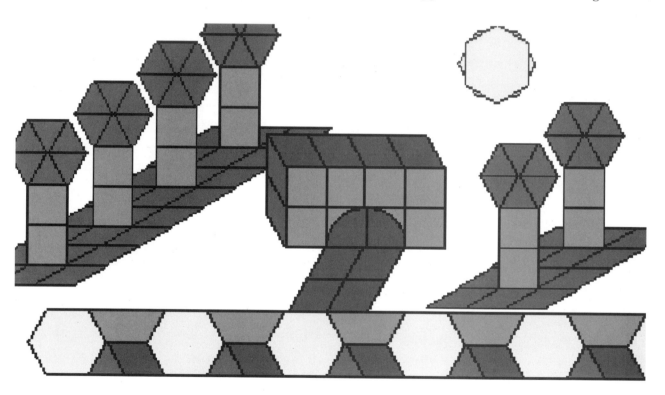

The picture is finished.

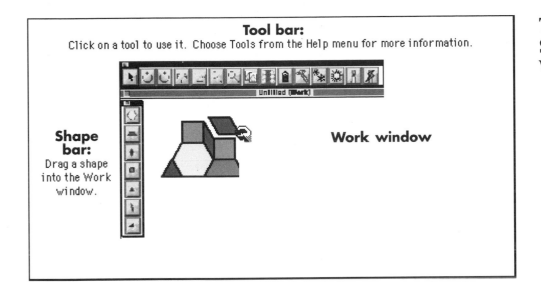

Tool Bar, Shape Bar, and Work Window

Begin by dragging a shape from the Shape bar (the vertical, "floating" bar on the left) to the Work window (the large blank window). Dragging means clicking on a shape and then holding the mouse button down while you move the mouse.

Move the cursor to a shape with the mouse. It becomes a hand.	Click the mouse button and hold it down . . .	. . . while you move the new shape where you want it.

Once the shape is placed in the Work window, you can slide it again by dragging it with the Arrow tool. If you place one shape so that one of its sides is close to a side of another shape, the two shapes will "snap" together.

You can change the position of the shape, or duplicate it, by using the tools in the Tool bar. The tool that is "active," or in use, is surrounded by a black outline (like the arrow tool shown in the diagram on p. 158). Another way to see which tool is active is by the shape of the cursor.

Only the most commonly used tools are available and displayed for each activity. All tools are available for Free Explore.

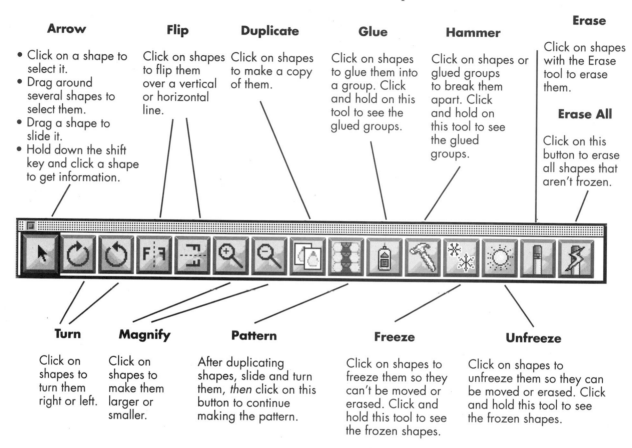

Arrow
- Click on a shape to select it.
- Drag around several shapes to select them.
- Drag a shape to slide it.
- Hold down the shift key and click a shape to get information.

Flip
Click on shapes to flip them over a vertical or horizontal line.

Duplicate
Click on shapes to make a copy of them.

Glue
Click on shapes to glue them into a group. Click and hold on this tool to see the glued groups.

Hammer
Click on shapes or glued groups to break them apart. Click and hold on this tool to see the glued groups.

Erase
Click on shapes with the Erase tool to erase them.

Erase All
Click on this button to erase all shapes that aren't frozen.

Turn
Click on shapes to turn them right or left.

Magnify
Click on shapes to make them larger or smaller.

Pattern
After duplicating shapes, slide and turn them, *then* click on this button to continue making the pattern.

Freeze
Click on shapes to freeze them so they can't be moved or erased. Click and hold this tool to see the frozen shapes.

Unfreeze
Click on shapes to unfreeze them so they can be moved or erased. Click and hold this tool to see the frozen shapes.

To use most tools (except Pattern and Erase All, which are buttons):

☞ 1. Click on a tool in the Tool bar to make it active. The cursor will change to look like the tool.

☞ 2. Click in the middle of a shape to perform the action. If you click one of several shapes that are "selected," the action is performed on each of the selected shapes. See the following section, The Arrow Tool, for more information about selecting shapes.

Pattern and Erase All are **buttons**. Simply clicking on a button will perform the action immediately.

The following sections discuss the tools in more detail.

With the Arrow tool, you can drag shapes to slide them. This is the most important use of the Arrow tool.

1. Click in the middle of a shape and hold the mouse button down . . .

2. . . . while you move the mouse, sliding the shape.

3. Release the button to stop sliding.

You can also select shapes with the Arrow tool.

Note: You can do most tasks in *Shapes*, including sliding, without ever selecting shapes. It's usually just a convenience for taking some action on several shapes at once. Before we discuss how to select shapes, let's describe what "selecting" means.

Selected shapes are shown surrounded with small gray squares.

Selected shapes can be copied to the clipboard (a place in computer memory for temporary, invisible storage) or cut—copied to the clipboard *and* removed from the Work window—using commands on the **Edit** menu. Also, if you apply a tool to one shape that is part of a group of selected shapes, the tool will automatically be applied to each shape in the group.

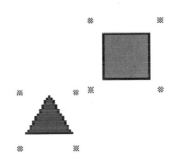

There are two ways to select shapes. First, you can click on any shape with the Arrow tool. That selects the shape. (If it is *already* selected, this will "unselect" the shape.) Second, you can select multiple shapes that are near one another:

1. Place the arrow at one corner of the group of shapes. Press the mouse button.

2. Drag diagonally to enclose the shapes in a dotted rectangle . . .

3. . . . and release the mouse button.

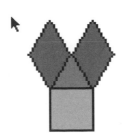

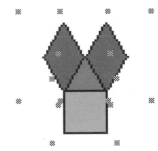

Now you can do something to all these shapes at once; for example, copy or cut them, slide them all together, or flip them all. Note that if you click on one of the selected group and slide the whole group, there may be a delay while the *Shapes* program builds an outline. Hold the mouse button down without moving the mouse until the outline appears.

You can use the Arrow tool to shift-click on a shape to get information about it. To shift-click, hold the shift key down while clicking on a shape. Click again to clear the message.

One final feature: If you're using any other tool and you want to use the Arrow tool for a quick selection or slide, just hold down the Command ⌘ key. *Shapes* will know to use the Arrow tool while the Command key is held down. When you let go of the Command key, *Shapes* will return to the previous tool.

Turn, Flip, and Magnifying Tools: Moving and Sizing

You can use these tools to turn or flip shapes:

One shape: Click on a shape with the tool. For example, if you click on the shape with the first flip tool, the shape flips over a vertical line through the center of the shape.

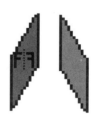

Several shapes: After the shapes have been selected, click on one of them with the tool. For example, if you click on one with the first Turn tool, each shape turns right around its center.

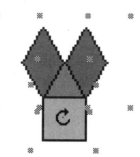

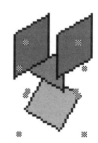

To magnify shapes: If you click on a shape with the first Magnify tool, the shape gets bigger. The second Magnify tool will make it smaller. Shapes that are different sizes will not snap to each other.

You can use the Glue tool to glue several shapes together into a group. This group is a new shape you have created. You can slide, turn, and flip it as a unit—that is, as if it were a single shape. For example, you can glue several shapes and then move them or duplicate them.

To use the Glue tool,

☞ 1. Click on Glue tool in the Tool bar to make it active.

☞ 2. Click on each shape you wish to glue together into a group.

   If there are only two shapes, or if two or more shapes are "snapped" or touching, you still have to click on each of them. Click in the middle of each shape and the computer glues them together. Similarly, if you select a group of shapes, and click on one shape, the group will be glued.

   You can add more shapes to an already glued group. Click on one shape in the glued group, then click on one shape in the new group. The two groups will now be glued.

☞ 3. Click on the Arrow tool or any other tool. All the shapes you glued will become a single, new group.

The small gray "selection" squares will surround a whole group instead of each individual shape.

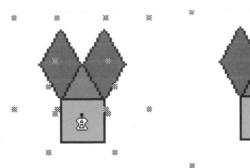

Glue and Hammer Tools: Combining and Breaking Apart

The group will now act as a single unit. For example, if you click on the group with the Right Turn tool, the group turns *as one shape* around the center of the group.

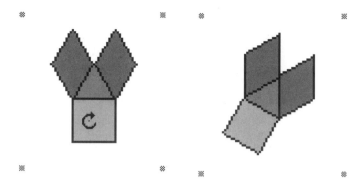

What if you want to make two separate groups? Suppose you made two different kinds of houses and you want each to be glued in a different group. You can't glue all the shapes in each of the houses at once; that would make one two-house group. Instead, you must glue one house, clicking on the Arrow tool to end the gluing process and glue that group. Then you must choose the Glue tool again and glue the second house.

Sometimes it helps to know what shapes are already glued into groups. Hold the mouse button down on either the Glue or Hammer tool on the Tool bar to see which shapes are in which groups.

☞ 1. Hold the button down on the Glue (or Hammer) tool to see the group number on each shape.

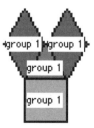

Use the Hammer tool to break apart glued shapes. Click on any shape in the group with the hammer to break apart the group.

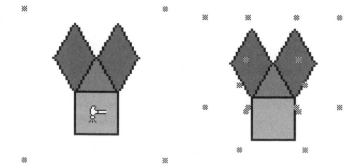

The Pattern tool is a **button**. You just click on it to perform the action (the Erase All button works the same way). To use the Pattern button, you must first make a pattern.

☞ 1. Make a basic unit for the pattern. Any shape or combination of shapes can be used as this unit. If you wish to turn the unit later to start the pattern, you must glue the shapes in the basic unit to form a group. Turn patterns must have a single glued group as the basic unit.

☞ 2. Duplicate this unit with the Duplicate tool. (You can also choose **Copy** and then **Paste** from the **Edit** menu.)

☞ 3. Move the duplicate of the unit where you want it to be for the start of the pattern by using the tools. You can slide the duplicate or turn it. (Remember, if you turn it as in this example, all the shapes in the duplicate must have been glued into one group.)

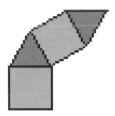

☞ 4. Now, click on the Pattern button as many times as you wish to continue the pattern. If a duplicate goes off the Work window, you will hear a beep and the Pattern button will not make any more copies.

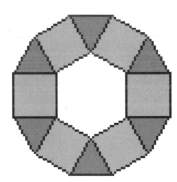

The pattern below was made by sliding the duplicate and then clicking on the Pattern button.

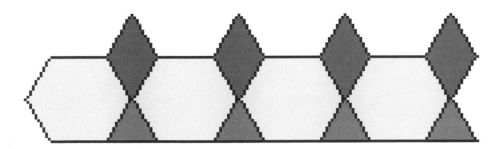

The Pattern tool makes patterns composed of slides and turns. If you want flipped shapes in your pattern, use these steps to make a basic unit (Step 1, p. 163):

a. Glue a group.

b. Duplicate the group.

c. Use the Flip tool to flip the duplicate.

d. Glue the two groups (the original and its flipped [mirror] image) together to make the basic unit for the pattern.

e. Continue with Step 2 (p. 163).

Freeze and Unfreeze Tools: Combining and Breaking Apart

You can use the Freeze tool to "freeze" shapes. Frozen shapes can't be moved or erased. They are frozen in place (in comparison, the Glue tool glues shapes to each other; however, the glued group can still be moved).

Freezing shapes allows you to manipulate other shapes without accidentally moving or erasing those that are frozen. Click on a shape with the Unfreeze tool to unfreeze it. Click and hold either tool on the Tool bar to see the frozen shapes.

Using Menu Commands

To use any menu commands, do the following:

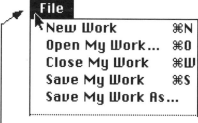

Point to the menu you want and press the mouse button . . .

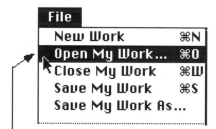

. . . then drag the selection bar to your choice and release the button.

About Menus

The **File** menu deals with documents and quitting.

New Work starts a new document. The ⌘N indicates that, instead of selecting this from the menu, you could enter ⌘N or **Command N** by holding down the **Command** key (with the ⌘ and symbols on it) and then pressing the N key.

Open My Work opens previously saved work.

Close My Work closes present work.

Save My Work saves the work.

Save My Work As saves the work with a new name or to a different disk or folder.

Change Activity lets you choose a different activity.

Page Setup allows you to set up how the printer will print your work.

Print prints your work.

Quit quits *Shapes*.

When you save your work for the first time, a dialogue box opens. Type a name. You may wish to include your name or initials, your work, and the date. For the remainder of that session, you can save your work simply by selecting the **Save** menu item or pressing ⌘S (**Command S**).

To share the computer with others, save your work then choose **Close My Work**. Later, to resume your work, choose **Open My Work** and select the work you saved.

When you **Quit**, you are asked whether you wish to save your work. If you choose to save at that time (you don't have to if you just saved), the same steps are followed.

File	
New Work	⌘N
Open My Work...	⌘O
Close My Work	⌘W
Save My Work	⌘S
Save My Work As...	
Change Activity...	
Page Setup...	
Print...	⌘P
Quit	⌘Q

The **Edit** menu contains choices to use when editing your work.

Cut deletes the selected object and saves it to a space called the clipboard.

Copy copies selected object on the clipboard.

Paste puts the contents of the clipboard into the Work window.

Clear deletes the selected object but does not put it on the clipboard.

Select All selects all shapes. This is not only a fast and handy shortcut, it also helps when some shapes are nearly or totally off the Work window.

Bring To Front puts the selected shapes "in front of" unselected shapes. That is, each new shape you create will be "in front of" the shapes already on the Work window. If you want to change this, select a shape that is in the "back," hidden by other shapes, and choose **Bring To Front**.

Edit	
Undo	⌘Z
Cut	⌘X
Copy	⌘C
Paste	⌘V
Clear	
Select All	⌘A
Bring To Front	

The **Font** menu is used to change the appearance of text in the Show Notes window. In order for any command in the **Font** menu to be highlighted, the Show Notes command in the **Windows** menu must be open.

The first names are choices of typeface.

Size and **Style** have additional choices; pull down to select them and then to the right. See the example for **Style** shown at left. The **Size** choice works the same way.

All Large changes all text in all windows to a large-size font. This is useful for demonstrations. This selection toggles (changes back and forth) between **All Large** and **All Small**.

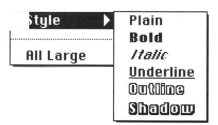

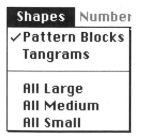

The **Windows** menu shows or hides the windows. If you hide a window such as the Tool bar, the menu item changes to **Show** followed by the name of the window—for example, **Show Tools**. You can also hide a window by clicking in the "close box" in the upper-left corner of the window.

The **Notes** Window is designed to be a word processor. Students might use this to record a strategy they used to solve a problem, or to write notes to themselves as reminders of how they plan to continue in the next math session.

The **Shapes** menu contains several commands to change the shapes.

Pattern Blocks and **Tangrams** chooses one of the shape sets for the Shape bar.

All Large, **All Medium**, and **All Small** changes the size of all the shapes. Use the Magnify tools to change the size of some of the shapes. Note that shapes of different sizes do not snap to each other.

The **Number** menu is available for only certain activities that have more than one task. Select a number off the submenu to work on that number task.

```
┌─────────────┐
│ Number      │
├─────────────┤
│ Number 1    │
│✓Number 2    │
│ Number 3    │
│ Number 4    │
│ Number 5    │
│ Number 6    │
│ Number 7    │
│ Number 8    │
│ Number 9    │
│ Number 10   │
└─────────────┘
```

The **Options** menu allows you to customize *Shapes*.

> **Vertical Mirror** and **Horizontal Mirror** toggle (turn on and off) the Work windows mirrors, which reflect any action you take.

> **Snap** toggles the "snap" feature, in which shapes, when moved, automatically "snap" or move next to, any other shape they are close to. You may want to turn that feature off if you have lots of shapes on the Work window, or if you are copying many shapes. This feature can slow down moving the shapes. You can turn it off temporarily to speed things up.

```
┌──────────────────────┐
│ Options │ Help       │
├──────────────────────┤
│ Vertical Mirror      │
│ Horizontal Mirror    │
├──────────────────────┤
│✓Snap                 │
└──────────────────────┘
```

The **Help** menu provides assistance.

> **Windows** provides information on the three main windows: the Tool bar, the Shape bar, and the Work window.

> **Tools** provides information on tools (represented on the Tool bar as icons, or pictures).

> **Directions** provides instructions for the present activity.

> **Hints** gives a series of hints on the present activity, one at a time. It is dimmed when there are no available hints.

```
┌──────────────────────┐
│ Help                 │
├──────────────────────┤
│ Windows...           │
│ Tools...             │
│ Directions...    ⌘D  │
│ Hints...         ⌘H  │
└──────────────────────┘
```

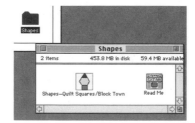

This section contains suggestions for how to correct errors and what to do in some troubling situations.

If you are new to using the computer, you might also ask a computer coordinator or an experienced friend for help.

No *Shapes* Icon to Open

■ Check that *Shapes* has been installed on your computer by looking at a listing of the hard disk.

■ Open the folder labeled *Shapes* by double-clicking on it.

■ Find the icon for the *Shapes* application and double-click on it.

Shapes—Quilt Square/Block Town

Nothing Happened After Double-Clicking on the *Shapes* Icon

■ If you are sure you double-clicked correctly, wait a bit longer. *Shapes* takes a while to open or load and nothing new will appear on the screen for a few seconds.

■ On the other hand, you may have double-clicked too slowly, or moved the mouse between your clicks. In that case, try again.

In the Wrong Activity

■ Choose **Change Activity** from the **File** menu.

A Window Closed by Mistake

■ Choose **Show Window** from the **Windows** menu.

Windows or Tools Dragged to a Different Position by Mistake

■ Drag the window back into place by following these steps: Place the pointer arrow in the stripes of the title bar. Press and hold the button as you move the mouse. An outline of the window indicates the new location. Release the button and the window moves to that location.

I Clicked Somewhere and Now *Shapes* Is Gone! What Happened?

You probably clicked in a part of the screen not used by *Shapes* and the computer therefore took you to another application, such as the "desktop."

■ Click on a *Shapes* window, if visible.

■ Double-click on the *Shapes* program icon.

How Do I Select a Section of Text?

In certain situations, you may wish to copy or delete a section or block of text.

■ Point and click at one end of the text. Drag the mouse by holding down the mouse button as you move to the other end of the text. Release the mouse button. Then use the **Edit** menu to **Copy**, **Cut**, and **Paste**.

System Error Message

Some difficulty with the *Shapes* program or your computer caused the computer to stop functioning.

■ Turn off the computer and repeat the steps to turn it on and start *Shapes* again. Any work that you saved will still be available to open from your disk.

I Tried to Print and Nothing Happened

■ Check that the printer is connected and turned on.

■ When printers are not functioning properly, a system error may occur, causing the computer to "freeze." If there is no response from the keyboard or when moving or clicking with the mouse, you may have to turn off the computer and start over.

I Printed the Work Window but Not Everything Printed

■ Choose the Color/Grayscale option for printing.

■ If your printer has no such option (e.g., an older black-and-white printer), you need to find a different printer to print graphics in color.

If the *Shapes* program does not understand a command or has a suggestion, a dialogue box may appear with one of the following messages. Read the message, click on **[OK]** or press **<return>** from the keyboard, and correct the situation as needed.

Disk or directory full.

The computer disk is full.

- Use **Save My Work As** to choose a different disk.

I'm having trouble with the disk or drive.

The disk might be write-protected, there is no disk in the drive, or some similar problem.

- Use **Save My Work As** to choose a different disk.

Out of space.

There is no free memory left in the computer.

- Eliminate shapes you don't need.
- Save and start new work.

The *Shapes* disk that you received with this unit contains the *Shapes* program and a Read Me file. You may run the program directly from this disk, but it is better to put a copy of the program and the Read Me file on your hard disk and store the original disk for safekeeping. Putting a program on your hard disk is called *installing* it.

Note: *Shapes* runs on a Macintosh II computer or above, with 4 MB of internal memory (RAM) and Apple System Software 7.0 or later. (*Shapes* can run on a Macintosh with less internal memory, but the system software must be configured to use a minimum of memory.)

To install the contents of the *Shapes* disk on your hard drive, follow the instructions for your type of computer or these steps:

Slide tab→
up to lock

Back of disk

1. Lock the *Shapes* program disk by sliding up the black tab on the back, so the hole is open.

   The *Shapes* disk is your master copy. Locking the disk allows copying while protecting its contents.

2. Insert the *Shapes* disk into the floppy disk drive.

3. Double-click on the icon of the *Shapes* disk to open it.

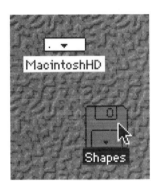

4. Double-click on the Read Me file to open and read it for any recent changes in how to install or use *Shapes*. Click in the close box after reading.

5. Click on and drag the *Shapes* disk icon (the outline moves) to the hard disk icon until the hard disk icon is highlighted, then release the mouse button.

   The message appears indicating that the contents of the *Shapes* disk are being copied to the hard disk. The copy is in a folder on the hard disk with the name *Shapes*.

6. Eject the *Shapes* disk by selecting it (clicking on the icon) and choosing **Put Away** from the **File** menu. Store the disk in a safe place.

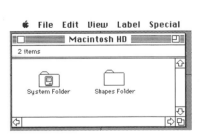

7. If the hard disk window is not open on the desktop, open the hard disk by double-clicking on the icon.

   When you open the hard disk, the hard disk window appears, showing you the contents of your hard disk. It might look something like this. Among its contents is the folder labeled *Shapes* holding the contents of the *Shapes* disk.

☞ 8. Double-click the *Shapes* folder to select and open it.

When you open the *Shapes* folder, the window contains the program and the Read Me file.

To select and run *Shapes,* double-click on the program icon.

Optional

For ease at startup, you might create an alias for the *Shapes* program by following these steps:

☞ 1. Select the program icon.

☞ 2. Choose **Make Alias** from the **File** menu.

The alias is connected to the original file that it represents, so that when you open an alias, you are actually opening the original file. This alias can be moved to any location on the desktop.

☞ 3. Move the *Shapes* alias out of the window to the desktop space under the hard disk icon.

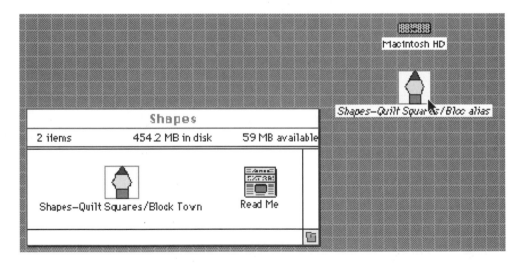

For startup, double-click on the *Shapes* alias instead of opening the *Shapes* folder to start the program inside.

For classroom management purposes, you might want to save student work on a disk other than the hard drive. Make sure that the save-to disk has been initialized (see instructions for your computer system).

Saving Work on a Different Disk

☞ 1. Insert the save-to disk into the drive.

☞ 2. Choose **Save My Work As** from the **File** menu.

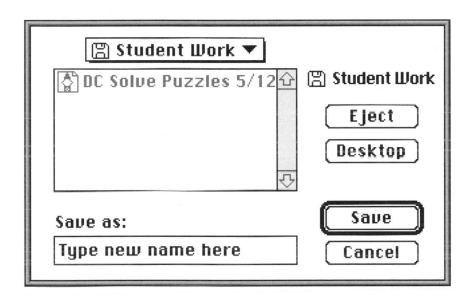

The name of the disk the computer is saving to is displayed in the dialogue box. To choose a different disk, click the **[Desktop]** button and double-click to choose and open a disk from the new menu.

☞ 3. Type a name for your work if you want to have a new or different name from the one it currently has.

☞ 4. Click on **[Save]**.

As students no longer need previously saved work, you may want to delete their work (called "files") from a disk. This cannot be accomplished from inside the *Shapes* program. However, you can delete files from disks at any time by following directions for how to "Delete a File" for your computer system.

Deleting Copies of Student Work

Blackline Masters

_____, 19____

Dear Family,

Our class is beginning a new mathematics unit called *Quilt Squares and Block Towns*. For the next few weeks we will be studying 2-D and 3-D geometry.

Geometry is about shapes and the way shapes are related. First the children will be using 2-D shapes, both on and off the computer, to make designs and fill in outlines. They will investigate the relationships between shapes and notice how shapes are alike and different. We will play Quick Images, a game that helps the children look carefully at shapes, and your child will bring home a version of this game to play with the family. We will also be making quilt patterns with squares and triangles.

Later we will focus on 3-D shapes, using a set of blocks called Geoblocks. One focus will be *rectangular prisms*—shapes like rectangular boxes. We will be asking for small boxes from home, and the children will also construct their own boxes from rectangles. The children will explore how to draw 3-D shapes when they design buildings for a block town.

During this unit, you can help your child by looking for and talking about shapes around your home and in your neighborhood.

■ Look for patterns or designs made from different shapes. Can you find floor patterns or wallpaper patterns made from squares, rectangles, triangles, circles, hexagons, and other shapes?

■ Take walks with your child to look at the shapes of buildings in your neighborhood. On longer trips, talk about the shapes in the buildings you see.

■ Look at boxes you have at home. What shapes are they? How many sides do they have?

■ Find books about shapes in the children's section of your public library. Read them with your child.

■ If you enjoy drawing, spend some time with your child drawing shapes you see around your home.

If you have a job or hobbies that use patterns or shapes, please let us know. We'd love to have you share with our class how you use shapes.

Sincerely,

Draw an Object

Find something at home that has
a special shape. Draw a picture of it.
Write about its shape.

This is a _____

I can tell you this about its shape:

_____

_____

_____

_____

Pattern Block Fill-In, Shape A

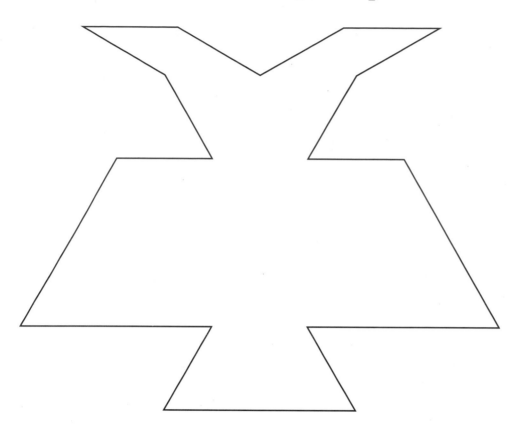

How many blocks did you use?

Shape	⬡	⬟	▱	▢	▱	△	Total blocks
How many?							

Investigation 1 • Session 2
Quilt Squares and Block Towns

Pattern Block Fill-In, Shape B

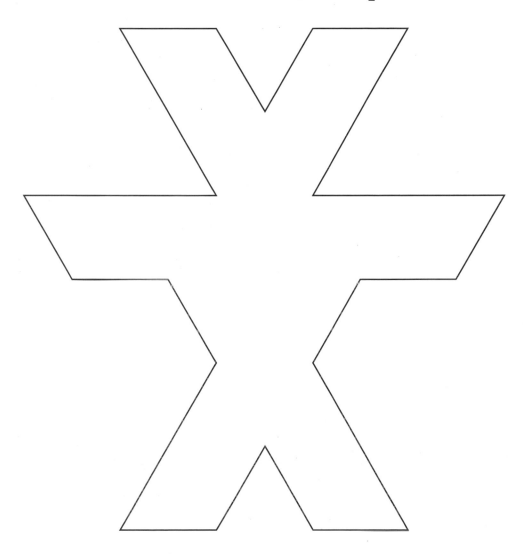

How many blocks did you use?

Shape	⬡	⏢	▱	◻	⟋	△	Total blocks
How many?							

Pattern Block Fill-In, Shape C

How many blocks did you use?

Shape	⬡	⬟	▱	▢	▱	△	Total blocks
How many?							

Pattern Block Fill-In, Shape D

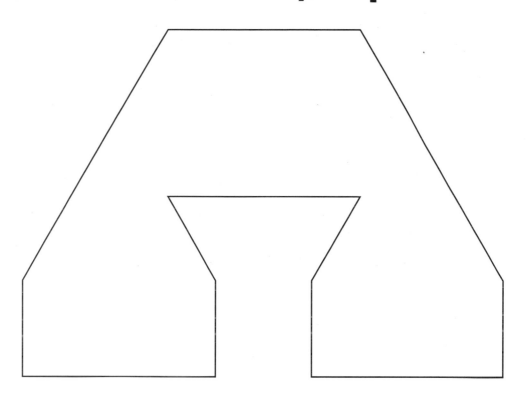

How many blocks did you use?

Shape	⬡	⬡	▱	▢	▱	△	Total blocks
How many?							

Investigation 1 • Sessions 3–6
Quilt Squares and Block Towns

Pattern Block Fill-In, Shape E

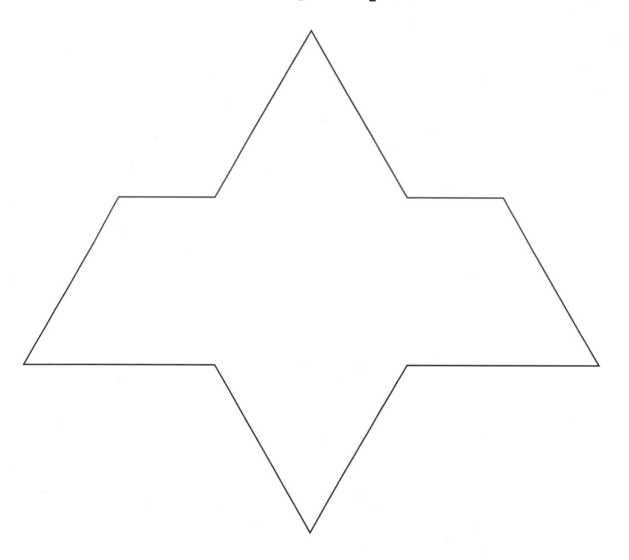

How many blocks did you use?

Shape	⬡	⬠ trapezoid	▱	▢	╱╱	△	Total blocks
How many?							

Pattern Block Counts A

Make a design with 12 pattern blocks.

How many blocks did you use?

Shape	⬡	▱	▱	◻	╱	△
How many?						

Pattern Block Counts B

Make a design with 18 pattern blocks.

How many blocks did you use?

Shape	⬡	⬠	▱	▢	▱	△
How many?						

Pattern Block Counts C

Make a design with 25 pattern blocks.

How many blocks did you use?

Shape	⬡	⬭	▱	▢	▱	△
How many?						

Pattern Block Counts D

Make a design with 28 pattern blocks.

How many blocks did you use?

Shape	⬡	⬠	▱	▢	▱	△
How many?						

Different Ways to Fill, Shape A

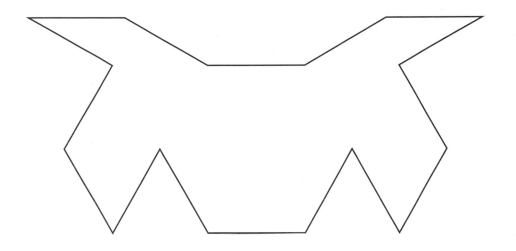

Number
of blocks

_____

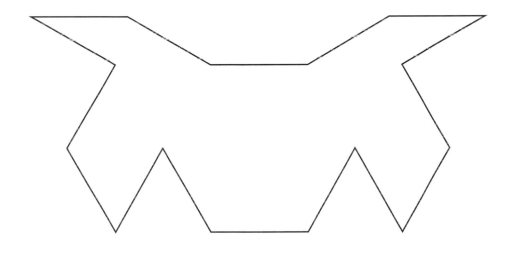

Number
of blocks

_____

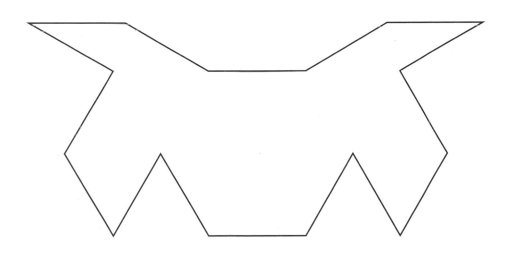

Number
of blocks

_____

Different Ways to Fill, Shape B

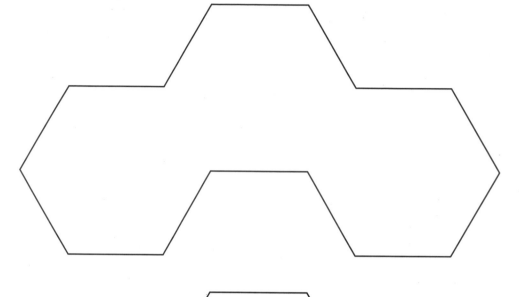

Number
of blocks

_____

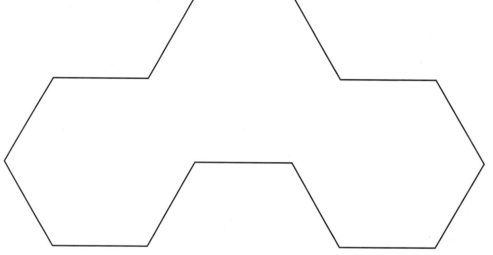

Number
of blocks

_____

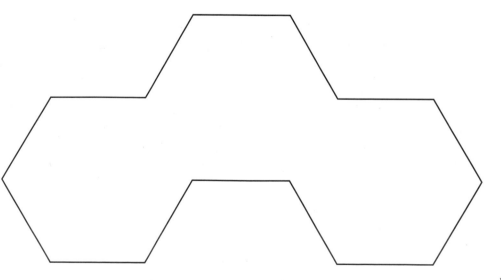

Number
of blocks

_____

Different Ways to Fill, Shape C

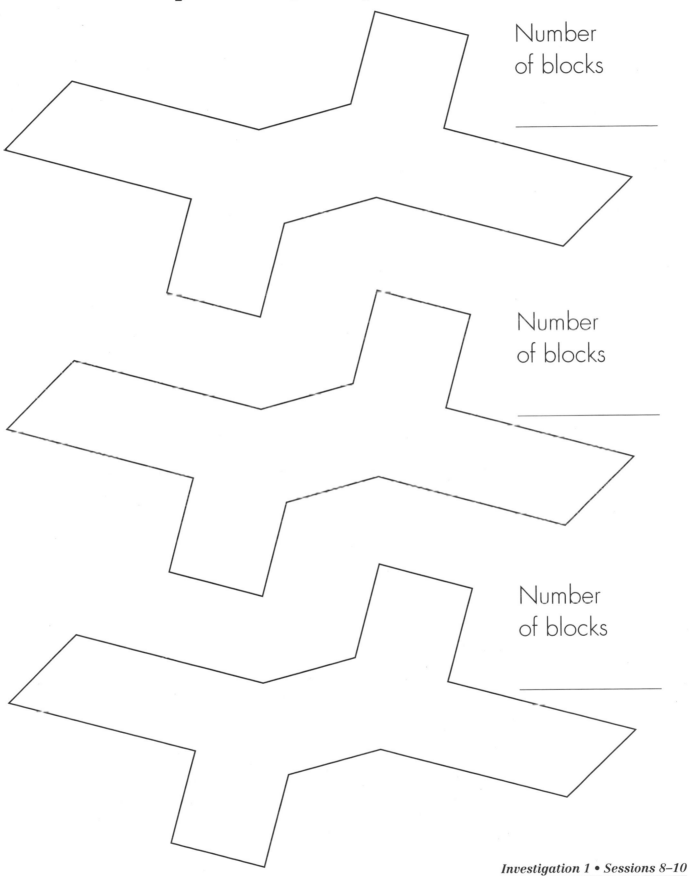

Number
of blocks

_____

Number
of blocks

_____

Number
of blocks

_____

Different Ways to Fill, Shape D

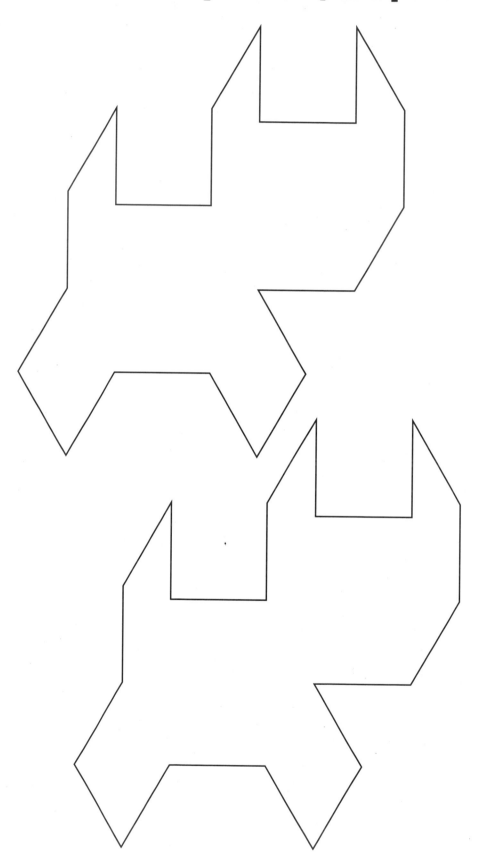

Number
of blocks

_____

Number
of blocks

_____

Different Ways to Fill, Shape E

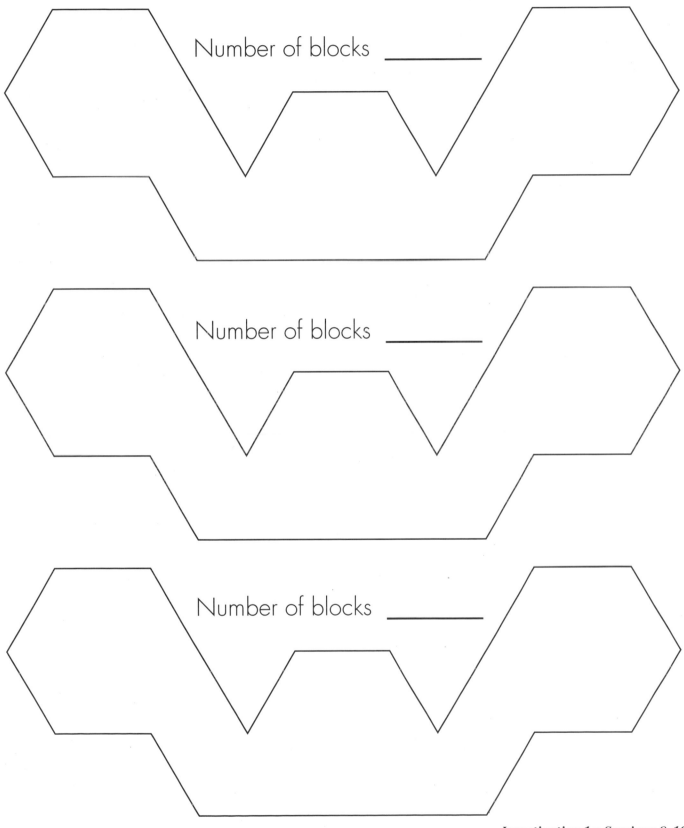

Number of blocks _____

Number of blocks _____

Number of blocks _____

Quick Images

Play Quick Images with your family. You need at least one other person. Any number can play.

1. Choose one of the shapes for Quick Images. Cut or fold the page on the dotted lines, so that only one shape can be seen.

2. Show the shape while you count slowly to 5. Then hide the shape. The other people try to draw the shape you showed them.

3. When they are ready, give them another look. Count to 5 again. (No one should draw while looking at the picture!) Then hide the shape. Give them time to change their drawings if they want to.

4. Then let everyone look at the shape. Talk about the ways people tried to remember it.

Choose another shape, or make up your own shape. Take turns being the person to show the shape and the person to draw it.

Shapes for Quick Images

Cut or fold on the dotted lines.
Show one shape at a time.

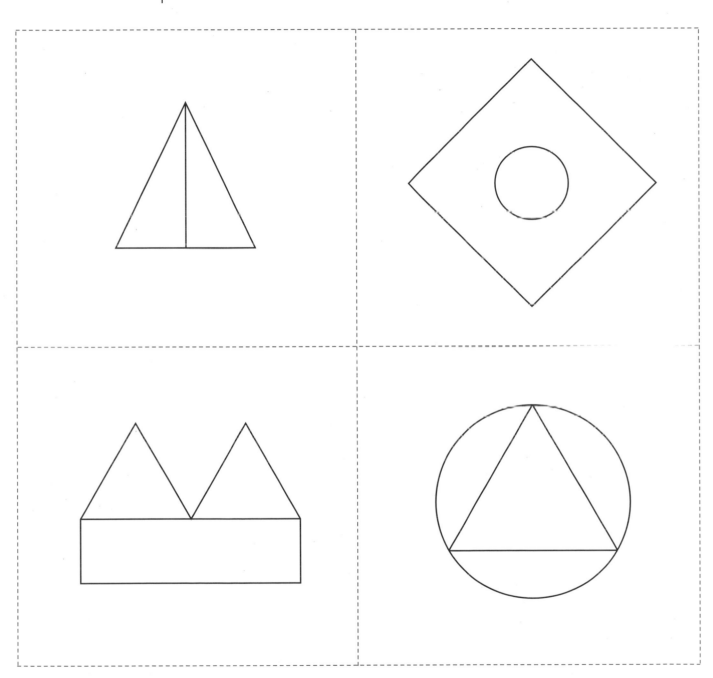

Quilt Squares

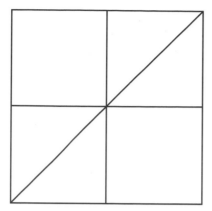

Quilt Pattern A

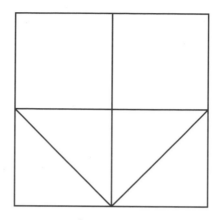

Quilt Pattern B

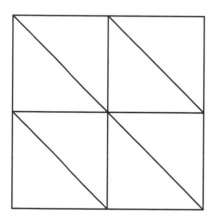

Quilt Pattern C

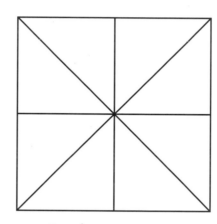

Quilt Pattern D

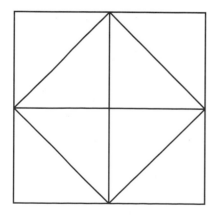

Quilt Pattern E

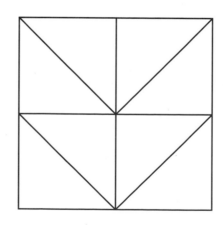

Quilt Pattern F

Name _____

Date _____

Quilt Pattern A

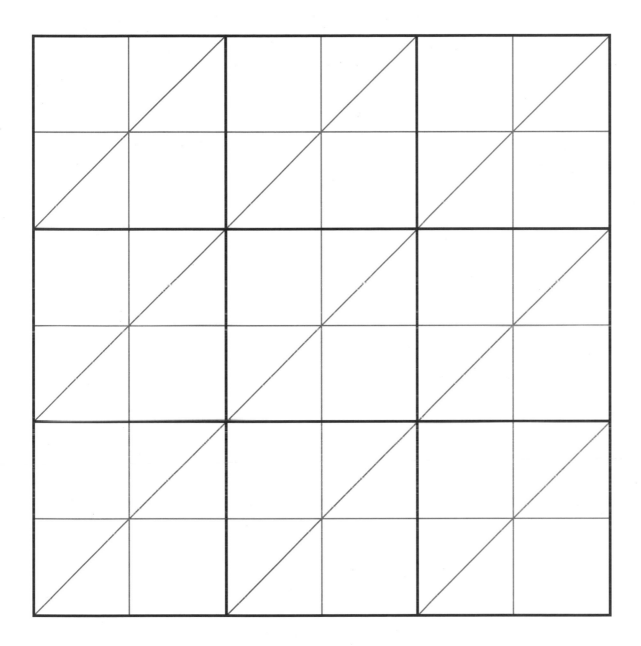

Quilt Pattern B

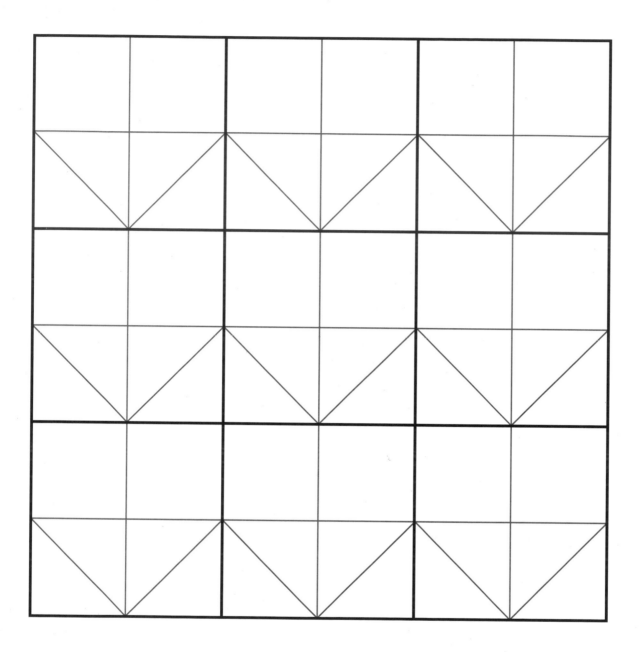

Quilt Pattern C

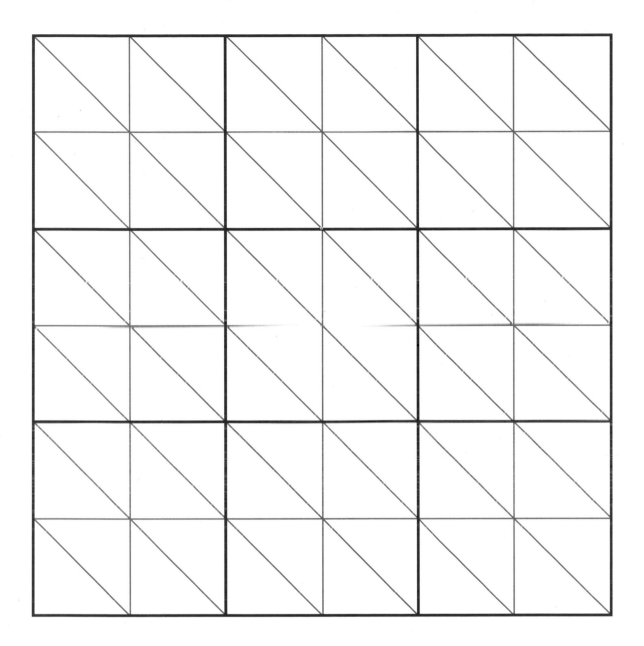

Investigation 1 • Sessions 11–12
Quilt Squares and Block Towns

Quilt Pattern D

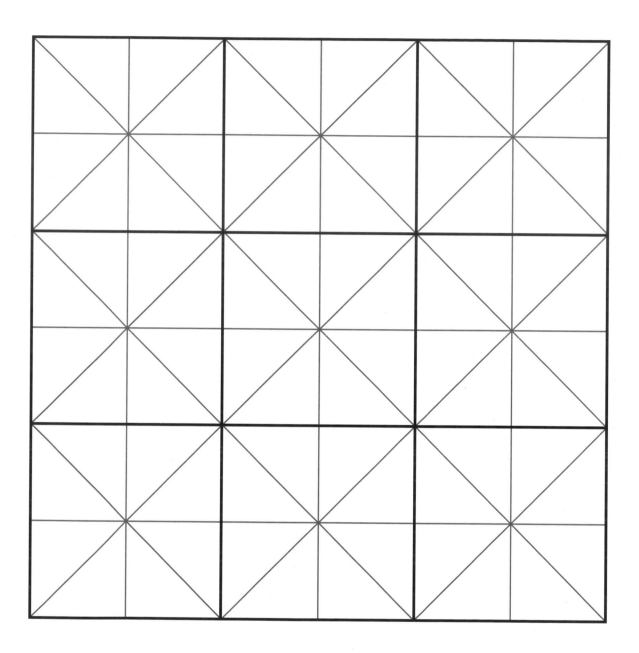

Quilt Pattern E

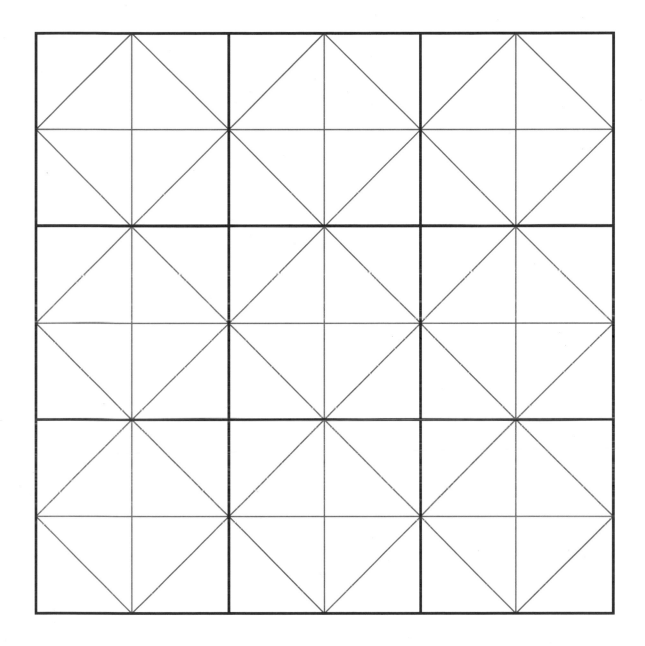

Quilt Pattern F

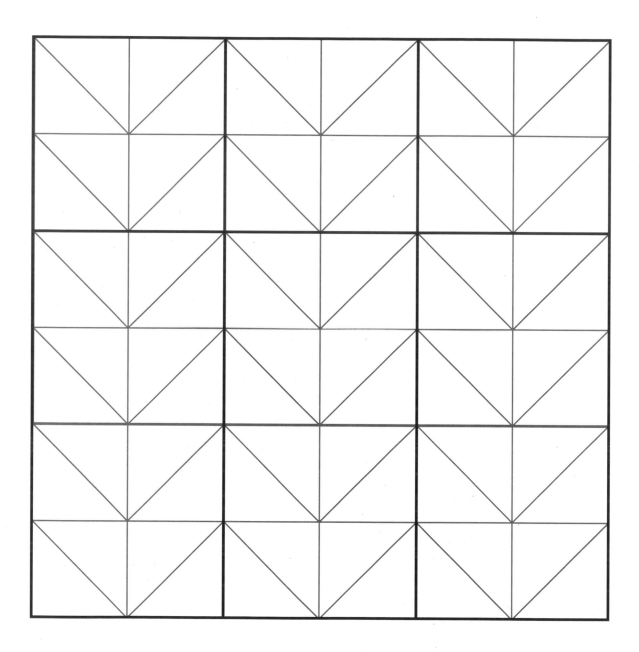

PATTERN BLOCK CUTOUTS (page 1 of 6)

Duplicate these hexagons on yellow paper and cut apart.

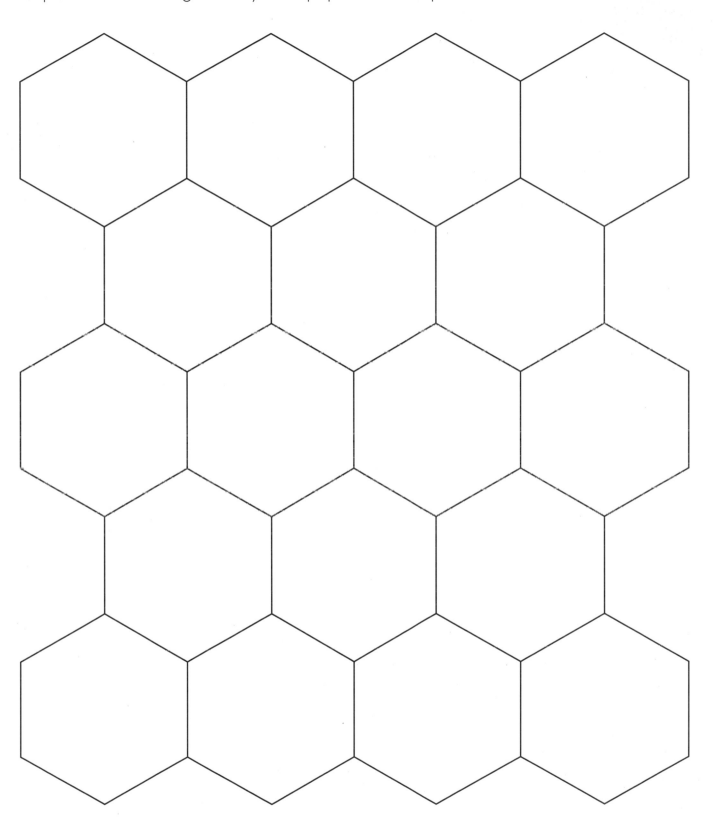

PATTERN BLOCK CUTOUTS (page 2 of 6)

Duplicate these trapezoids on red paper and cut apart.

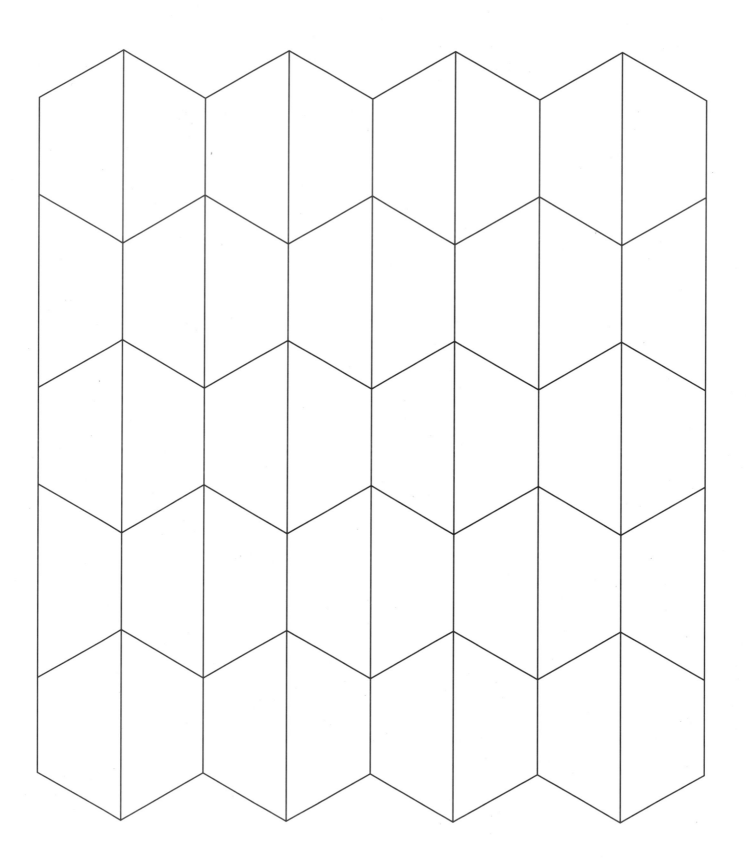

PATTERN BLOCK CUTOUTS (page 3 of 6)

Duplicate these triangles on green paper and cut apart.

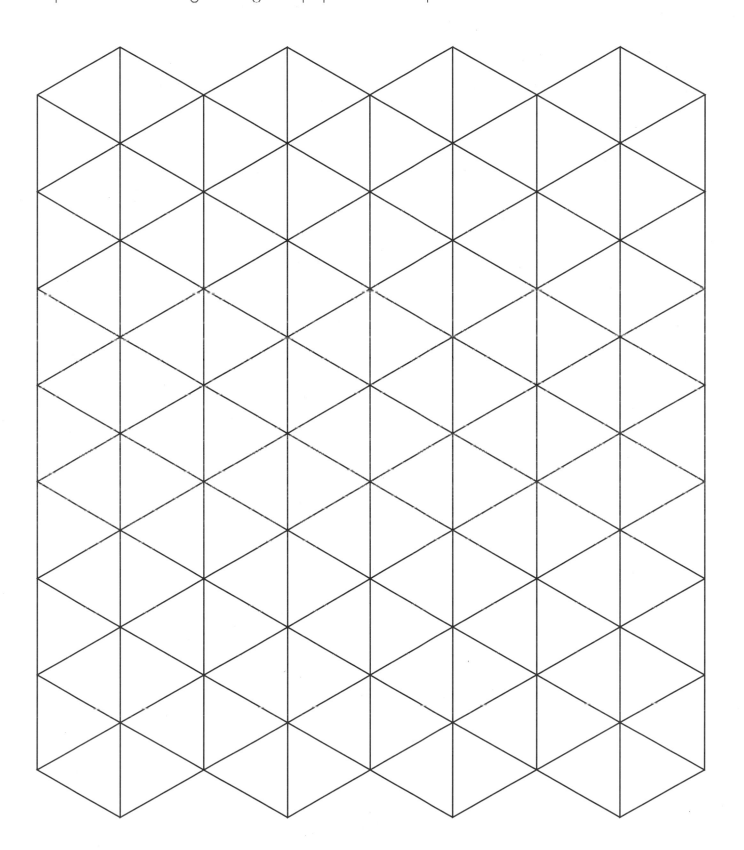

PATTERN BLOCK CUTOUTS (page 4 of 6)

Duplicate these squares on orange paper and cut apart.

Duplicate these rhombuses on blue paper and cut apart.

205

PATTERN BLOCK CUTOUTS (page 6 of 6)

Duplicate these rhombuses on tan paper and cut apart.

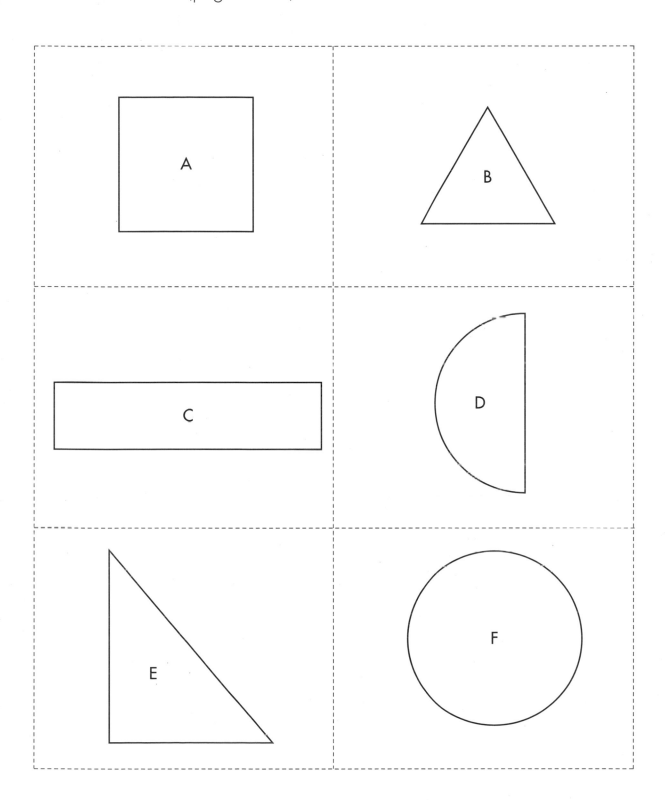

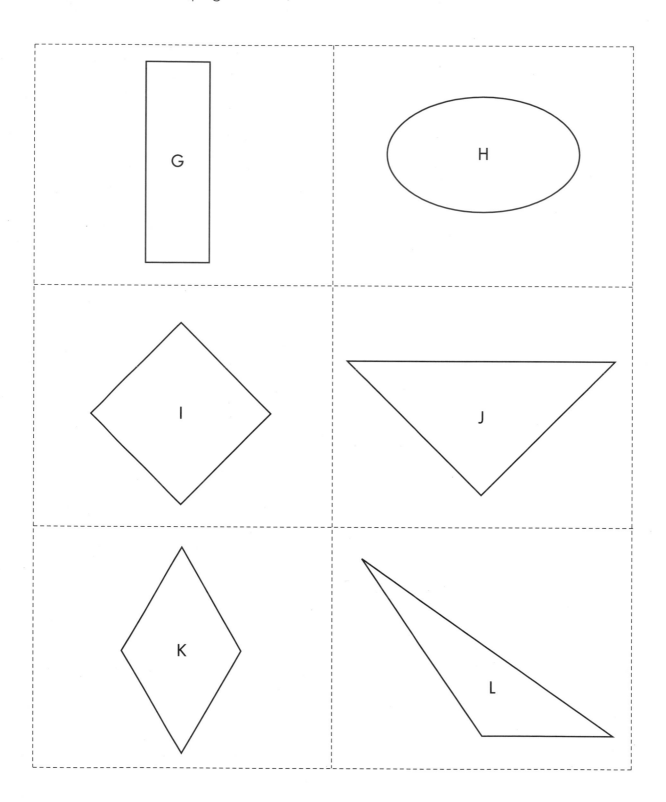

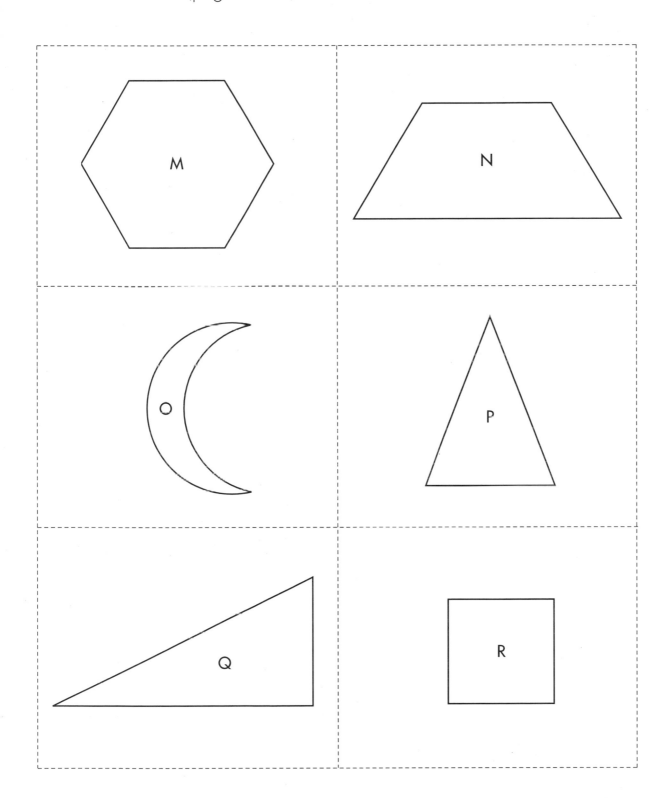

COMBINATION SHAPES

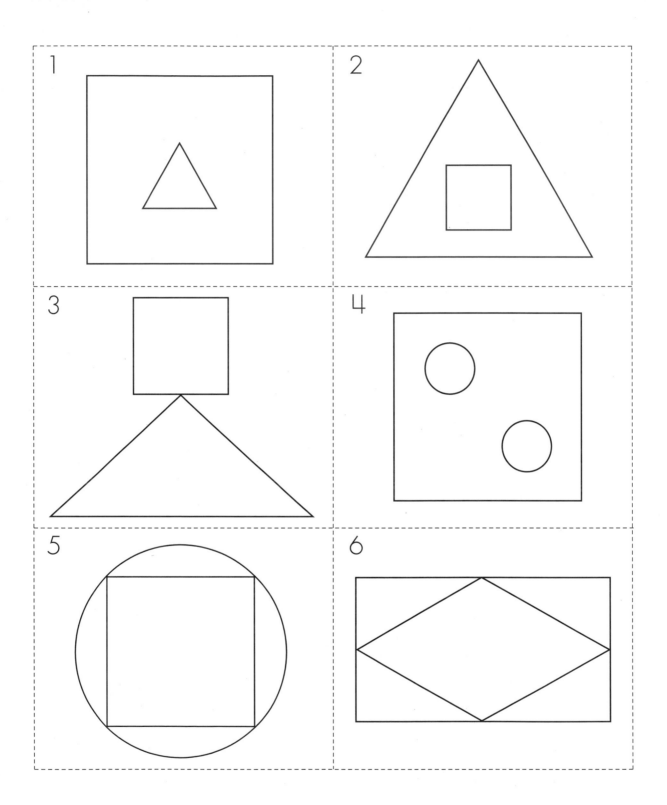

Investigation 1 Resource
Quilt Squares and Block Towns

Mystery Footprints

Find one or two things at home that have a special shape. Draw the "footprint" (or outline) of each shape by tracing around it. Bring your drawings to school.

Don't write the names of your objects on your drawings. The class will try to guess what your objects are.

Boxes for Our Collection

As we study 3-D shapes, we are exploring boxes of different sizes and shapes.

In one activity, we will look at covered boxes and try to guess what they might have held.
For this activity, we need a collection of boxes.

Look at home for at least two empty boxes. We need both ordinary box shapes and unusual box shapes. Boxes should be small—no bigger than a shoe box or a cereal box.

The boxes need to tell what came in them.
If that information is not printed on the box, please write it on.

Then, cover each box with plain paper or newspaper. Cover it well so that no one can tell what came in the box.

Please bring in your boxes by this date:

_____

Mystery Objects

Note to Families
We played this game in class with blocks of different shapes. Help your child find suitable objects at home. Also, please help your child with the writing step.

1. Find about five different small objects. You will need two of each object.

2. Put one of each object in a bag or sock. Leave the other one out where everyone can see it.

3. Point to one of the objects. The other person must reach in the bag, without looking, and try to pull out the matching object.

4. To make the game easier, choose objects that are very different. For a harder game, choose objects that are a lot alike. For example, a difficult game might use a penny, a dime, a nickel, a bottle cap, and a checker.

5. After playing the game, write about what you did. Tell what objects you used. Tell what was easy or hard.

GEOBLOCK FOOTPRINTS, SET A

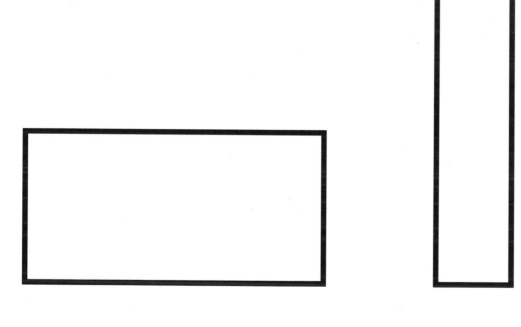

GEOBLOCK FOOTPRINTS, SET B

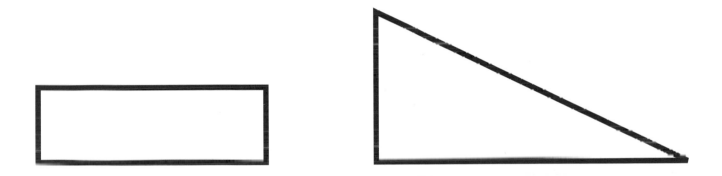

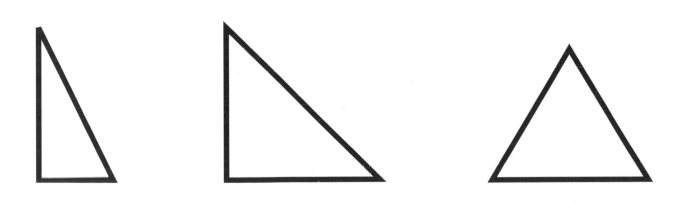

Investigation 2 Resource
Quilt Squares and Block Towns

© Dale Seymour Publications®

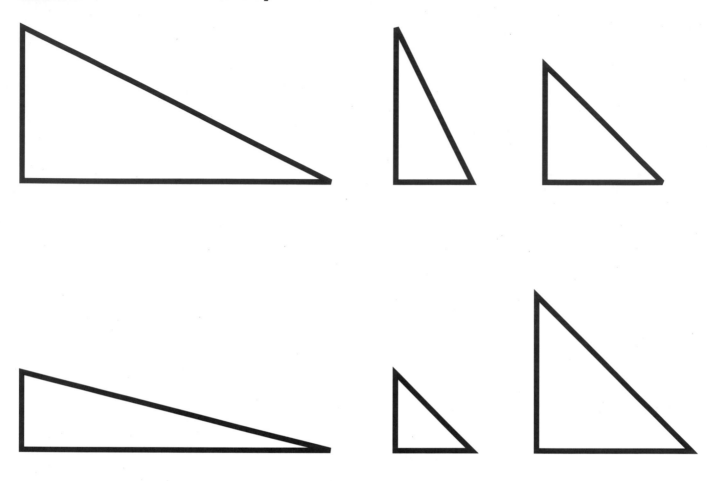

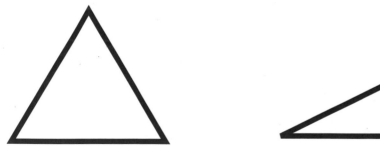

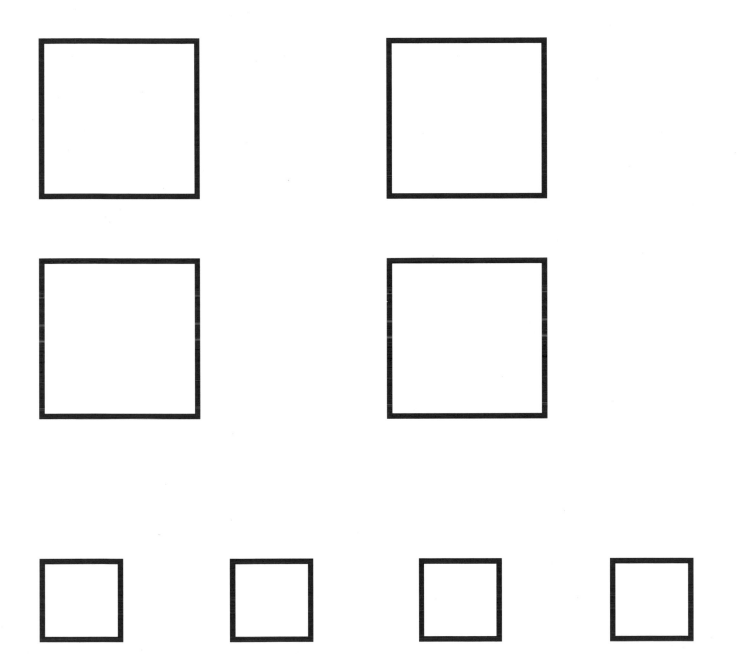

GEOBLOCK FOOTPRINTS, SET E

GEOBLOCK FOOTPRINTS, SET F

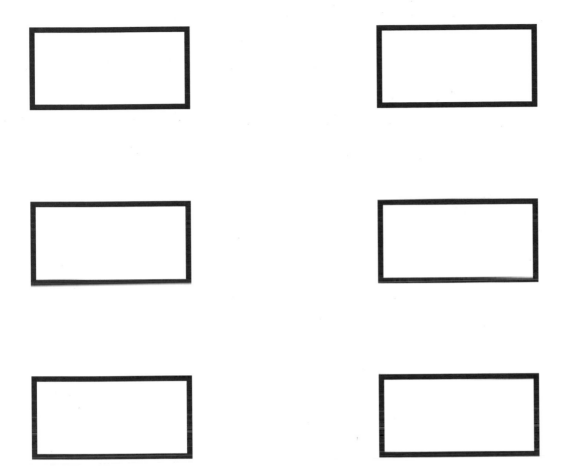

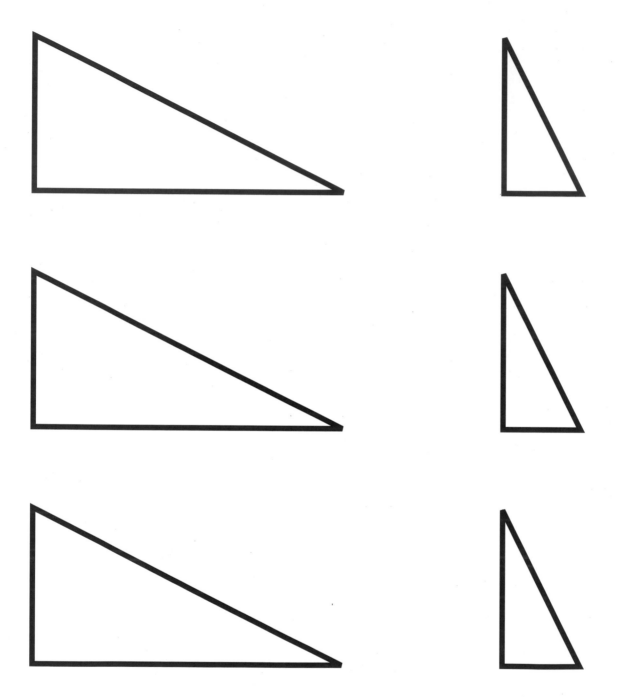

GEOBLOCK PICTURES, SHEET A

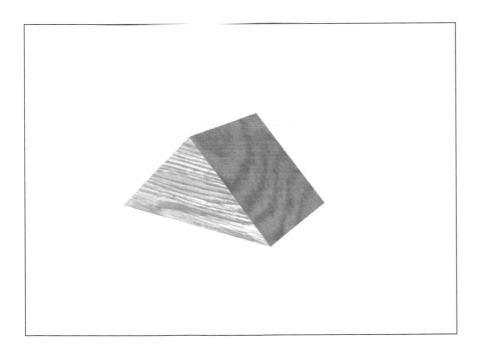

GEOBLOCK PICTURES, SHEET B

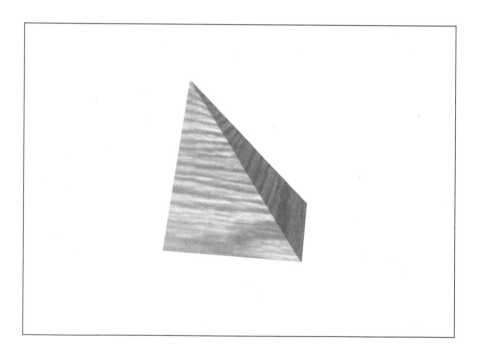

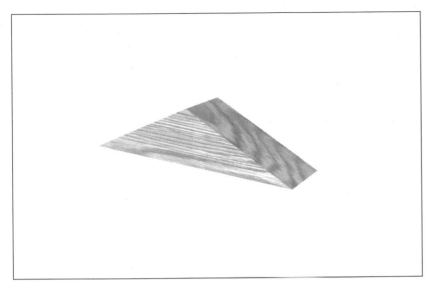

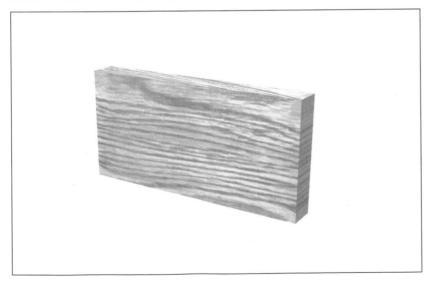

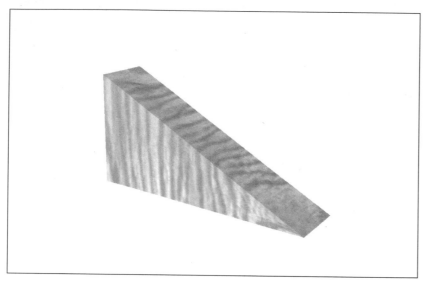

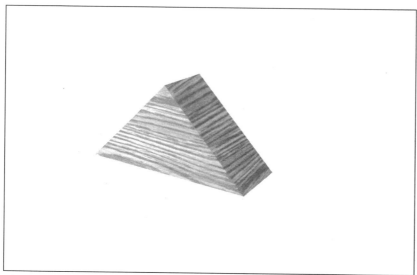

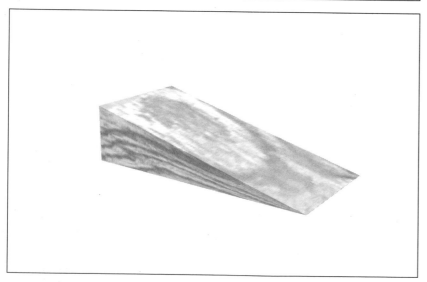

224

Draw a Building

Think of a building that you have seen.
It may be a building near where you live. Or it
may be a building you saw somewhere else.

Try to think of a building that has an interesting
shape. Draw a picture of the building.
If you have a picture of the building,
you can paste it on this sheet instead of drawing.

Write one or two sentences about the building.

Robot Paces

This activity takes two people. One person gives directions. The other person is a robot who walks a path from one place to another.

Choose a starting and ending point. They can be in your house or outside. For example, you could start at the stove and end up at the front door.

The robot can do only two things: walk straight ahead for so many paces, and turn. So, a robot can follow directions like these:

Walk 4 paces.
Walk 5 paces.
Turn toward the table.
Walk 6 paces.
Turn toward the front door.
Walk 8 paces.

A pace is a normal walking step.

Try this several times. Always choose a starting and ending point before you begin. Take turns being the robot.

Write a few sentences about one of your paths.

WAYS TO DRAW BLOCKS

E

N

S

W

STREET GRID

Practice Pages

This section provides optional homework for teachers who want or need to give more homework than is suggested to accompany the activities in this unit. With the games and problems included here, students get additional practice in learning about number relationships and solving number problems. Whether or not the *Investigations* unit you are presenting in class focuses on number skills, continued work at home on developing number sense will benefit students. In this unit, optional practice pages include the following:

Double Compare This game is introduced in the grade 1 units *Mathematical Thinking at Grade 1* and *Building Number Sense*. If your students are familiar with the game, simply send home the directions and the Number Cards. If your students have not played this game before, you will probably want to introduce it in class and help students play once or twice before sending it home. If they are very familiar with the game, you might suggest one of the listed variations. Some teachers send home a Game Record Sheet, which asks for the date students played, who they played with, and something about what happened when they played the game. Students fill out the sheet with help from their families and bring it back to class.

Missing Numbers Students fill in the missing numbers on 100 charts with some of the numbers left blank. This activity is introduced in the grade 1 unit, *Building Number Sense*. Two different 100 charts with missing numbers are provided here. Use the blank 100 chart to make up your own Missing Numbers sheets. For extra challenge, ask students to fill in an entire blank chart. Briefly introduce this activity in class before sending it home.

Double Compare

Note to Families
In this game, your child will be finding the totals of pairs of numbers. You will need a set of Number Cards to play this game.

Materials: Deck of Number Cards 0–10
(remove the wild cards)

Players: 2

Object: Decide which of two totals is greater.

How to Play

1. Mix the cards and deal them evenly to each player. Place your stack of cards facedown in front of you.

2. At the same time, both of you turn over the top two cards in your stack. Look at your two numbers and find the total. Then find the total of the other player's numbers.

   If your total is more than the other player's, say "Me!" If the two totals are the same, turn over the next two cards.

3. Keep turning over two cards. Say "Me!" each time your total is more.

4. The game is over when you have both turned over all the cards in your stack.

Variations

a. If your total is **less,** say "Me."

b. Play with three people. Find all three totals. If yours is the most, say "Me."

c. Add the four wild cards to the deck. A wild card can be any number.

Name _______________ Date _______________

Game Record Sheet

Game:

____

Play this game at home. You should have the directions and other things you need. After you play, fill out and return this sheet.

Who played the game?

____

Write about what happened when you played the game.

____

____

____

____

____

____

Note to Families

Please play this game with your child, then help fill out and return this sheet. The more times children play a mathematical game, the more practice they get with important skills and with reasoning mathematically.

0	0	0	0
1	1	1	1
2	2	2	2

232

3	3	3	3
4	4	4	4
5	5	5	5

Practice Page
Quilt Squares and Block Towns

6	6	6	6
7	7	7	7
8	8	8	8

234

9	9	9	9
10	10	10	10
Wild Card	Wild Card	Wild Card	Wild Card

Practice Page
Quilt Squares and Block Towns

Practice Page A

What are the missing numbers? Write them on the chart.

	2	3	4			7	8	9	
		13			16	17			20
31	32	33	34		36	37	38	39	40
			44			47	48	49	
			54		56				60
			64			67		69	
71	72	73	74		76		78		
	82		84			87	88	89	
	92	93	94		96				100

Practice Page
Quilt Squares and Block Towns

Practice Page B

What are the missing numbers? Write them on the chart.

				5			8		
	13								20
	22			26					
31			34					39	
					47				
	53								60
			65					69	
		74			77				
81				86					90
	93						98		

_____ Date _____

Practice Page C

What are the missing numbers? Write them on the chart.

Practice Page
Quilt Squares and Block Towns